The Practice of Prophecy

The Practice of Prophecy

An Empirical-Theological Study
of Pentecostals in Singapore

LUM LI MING DENNIS
Foreword by William K. Kay

⌒PICKWICK *Publications* • Eugene, Oregon

THE PRACTICE OF PROPHECY
An Empirical-Theological Study of Pentecostals in Singapore

Copyright © 2018 Lum Li Ming Dennis. All rights reserved. Except for brief quotations in critical publications or reviews, no part of this book may be reproduced in any manner without prior written permission from the publisher. Write: Permissions, Wipf and Stock Publishers, 199 W. 8th Ave., Suite 3, Eugene, OR 97401.

Pickwick Publications
An Imprint of Wipf and Stock Publishers
199 W. 8th Ave., Suite 3
Eugene, OR 97401

www.wipfandstock.com

PAPERBACK ISBN: 978-1-5326-1840-6
HARDCOVER ISBN: 978-1-4982-4395-7
EBOOK ISBN: 978-1-4982-4394-0

Cataloguing-in-Publication data:

Names: Lum, Li Ming Dennis. | Kay, William K., foreword writer

Title: The practice of prophecy : an empirical-theological study of Pentecostals in Singapore / Lum Li Ming Dennis.

Description: Eugene, OR: Pickwick Publications, 2018 | Includes bibliographical references.

Identifiers: ISBN 978-1-5326-1840-6 (paperback) | ISBN 978-1-4982-4395-7 (hardcover) | ISBN 978-1-4982-4394-0 (ebook)

Subjects: LCSH: Pentecostalism | Prophecy—Christianity | Christian sociology | Christianity—Singapore

Classification: BR1644 L85 2018 (paperback) | BR1644 (ebook)

Manufactured in the U.S.A.   03/13/18

Scriptures taken from the Holy Bible, New International Version®, NIV®. Copyright © 1973, 1978, 1984, 2011 by Biblica, Inc.™ Used by permission of Zondervan. All rights reserved worldwide. www.zondervan.com The "NIV" and "New International Version" are trademarks registered in the United States Patent and Trademark Office by Biblica, Inc.™

This book is dedicated to my wife and children.

Contents

List of Figures and Tables | viii
Foreword by William K. Kay | xi
Acknowledgements | xiii
Abbreviations | xiv

1 Introduction and Background | 1
2 An Empirical Approach to Practical Theology | 11
3 A Qualitative Study on Prophecy | 56
4 The Nature and Purpose of Prophecy | 86
5 The Practice of Prophecy | 124
6 A Quantitative Study on Prophecy | 158
7 Theological Reflection and Conclusion | 211

Appendix A: Qualitative Interview Questions | 237
Appendix B: Survey Instruments | 239

Bibliography | 245

Figures and Tables

FIGURES

Figure 6.1 The theological-conceptual model for the practice of prophecy | 161
Figure 6.2 Path diagram for ProphAct | 204
Figure 6.3 Path diagram for EvangAct | 207

TABLES

Table 6.1 Age distribution of respondents | 167
Table 6.2 Highest educational level of respondents | 168
Table 6.3 Respondents' role in their churches | 168
Table 6.4 Reliability analysis of prayer scales | 171
Table 6.5 Reliability analysis for DevoFreq | 172
Table 6.6 Reliability analysis for ProphAct | 172
Table 6.7 Component matrix for ProphAct | 173
Table 6.8 Rotated component matrix for ProphAct | 174
Table 6.9 Reliability analysis for CharExp | 175
Table 6.10 Component matrix for CharExp | 176
Table 6.11 Reliability analysis for EvangAct | 176
Table 6.12 Component matrix for EvangAct | 177
Table 6.13 Experience with prophecy | 178
Table 6.14 Understanding of prophecy | 179
Table 6.15 Cross-tab for prophecy and the authority of the Bible | 180
Table 6.16 Cross-tab for prophecy contradicts the Bible | 181

Table 6.17 Spiritual experiences initiating prophecy | 182
Table 6.18 Reception of prophecy | 183
Table 6.19 One-way ANOVA: Receiving entire prophetic message by ProphAct | 184
Table 6.20 Hochberg GT2 post-hoc: Receiving entire prophetic message by ProphAct | 184
Table 6.21 Delivery of prophecy | 185
Table 6.22 Judging of prophecy | 186
Table 6.23 Criteria for judging prophecy | 186
Table 6.24 Evaluation of congregational prophecy | 187
Table 6.25 Evaluation of personal prophecy | 187
Table 6.26 Content of congregational prophecy | 188
Table 6.27 Content of personal prophecy | 189
Table 6.28 Influence of prophecy on gratitude | 190
Table 6.29 Influence of prophecy on compassion | 190
Table 6.30 Influence of prophecy on courage | 190
Table 6.31 Items for quality control | 190
Table 6.32 Independent-sample t-test: ProphAct and CharExp by sex | 191
Table 6.33 Independent-sample t-test: ProphAct and CharExp by marital status | 192
Table 6.34 One-way ANOVA: ProphAct and CharExp by educational level | 192
Table 6.35 One-way ANOVA: ProphAct and CharExp by role in church | 193
Table 6.36 Pearson correlation matrix | 195
Table 6.37 Variables for multiple regression with ProphAct and EvangAct | 203
Table 6.38 Stepwise multiple regression with ProphAct | 203
Table 6.39 Stepwise multiple regression with EvangAct | 206

Foreword

WHEN THE PENTECOSTAL MOVEMENT began at the start of the twentieth century, it burst into life with the sound of speaking in other tongues—a controversial and distinctive vocal flow that signaled the belief that charismatic gifts were once again restored to the church. Less prominent and less noticed at the time was also a belief that New Testament prophecy should now be heard in the churches. Here was a belief that ordinary Christians might be inspired by the Holy Spirit to bring spontaneous declarations to their meetings. This was something separate from preaching because it was unpremeditated and erupting from within the congregation without the sanction of clerical training. Anyone might stand up in a meeting and say, "Thus saith the Lord . . ."

But the Pentecostals struggled with this spiritual spontaneity. They recognized the phenomenon was to be found in the pages of the New Testament and believed today's churches would benefit immensely from free, unfettered revelations given by the Spirit. At the same time, they noted all kinds of problems might arise if these utterances were placed on a level with the canonical Scriptures or if they were used as a way of giving uncontrolled and untested direction to uninformed Christians. There was a danger of exploitation, manipulation, or peculiar doctrine. So Pentecostal congregations began to develop a body of teaching and practice about prophecy that enabled it to be weighed or judged. Somewhere between spiritual wildfire and legalistic control was a space for prophetic utterance that would accompany or complement preaching and which might or might not be given privately to individuals as well as publicly to large congregations.

The emergence of prophecy within contemporary churches is an inviting subject for research. There is evidently an exegetical and hermeneutical side to the investigation and, equally, there is an empirical side which can be carried out by listening to prophecies, talking to people who prophesy, understanding the role of the practice within the church, and seeking to penetrate to the psychological and spiritual features underlying the phenomenon. This book makes a wonderful contribution to our understanding of contemporary prophecy, and it does so within the context of Asian churches in the country of Singapore.

This book began its life as a prize-winning doctoral dissertation. Information on prophetic utterance was gathered through interviews and by survey, and to each method the appropriate analytic method was applied. This gives the reader a rich and rounded appreciation of prophecy in Singaporean Pentecostal churches and enables us to see how such a gift is handled in the setting of congregational worship and service. At what stage in a public meeting may prophecy be given? What sort of things are said in prophecy? How are prophecies assessed? How do those who prophesy feel prompted to do so? Is prophecy always given to a large group or may it be given to individuals? And then what are the effects of prophecy on a congregation and how is it linked with other spiritual disciplines like intercessory prayer?

These important questions come within the scope of this book. One of the surprising findings of this enquiry is that there is a firm connection between prophecy and love. Much Pentecostal emphasis has been upon the power of the Holy Spirit, and early Pentecostals believed they were divinely equipped for service by their remarkable experiences of the Spirit. Some thought they needed no training or other preparation for ministry apart from what they received directly through their encounters with the Spirit. This book reveals that love is one of the prime motivations for prophecy. It is out of concern for other people that prophecy is given. Prophecy then becomes an expression of God's love personally and verbally imparted to an individual or congregation in need of reassurance: it is intended to lift up the disconsolate and weary, and to encourage those who are in a dark place. It is not intended to open up new avenues of doctrine but rather to meet many of the emotional needs of Christians in their daily lives and struggles. Yes, the power of the Spirit leads to miracles and signs and wonders, but also to the more unobtrusive uplift imparted by a well-timed word of prophecy. These and other findings are evidenced by the data discussed here and will help biblical and systematic theologians as well as pastors and preachers understand this vital gift to the church. That is, after all, how the Holy Spirit has been understood by Pentecostals: as a gift to the church by Christ to enable the conditions of a fallen and sometimes hostile world to be addressed and surmounted.

William K. Kay
Emeritus Professor of Theology, Wrexham Glyndŵr University
Honorary Professor of Pentecostal Studies, Chester University

Acknowledgements

THIS BOOK IS BASED on my doctoral dissertation and so I wish to acknowledge the many people who have contributed to this work. First, I want to thank the Assemblies of God of Singapore for facilitating and supporting the empirical study. I am grateful to the senior pastors who availed themselves for the interviews and the ministers who patiently completed the surveys. Their participation has made a significant contribution to the understanding of prophecy.

I wish to thank my school, TCA College, and my church, Trinity Christian Centre, for the opportunity to pursue my studies and engage in ministry. I joined my church as a youth and grew up being blessed by many within the community of faith. In particular, I deeply appreciate Rev. Dominic Yeo and Rev. Dr Wilson Teo for their relentless belief, encouragement, and support throughout my life, ministry, and academic pursuits.

I am indebted to my doctoral supervisors, Prof. William K. Kay and Prof. Christopher Alan Lewis, for their wise guidance and generous feedback. I especially appreciate the warm friendship and constant encouragement of Prof. Kay. He has been a wonderful model of a scholar, practical theologian, and Christian minister.

I am a second-generation Christian and owe much to my parents for raising me in the Christian faith. It is through their efforts that I learned to study the Bible, pray, and serve the Lord. I am forever thankful for their love, wisdom, discipline, and countless prayers. This book would also not be possible without the support of my wife and two children. Their love and laughter have brightened much of this journey and it is to them that this book is dedicated.

Abbreviations

AG	Assemblies of God
AGBC	Assemblies of God Bible College in Singapore
AGS	Assemblies of God of Singapore
AGUSA	Assemblies of God in the United States of America
ANOVA	Analysis of variance
BDAG	Walter Bauer, Frederick W. Danker, W. F. Arndt, and F. W. Ginrich. *Greek-English Lexicon of the New Testament and Other Early Christian Literature.* 3rd ed. Chicago: University of Chicago Press, 2000.
CharExp	Personal Charismatic Experience Scale
DevoFreq	Devotion Frequency Scale
EPQ	Eysenck Personality Questionnaire
EPQR-S	The short-form of the Revised Eysenck Personality Questionnaire
EvangAct	Evangelistic Activity Scale
ExamPray	Examination Prayer Scale
FMS	Faith Maturity Scale
FMS-H	Horizontal sub-scale of the Faith Maturity Scale
FMS-V	Vertical sub-scale of the Faith Maturity Scale
InterPray	Intercession Prayer Scale
JET	*Journal of Empirical Theology*
JPT	*Journal of Pentecostal Theology*
KMO	Kaiser-Meyer-Olkin measure

PetPray	Petition Prayer Scale
ProphAct	Prophetic Activity Scale
RadPray	Radical Prayer Scale
RestPray	Rest Prayer Scale
SacraPray	Sacramental Prayer Scale
SPSS	Statistical Package for Social Sciences
SuffPray	Suffering Prayer Scale
TearsPray	Tears Prayer Scale
TDNT	*Theological Dictionary of the New Testament.* 10 vols. Edited by Gerhard Kittel and Gerhard Friedrich. Translated by Geoffrey William Bromiley. Grand Rapids: Eerdmans, 1964–76.

1

Introduction and Background

1.1 INTRODUCTION

THE PHENOMENON OF PROPHECY is widely observed throughout the history of the Pentecostal movement.[1] A survey conducted by the Pew Research Center showed that prophecy remains common among contemporary Pentecostal congregations worldwide.[2] The report revealed that prophecy is extensively practiced within Asia, with 29 percent in the Philippines, 41 percent in India, and 43 percent in South Korea responding to say they had given or interpreted prophecy. It would be reasonable to infer that an even greater percentage of believers have heard or received a prophecy in these congregations. Similarly, a survey of Pentecostals in Singapore, Malaysia, and Hong Kong showed that 60 percent of the respondents were engaged in prophesying.[3] This widespread occurrence of the phenomenon highlights its important place within the Pentecostal movement. The great value of prophecy is highlighted by early Pentecostal statesman Donald Gee when he writes: "It [prophecy] can sweep the assembly up into heights of glory and enthusiasm, melt with tenderness, and make to tremble with awe.

---

1. Alexander, *Signs and Wonders*, 115–30; Anderson, *Introduction to Pentecostalism*, 19–38; Kay, *Pentecostals in Britain*, 63–69; Sheppard, "Prophecy."

2. Pew Research Center, "Spirit and Power," 19. The report defined prophecy as a "spontaneous utterance spoken in worship settings believed to be inspired by the Holy Spirit; not necessarily a prediction of future events as the term is commonly understood." Ibid., 12.

3. Kay, "Empirical and Historical Perspectives," 22.

It truly ministers to the believer 'exhortation, edification and comfort' (1 Corinthians 14:3); and in the unbeliever can produce deep conviction (verse 24)."[4]

Prophecy is one of the spiritual gifts or *charismata* listed by Paul in 1 Corinthians 12:8–10. Pentecostals generally consider prophecy to be the reception and communication of a spontaneous revelation through a divinely inspired human intermediary.[5] This is often described as comprising of either forth-telling or fore-telling.[6] Forth-telling consists of communicating a message believed to originate from God whereas fore-telling comprises the prediction of future events; the former function being more common of the two. The prophetic message is usually directed to a congregation though it may also be directed specifically at individuals.

The purpose of prophecy is understood to be primarily for the strengthening, encouragement, and comfort of the community of faith (1 Cor 14:3).[7] The literature review will later demonstrate that prophecy is widely discussed within Pentecostal literature at both the popular level as well as in academic discourse. However, most discussions examine prophecy from a historical or biblical-theological perspective. While there are popular handbooks on how Pentecostal prophecy should be practiced in the church today, there is a somewhat surprising dearth of academic studies on the practice of contemporary prophecy within the Pentecostal movement, particularly from the empirical perspective.[8] A significantly larger number of studies have focused on the phenomenon of *glossolalia*.[9] Furthermore, Pentecostal literature is strongly dominated by Western scholarship and

---

4. Gee, *Concerning Spiritual Gifts*, 61.

5. Ibid., 57; Lim, *Spiritual Gifts*, 79; Palma, "Prophecy: Nature and Scope," 11; Robeck, "Gift of Prophecy in Acts and Paul Part 2," 42. This understanding of prophecy will be discussed further in chapter 4.

6. Robeck, "Prophecy, Gift of," 999.

7. All Scripture quotations, unless otherwise indicated, are taken from the Holy Bible, New International Version®, NIV®.

8. This point is noted by Turner. See Turner, *Holy Spirit and Spiritual Gifts*, 306. Recent practical-theological research on contemporary prophecy include Cartledge, "Charismatic Prophecy," *JET*; Muindi, "Nature and Significance of Prophecy." Both of these were qualitative investigations that sought to describe the phenomenon.

9. Cartledge, *Charismatic Glossolalia*; Cartledge, *Speaking in Tongues: Multidisciplinary Perspectives*; Friesen, *Norming the Abnormal*; Holm, Wolf, and Smith, "New Frontiers in Tongues Research"; Mills, *Speaking in Tongues*. There are also several studies on Pentecostalism as a global movement from various sociological and psychological perspectives. For a discussion on some of these studies, see Anderson et al., *Studying Global Pentecostalism*.

studies on prophecy are mostly focused on the Western context.[10] This is despite the fact that the majority of Pentecostals reside in Asia, Africa, and Latin America.[11] There is thus a lack of studies on the contemporary practice of prophecy in the Pentecostal movement, particularly in the majority world. This study hopes to fill this lacuna in the literature through an empirical-theological investigation of prophecy in the Asian city-state of Singapore.

1.2 PURPOSE OF THE STUDY

The purpose of this study is to investigate the contemporary practice of prophecy within the Pentecostal church. Specifically, the study hopes to answer the following research questions: What is the nature, purpose, significance, and characteristics of contemporary prophecy? How does contemporary prophecy compare with literature on this subject? What variables are correlated with the practice of prophecy and what is their relationship? What practical-theological understanding can be gained from this study and what are its implications? The study will conduct an empirical-theological examination of the practice of prophecy within the Assemblies of God of Singapore (AGS) to address these questions.

1.3 CONTEXT OF THE STUDY

The beginning of the Pentecostal movement is usually traced back to the revivals that took place globally at the beginning of the twentieth century.[12] Perhaps the most prominent and significant of these revivals were those that occurred at Topeka, Kansas and at Azusa Street in the United States.[13] These revivals were marked by believers seeking a spiritual experience, subsequent to conversion, termed as the Baptism of the Holy Spirit. This experience

---

10. One recent welcome exception is the study by Muindi on the Redeemed Gospel Church in Kenya. See Muindi, "Nature and Significance of Prophecy."

11. Anderson and Tang, *Asian and Pentecostal*, 2–3; Ma and Anderson, "Pentecostals (Renewalists), 1910–2010"; Kay, *Pentecostalism*, 11–15.

12. Anderson, *Introduction to Pentecostalism*, 35–38; Kay, *Pentecostalism*, 42–72.

13. Anderson, *Introduction to Pentecostalism*, 33–35, 39–45; Hollenweger, *Pentecostalism*, 18–24; Synan, *Century of the Holy Spirit*, 39–68. Without seeking to minimize the revivals taking place elsewhere, Kay points out that Pentecostalism spread out globally from the United States through the dynamism of American capitalism and entrepreneurship. This resulted in the increased influence of North American Pentecostalism over the global movement. See Kay, *Pentecostalism*, 25.

was marked by the utterance of tongues or *glossolalia*.[14] The revivals were also characterized by the fervent activity of *charismata* such as prophecy and divine healing. These supernatural phenomena were, in fact, exhibited throughout the New Testament and much of church history.[15] However, the Pentecostal movement has placed far greater emphasis on the activity of the *charismata* than other modern Christian movements.

The Pentecostal movement is commonly categorized into three groups within the literature.[16] Classical Pentecostal churches form the first group and this consists of denominations and churches that originated from the revivals mentioned above at the start of the twentieth century and the subsequent missionary endeavors of these churches. The second group comprises of Charismatic churches within the older, historical denominations which have been impacted by Pentecostal teaching and experience. These churches hold to the Pentecostal emphases of the supernatural activity of the Holy Spirit and the *charismata* while incorporating them into their traditional doctrinal positions. Neo-charismatic churches form the third and largest group. This group includes a wide variety of churches that are independent, indigenous, or part of post-denominational networks. These churches likewise stress the activity of spiritual gifts while placing greater emphasis on "signs and wonders," deliverance, and power encounters. The practice of *glossolalia* is much less emphasized within this last group.

This present study is limited to examining the practice of prophecy within the Assemblies of God (AG) denomination in Singapore. There are various reasons for limiting the scope to this group. First, the AG is the largest, most visible, and well-known Classical Pentecostal denomination in the world.[17] The denomination stresses a supernatural worldview with the activity of miraculous spiritual gifts. The most distinctive characteristic of the AG is its belief in the baptism of the Holy Spirit as a distinct experience, separate and subsequent to conversion, evidenced by the utterance of *glossolalia*.[18] A study on the phenomenon of prophecy within the AG will

---

14. This became the dominant view within Classical Pentecostalism though there are differences within the movement. For a full discussion, see McGee, *Initial Evidence*.

15. Anderson, *Introduction to Pentecostalism*, 19–38.

16. Burgess and Van der Maas, "Introduction"; Synan, *Century of the Holy Spirit*, 8–10. For further discussion on the challenges of classifying Pentecostals, see Anderson, "Varieties, Taxonomies, and Definitions"; Hwa, "Endued with Power."

17. Rodgers, "Assemblies of God," 86; Synan, *Century of the Holy Spirit*, 124. For an extensive history of the Assemblies of God in the United States, see Blumhofer, *Assemblies of God*.

18. Menzies and Horton, *Bible Doctrines*, 123–30; Rodgers, "Assemblies of God," 87; Wyckoff, "Baptism in the Holy Spirit."

contribute to an increased understanding of the theology and practices of this historical movement.

Second, a global perspective on the AG is still lacking. Darrin Rodgers, Director of the Flower Pentecostal Research Center, acknowledges this need when he writes:

> It should be noted that a history or theology of the Assemblies of God from a global perspective has not been written. While most Assemblies of God adherents reside in Third-World nations, scholars lack enough up-to-date information to begin to form a comprehensive picture. Most scholarship, including this brief introduction, relies almost exclusively on Western (North American) sources.[19]

The literature review will later reveal a lack of scholarly studies on the AG in Asia, particularly in the Singaporean context.[20] The few significant studies in Singapore are limited to the history of the movement and there are no known empirical data on the practice of the *charismata*.[21] Furthermore, the AGS has never been investigated from an empirical-theological perspective. This is surprising since the charismatic nature of the AG is its most distinctive feature. Therefore, this study is able to make an original and significant contribution to knowledge through an investigation of prophecy in the AGS. Furthermore, it provides an opportunity for practical-theological reflection and transformation of actual Christian praxis.

Third, the AGS is the main Pentecostal denomination in Singapore.[22] In 2009, the AGS had forty-nine churches with a combined weekly attendance of 21,809 people.[23] The AGS is also one of the largest protestant denominations in Singapore.[24] Hence, the results of this study may be considered as

19. Rodgers, "Assemblies of God," 87.

20. Anderson observes that there is an overall lack of academic studies on Pentecostalism in Asia despite the huge numbers of Pentecostals in the region. See Anderson and Tang, *Asian and Pentecostal*, 3.

21. For historical studies on the AGS, see Abeysekera, *History of the Assemblies of God of Singapore*; Ong, "Historical Analysis of the Factors of Growth." Kay has conducted an empirical study on the growth of Pentecostal churches in Singapore, Malaysia, and Hong Kong. The research includes some data on the AGS and on *charismata* but it is difficult to isolate specific statistics from the data-set. See Kay, "Where the Wind Blows"; Kay, "Empirical and Historical Perspectives"; Kay, "Dynamics of the Growth of Pentecostal Churches."

22. Tan, "Singapore," 224.

23 The Assemblies of God of Singapore, *Directory 2010*, 49.

24. In comparison, the largest protestant denomination in Singapore is the Methodist Church which has forty-four churches, six preaching points, and membership of more than 38,000. National Council of Churches of Singapore, *Guide to Churches and*

representative of Pentecostals in Singapore. Other Charismatic and Neo-charismatic churches in Singapore also believe in and practice prophecy in a manner similar to the AGS. However, they are excluded from this study so as to maintain greater doctrinal homogeneity within the research population.

Fourth, access to data and the feasibility of data collection is an important consideration for empirical studies. The AGS was chosen partly due to the confidence in accessing the research population. There are 341 credentialed workers in the AGS in 2010 and this presents a reasonable population for investigation.[25] A wider research context that includes the AG churches from other Southeast Asian countries would allow for broader generalizations from the empirical data. However, this would bring challenges in data collection and also introduce political, social, and cultural factors into the analysis.

1.4 RESEARCH METHOD

This research is an empirical-theological investigation within the field of practical theology. The study will discuss, augment, and adopt the empirical approach of Johannes van der Ven for its purpose.[26] The approach uses the empirical tools of the social sciences in the service of theology. The endeavor, however, remains wholly theological in that the hypothesis for testing and the subsequent reflection take place within a theological framework. This approach has been successfully employed in other studies in practical theology, examining phenomena such as prophecy, *glossolalia*, and healing.[27] These studies demonstrate that the approach is a valid and accepted method within practical theological research.[28]

Van der Ven's approach centers around the empirical-theological cycle consisting of five phases. These phases are: development of the theological problem and goal, theological induction, theological deduction, empirical-theological testing, and theological evaluation. The approach involves two stages of field investigation. The first stage consists of a qualitative study conducted within the phase of theological induction whereas the second stage involves a quantitative study in the phase of empirical-theological

---

Christian Organisations, 116.

25. The Assemblies of God of Singapore, *Directory 2010*, 49.

26. Van der Ven, *Practical Theology: An Empirical Approach*.

27. Cartledge, *Charismatic Glossolalia*; Friesen, *Norming the Abnormal*; Muindi, "Nature and Significance of Prophecy"; Thomas, "Pathways to Healing."

28. For a discussion on Van der Ven's contribution to practical theology, see Hermans and Moore, *Hermeneutics and Empirical Research*.

testing. The use of both qualitative and quantitative methods as complementary approaches allows the inclusion of both participant and observer perspectives to the research.[29] Furthermore, the use of both induction and deduction addresses the issues of objectivism, positivism, and empiricism.[30] The field of practical theology and Van der Ven's model will be discussed and evaluated in detail in chapter 2. This study will demonstrate that the model is an intradisciplinary approach and will locate the method within a theo-dramatic hermeneutical model.

The research design employed by this study resembles a mixed-method approach commonly utilized in social science studies.[31] In particular, it resembles the sequential exploratory strategy that involves a first stage of qualitative data collection and analysis followed by a second stage of quantitative data collection and analysis. This design is advocated when the primary focus is to initially explore a phenomenon inductively before testing elements of an emergent theory deductively.[32] The design also enables the development of instruments from the qualitative data to enable proper measurement of variables in the quantitative stage. Thus, the research design is justified for the current research study since it seeks to explore the phenomenon of prophecy within a context not found in literature. The initial qualitative study also enables the identification of themes for further exploration in the quantitative study and the development of instruments for measuring prophecy and other variables.

1.5 REFLEXIVITY

The need for the researcher to maintain objectivity is often emphasized in social science research.[33] This requires the researcher to remain detached and distant from the research subject so as not to influence the collection, interpretation, and analysis of data. In reality, however, a researcher will always possess some pre-judgments and presuppositions that affect the research. Furthermore, detached observation may actually limit openness and awareness of the phenomenon under investigation. Van der Ven points

---

29. Van der Ven, *Practical Theology: An Empirical Approach*, 106.

30. Ibid., 114.

31. Creswell, *Research Design*, 211–12. For a discussion on trends in mixed methods research, see Small, "How to Conduct a Mixed Methods Study."

32. Creswell, *Research Design*, 211–12; Small, "How to Conduct a Mixed Methods Study," 67–68.

33. Neuman, *Social Research Methods*, 86; VanderStoep and Johnston, *Research Methods for Everyday Life*, 171–73.

out that empirical theology is often practiced within a commitment to the Christian faith that implies that the researcher is an insider rather than a detached outsider.[34] The researcher is personally affected by the results since the research seeks to transform Christian praxis. Critical realism within empirical theology is noted to be a relational epistemology recognizing the covenantal relationships that humans have with God and with the world.[35] Furthermore, the researcher is often motivated to conduct research due to personal engagement with the issue in ministry. Thus, research methods must critically consider the role of the researcher in the research process.

Swinton and Mowat have emphasized that reflexivity is the most crucial aspect of the research process.[36] They describe reflexivity as critical self-awareness and self-reflection on how the researcher's values, beliefs, and experiences influence and shape the research process. Within the paradigm of critical realism, objectivity and subjectivity should not be viewed as diametric opposites on a continuum. Instead, objectivity in a world mediated through human sense data can only be achieved through authentic subjectivity or reflexivity.[37] This is especially important in qualitative approaches since the researcher functions as the key tool in accessing the meaning and significance accorded to a phenomenon. Therefore, reflexivity is an integral part of research rather than a mere tool. Researchers should make explicit their personal history, presuppositions on the research issue, and reasons for choices made in the research process.[38] This serves to enhance self-awareness and reflexivity in the researcher.

This study was conducted by an ordained minister within the AGS. Hence, the investigation was conducted as an insider rather than as an outsider. This permits greater understanding of AG beliefs and practices and also presents familiarity with the local context of ministry. However, it also presents challenges in ensuring objectivity in the research process. Bracketing was performed to enhance self-awareness and reflexivity in the researcher. Care was taken to ensure that the researcher's personal experience did not form part of the data. Personal, first-hand observation of the phenomenon was excluded from the study so as to reduce the researcher's participation and involvement in the data. Furthermore, the research design

---

34. Van der Ven, *Practical Theology: An Empirical Approach*, 106.

35. Middleton and Walsh, *Truth Is Stranger than It Used to Be*, 168–69; Wright, *New Testament and the People of God*, 45.

36. Swinton and Mowat, *Practical Theology and Qualitative Research*, 59. Also see Dowling, "Reflexivity."

37. Lonergan, *Method in Theology*, 265.

38. Patton, *Qualitative Research and Evaluation Methods*, 66; Swinton and Mowat, *Practical Theology and Qualitative Research*, 61.

opted to conduct the qualitative study before reviewing the extant literature on the subject. This reduces the influence of current literature on the conduct and initial interpretation of the qualitative data.

1.6 OVERVIEW OF THE STUDY

This study proceeds along the five phases of the empirical-theological cycle proposed by Van der Ven. Chapter 1 serves as the introduction to the research study and also explains the purpose of the investigation. This comprises the first phase of theological problem and goal development. The chapter also introduces the research context and the research method that will be employed.

Chapter 2 will discuss the field of practical theology and locate the present investigation within this field. The chapter will then describe the empirical approach of Johannes van der Ven before discussing and evaluating it. This study will adopt a revised empirical approach by augmenting the model with the Chalcedonian pattern and employing a theo-dramatic hermeneutical framework.

Chapter 3 will present the second phase of theological induction. A qualitative study utilizing the case study method will be performed to provide a thick description of prophecy within the AGS. The study will interview ten senior pastors of AGS churches to obtain their understanding of prophecy and how the phenomenon actually occurs within their congregations. The data will then be analyzed to identify themes that can be explored further in the rest of the study.

Chapters 4 and 5 continue the phase of theological induction through an extensive literature survey on the phenomenon of prophecy. The survey mainly focuses on the Classical Pentecostal position and practice of this phenomenon so that this can later be compared with the actual practice in AGS churches. Chapter 4 will focus on the nature and purpose of prophecy while chapter 5 will examine the actual practice of prophecy. The latter chapter will also include psychological aspects of prophecy and prophecy's relation with Pentecostal spirituality.

Chapter 6 deals with the phase of theological deduction and empirical-theological testing. A theological-conceptual model will be proposed based on the data gathered from the qualitative study and the literature review. The chapter will then present the descriptive aims of the quantitative study as well as the theological hypotheses that will be empirically tested. The chapter will continue to describe the process of conducting the quantitative survey of credentialed members of the AGS followed by the results and analysis.

Chapter 7 completes the empirical-theological cycle with the phase of theological reflection. This chapter will draw together all the data from the rest of the study and identify points of convergence that will then be reflected upon in terms of their theological meaning, significance, and relevance to the practice of prophecy. The chapter will also include a reflection and evaluation of the methodology adopted by the study.

2

An Empirical Approach to Practical Theology

2.1 INTRODUCTION

THE PRESENT STUDY IS an exercise in practical theology. This chapter aims to critically discuss and present the empirical approach adopted. The chapter seeks to do this in three main sections. The first section describes the field of practical theology by considering the relationship between theory and practice within theology. The second section summarizes the empirical approach of Johannes van der Ven, describing its basis, assumptions, and methodological aspects. The chapter moves to a third section which evaluates Van der Ven's approach and makes proposals for a revised empirical approach which this study will adopt. It will show that this empirical approach is a viable proposal to conduct practical theological research.

2.2 THE FIELD OF PRACTICAL THEOLOGY

Practical theology has been described as "a place where religious belief, tradition and practice meets contemporary experiences, questions and actions and conducts a dialogue that is mutually enriching, intellectually critical, and practically transforming."[1] It is a field which has seen considerable at-

---

1. Woodward, Pattison, and Patton, *Blackwell Reader in Pastoral and Practical Theology*, 7.

tention and growth through the last century. Activity and discussion has focused on its identity as a discipline, its place in the theological encyclopedia, its subject field, its main tasks, and how it should be practiced.[2] This section will seek to give a brief overview of the development of practical theology in recent history. The intent is to subsequently locate empirical theology within the field of practical theology and hence it will not seek to be an exhaustive survey of the developments within this field.

2.2.1 The Practical Nature of Theology

The early church was noted to possess a two-fold understanding of theology.[3] The first sense was that it concerned the *habitus* of believers; their worldview and orientation towards God, others, and the world. Believers' lives and practices were thus determined by this orientation. The second sense of theology was then directed towards forming this *habitus* within believers. The social setting for theological activity within Christian congregations also led to its focus on the practical needs for the Christian life. However, theological activity in the West subsequently shifted to a university setting resulting in questions surfacing about the identity of theology as a practical discipline. Thomas Aquinas viewed theology primarily as a speculative, theoretical science which was practical only in its application and this view gradually became the predominant position within universities in the West.[4]

The position that theology was primarily a theoretical science was subsequently challenged by theologians such as Duns Scotus. Scotus understood theology as concerned with the highest good and ultimate goal of life—God. In addition, Scotus held that theology must include the practical means toward reaching this goal and hence theology was *scientia practica*.[5] Following in this tradition, Martin Luther viewed theology as a practical discipline whereas the conception of it as merely speculative "belongs with the devil in hell."[6] Luther's understanding was that the proper study of theology was not God but rather the relationship between God and humanity. In discussing the nature of theology, Ballard and Pritchard have argued for theology to be considered a descriptive, normative, critical, and apologetic

---

2. For an overview of the developments within practical theology, see Maddox, "Practical Theology"; Dingemans, "Practical Theology in the Academy."
3. Maddox, "Recovery of Theology," 651.
4. Pannenberg, *Theology and the Philosophy of Science*, 232.
5. Ibid., 233.
6. Ibid., 235.

activity.[7] They point to Anselm's definition of theology as *"fides quaerens intellectum"* (faith seeking understanding) as encapsulating its nature, emphasizing that faith requires thought and explanation. Flowing from this understanding of the practical nature of theology, there cannot be a sharp divide between knowledge and action, theory and practice, the academic and the practical.

The practical focus and nature of theology brings into question the proper relationship between theory and practice. How are these two aspects related? Does theological theory guide Christian praxis or is the relationship governed in the opposite direction? Or should the relationship be understood as a dialectic? This question forms a central concern within practical theology and will be considered next.

2.2.2 Theory and Praxis

2.2.2.1 Human Action as Praxis

This section seeks to determine the proper relationship between theological theory and human action but first an appropriate understanding of human action must be established. Within practical theology, the term "praxis" is sometimes preferred over "practice."[8] The issue is that "practice" is often understood to focus on technical ability or skill and neglects the intent or theory behind and within the action. Within the study of practical theology, actions cannot be conceived as devoid of theory and hence Aristotle's understanding of human action may prove beneficial for consideration.

Aristotle distinguishes between three activities by which humans relate to the objective world and gain understanding.[9] The first activity is *theoria* which describes the speculative activity of non-engaged reflection. Next is *poiesis* which is knowing that comes from the activity of making or producing. The third is *praxis* which concerns rational and purposeful human activity within the social situation from which understanding arises. *Praxis* thus includes both action and reflection intertwined together; it is reflective-action. Browning highlights the importance of acknowledging our actions as theory-laden when he writes:

> All our practices, even our religious practices, have theories behind and within them. We may not notice the theories in our practices. We are so embedded in our practices, take them so

---

7. Ballard and Pritchard, *Practical Theology in Action*, 13.
8. Forrester, *Truthful Action*, 7; Groome, *Christian Religious Education*, 152.
9. Groome, *Christian Religious Education*, 152–77.

much for granted, and view them as so natural and self-evident that we never take time to abstract the theory from the practice and look at it as something in itself.[10]

This understanding of human actions as value and theory-laden is an important foundation within practical theology. Actions must not be studied as mere methods to carry out a task or to perform a skill. The theories and intentions behind and within the actions must be discerned and critically examined. Within this study, the terms "practice" and "praxis" will be used interchangeably to refer to theory-laden human action.

2.2.2.2 Relationship between Theory and Praxis

The theory-praxis relationship is complex and has been discussed elsewhere in relation to practical theology.[11] These discussions are based on a five-fold typology of theory-praxis relationships and this proves useful in classifying and examining various approaches within practical theology.[12] These theory-praxis paradigms will be briefly described followed by a description of how practical theology has evolved through its understanding of the theory-praxis relationship.

The first paradigm is where theory precedes praxis. This position sees that theory consists of truth and insight obtained independently from praxis. Once the theory is properly formulated, it then determines right praxis. Praxis is treated as the application of theory and becomes subordinate to it. Within this paradigm, praxis is not seen as a source of truth.

The second paradigm is where praxis precedes theory. This approach reduces theory to extrinsic reflection on praxis and assumes that theory is devoid of eternal truth. Instead, theory undergoes a constant revision in line with reflection upon contemporary praxis in its varied contexts. Forrester and Heitink observe this paradigm contains Marxist elements and assert that some social scientists operate within this paradigm.[13]

The third paradigm is described as the primacy of faith-love and is developed from Karl Barth's neo-orthodoxy. It stresses that Christian faith-love should be distinguished from mere human theory-praxis and that they

---

10. Browning, *Fundamental Practical Theology*, 6.

11. Fowler, "Practical Theology and Theological Education"; Groome, "Theology on Our Feet"; Parker, *Led by the Spirit*.

12. Lamb, *Solidarity with Victims*. Lamb develops his typologies from the basic models of contemporary theology put forward by Tracy. See Tracy, *Blessed Rage for Order*.

13. Forrester, *Truthful Action*, 26; Heitink, *Practical Theology*, 152.

should never be identified with each other. Neither theory nor praxis is understood to be normative. Instead, this view holds the revelation of Jesus Christ as the only source of theological understanding and that both theory and praxis are grounded within God's Word in revelation.[14]

The fourth paradigm may be termed critical theoretical correlation. It seeks the critical theoretical correlation of truth found within the Christian tradition and the exigencies of theory and praxis in history.[15] This approach seeks to take seriously both theory and practice, considering each of them as essential and important to theology. However, the approach still leads with theory in that it sees theory as the foundation for praxis.

The fifth theory-praxis paradigm is critical praxis correlation. Similar to the previous approach, this approach seeks to take seriously both theory and praxis as essential partners within theology. However, the approach draws from liberation theology in placing an emphasis on praxis by viewing historical praxis as the grounds for theorizing. Praxis is thus both the goal of theory as well as its foundation. Critical correlation should then occur at the level of praxis rather than the level of theory in the previous model.

2.2.2.3 Approaches to Practical Theology

Groome notes that the various theory-praxis models just described approximately trace the historical development of practical theology.[16] The paradigm where theory is accorded primacy over praxis is most often associated with Friedrich Schleiermacher, the "Father of Modern Theology." His conception of practical theology inadvertently turned it into applied theology and is historically significant due to its dominance in seminaries and the church till today. While at the University of Berlin, Schleiermacher set out to establish the position of theology amongst the academic disciplines of the university. His understanding of theology is laid out in his classic book *Brief Outline on the Study of Theology*.[17] Schleiermacher conceived of three levels within theological studies, namely, philosophical theology, historical theology and practical theology. His intent was to present the equal partnership of these three levels and to stress the necessary relationship between them. This relationship is likened to a tree where philosophical theology formed the roots, historical theology the trunk, and practical theology the crown of

---

14. Groome, "Theology on Our Feet," 64.
15. Fowler, "Practical Theology and Theological Education," 48.
16. Groome, "Theology on Our Feet," 65.
17. Schleiermacher, *Brief Outline on the Study of Theology*.

the tree.[18] Practical theology was thus seen as drawing from the insights of philosophical and historical enquiry and applying their fruit to the task of church leadership. This linear relationship between practical theology and philosophical and historical theology fits into the model of theory preceding praxis. The inherent weakness of this model is that it reduces praxis to technical skill of application and suggests that theory has nothing to learn from practice. In any case, Schleiermacher succeeded in securing theology as an academic discipline within the German University and resulted in the Berlin model of theological education as his legacy.

The model of applied theology that resulted from Schleiermacher produced two unfortunate results.[19] The first problem was that it resulted in a division between theory and practice. Theology became divided into speculative enquiry and practical application similar to the view held by Aquinas. While Schleiermacher's intent might have been to present the equality of philosophical, historical, and practical theology, it in fact led to the subordination of practical theology to the other two. Only philosophical and historical enquiries were understood to produce theological understanding whereas practical theology had nothing to contribute. Schleiermacher declares: "It is not among the aims of practical theology to teach the right conception of these tasks. Rather supposing this, it has only to do with the correct procedures for executing all the tasks which are to be included within the notions of 'Church leadership.'"[20] This led to a boundary being drawn between supposedly academic disciplines of systematic theology, biblical studies, historical studies, and the practice of the church that formed practical theology. Practical theology turned into pastoral theology, concerned with the formulation of ministerial "rules of art."[21]

The second problem was that the association of practical theology with church leadership meant it was a concern primarily for clergy. The focus became the professional equipping of ministers for preaching, worship, education, and pastoral care. This established the clerical paradigm within practical theology. Schleiermacher espouses this clerical paradigm when he writes:

> The purpose of leadership in the Christian Church is to hold the various concerns of the Church together and to build on them further, both in a comprehensive as well as in a concentrated way. The knowledge concerning this activity forms a kind of

18. Paver, *Theological Reflection*, 9.
19. Maddox, "Practical Theology," 60.
20. Schleiermacher, *Brief Outline on the Study of Theology*, 92.
21. Ibid., 93.

technology which, in combining all its different branches, we designate as practical theology.[22]

As a result, laity were rarely concerned with practical theology since it seemed the domain of the ordained. Its relegation to Christian instruction on ministry skills led to questions over its rightful identification as an academic discipline. It seemed to be a mere appendix at the end of the theological encyclopedia. The disembodiment of theory from practice further resulted in a sense that theology was irrelevant to the daily life of believers.

The paradigm of theory preceding praxis seems inadequate as it does not take into consideration the notion of praxis as value and theory-laden. It does not consider the complexity of the present situation in its application of theory and does not acknowledge praxis as a source of understanding. Historically, it created a disembodiment of theory and praxis and introduced the clerical paradigm. Hence there is a need to better define the theory-praxis relationship.

The second theory-praxis paradigm seeks to correct the first paradigm's low view of praxis. It is essentially a linear model like the first paradigm and has gained popularity in a pragmatic age. It is often associated with liberal socio-political reform and also with radical Marxist revolutionary praxis.[23] Forrester notes that Metz, Moltmann, and Marx affirm praxis as the ultimate criterion of theology and faith.[24] However, he criticizes this paradigm for suggesting that theory is able to arise somewhat spontaneously and effortlessly from human activity. Groome further levels three criticisms against this model.[25] First, it assumes that Christian tradition has nothing to contribute to theological understanding. Second, it ignores God's on-going revelation within history and, third, the approach refuses to value past theory that has arisen out of praxis. The inadequacy of this paradigm suggests that neither theory nor praxis can be held as precedent over each other. Instead, it suggests that a dialectic relationship best holds both theory and praxis in tension.

The fourth and fifth paradigms are the most contemporary and significant to the discussion of this study. Both see theory and praxis as mutual partners in the theological process and demand a critical correlation between Christian truth and contemporary praxis. The work of David Tracy and Don Browning are commonly considered as examples of the paradigm

---

22. Ibid., 25.
23. Pilario, *Back to the Rough Grounds of Praxis*, 264.
24. Forrester, *Truthful Action*, 26.
25. Groome, "Theology on Our Feet," 64.

of critical theoretical correlation.[26] Tracy's approach is itself developed from the correlational method of Paul Tillich.[27] Tillich holds that existential questions that emerge from common human experience may be correlated with answers provided by the Christian message.[28] Thus, questions that arise out of human praxis should find their answers in the theological theories drawn from Scripture and tradition. Unlike Tillich, Tracy sees both Christian texts as well as common human experiences as legitimate sources for theology. He acknowledges Tillich's significant contribution but criticizes the insistence that questions arise solely from human experience and answers may be found only within the Christian message. To Tracy, Tillich's method was "juxtaposition" and not "correlation."[29] Instead, Tracy contends that questions and answers may be found within both Christian texts and human experiences. His method is then to critically correlate the principal questions and answers from both these sources and describes his approach as a revised correlational method. Applying his method to practical theology, Tracy arrives at the following definition: "Practical theology is the mutually critical correlation of the interpreted theory and praxis of the Christian faith with the interpreted theory and praxis of the contemporary situation."[30]

Browning follows after Tracy in applying this revised correlational approach to theology.[31] Like Tracy, Browning sees the hermeneutical nature of all theology in that it seeks to correlate the pole of interpretation of Christian scripture and tradition with the pole of interpretation of the current cultural experience. He describes his approach as praxis-theory-praxis, moving from "present theory-laden practice to a retrieval of normative theory-laden practice to the creation of more critically held theory-laden practices."[32] Browning argues that all theology is fundamentally practical, beginning and ending in practical concerns. All theological disciplines (descriptive theology, historical theology, systematic theology, and strategic practical theology) then become sub-movements within the theological process.[33] In this approach, the classical church disciplines of preaching, education, pastoral care, and liturgy are found within the sub-movement of "strategic practical theology." He advocates a focus on theological ethics to

26. Browning, *Fundamental Practical Theology*; Tracy, *Blessed Rage for Order*.
27. Tillich, *Systematic Theology*.
28. Ibid., 62.
29. Tracy, *Blessed Rage for Order*, 46.
30. Tracy, "Foundations of Practical Theology," 76.
31. Browning, *Fundamental Practical Theology*.
32. Ibid., 7.
33. Ibid., 8.

guide strategic practical thinking; most notably positing five dimensions of practical moral reasoning.[34]

John Swinton and Harriet Mowat provide a more recent model of practical theology which uses Tracy's revised correlational method.[35] They cite the Wesleyan quadrilateral of Scripture, tradition, experience, and reason as possible sources of theological understanding. Applying Tillich's method would then see questions raised by human experience and reason finding answers in Scripture and Christian tradition. Swinton and Mowat have likewise noted the weaknesses in this approach as it seemingly prevents experience and reason from questioning interpretations of truth from Scripture or Christian tradition. Thus, they turn to Tracy and argue for a mutual critical correlation between the poles of Scripture and tradition and the poles of experience and reason. For them, practical theology serves to mediate between these poles resulting in practical theology taking the form of "critical, theological reflection on the practices of the Church as they interact with the practices of the world, with a view to ensuring and enabling faithful participation in God's redemptive practices in, to and for the world."[36] Their approach emphasizes practical theology as transformative action which enables Christian praxis of individuals and communities to be transformed to be ever more faithful.

Rebecca Chopp has strongly criticized the critical theoretical correlation paradigm of practical theology.[37] In particular, she disagrees with the assumption by Tracy and Browning of a universal unity between individuals and tradition and the belief that human experience may be reconciled to reality through understanding. Instead she asserts that when critical theoretical correlation speaks of the source of experience, it elevates the religious experiences of certain groups above others, claiming these experiences to be universal. Likewise, the approach uses select Christian texts favored by certain groups as sources of theology. For Chopp, the end result is inevitably that the agenda of white, educated, male theologians are given pre-eminence above others.[38] Chopp insists that a hermeneutic of suspicion should be brought to critically analyze theoretical formulations and the Christian tradition. Drawing from liberation theology, her solution is to propose a critical praxis correlation in line with the fifth paradigm of

---

34. The five dimensions are (1) the visional level (2) the obligational level (3) the tendency-need or anthropological dimension (4) the environmental-social dimension, and (5) the rule-role dimension. Ibid., 71.

35. Swinton and Mowat, *Practical Theology and Qualitative Research*.

36. Ibid., 6.

37. Chopp, "Practical Theology and Liberation."

38. Ibid., 130.

theory-praxis relationships. This would include the questioning of ideological presuppositions within traditional interpretations of Scripture as well as intrinsic religious experiences.[39] Her approach also holds a commitment to a critical theory of emancipation and works towards a social theory to transform praxis; a commitment that is much in line with liberation theology from which she draws much of her understanding and motivation.[40]

Chopp finds the past understanding of praxis as intentional human actions as too narrow. Praxis, to her, should be expanded to include the complex web of social interactions, thus moving the loci of practical theology beyond the clerical and church paradigms. Praxis then includes the struggle against oppression and theology is understood to guide this emancipatory praxis. Theology is viewed as possessing an emancipatory goal and the dialogue and critical correlation is not a rational dialogue between academic disciplines but rather a critical correlation of the emancipatory praxis of theology and the emancipatory praxis of real movements and communities. Groome provides this useful summary of critical praxis correlation:

> Authentic Christian praxis demands engagement in the historical struggles for conversion and transformation, both social and personal. Such emancipatory praxis is the locus for authenticating and reformulating theory which must be held in a dialectical unity, or critical correlation with praxis.[41]

Thus, the locus of practical theology grows outward from the praxis of the pastor to include praxis within the church, and enlarges even further to include the praxis of the church within society.[42]

2.2.2.4 Evaluation

The following points now emerge from the preceding discussion. The first conclusion is that practical theology involves a dialectical relationship between theory and praxis. The emergence of the fourth and fifth paradigms have helped to correct the problems caused by Schleiermacher's model of applied theology. They raise the position of praxis such that it is no longer subordinate to theory but rather an equal and mutual interlocutor. These paradigms also recognize that theory and praxis are necessarily intertwined in a dialectical relationship, informing, corroborating, and transforming

39. Ibid., 122.
40. Ibid., 132.
41. Groome, "Theology on Our Feet," 65.
42. Van der Ven, "Practical Theology: From Applied to Empirical Theology," 11–12.

each other. Perhaps the best representation of the dialectic between theory and praxis is the hermeneutical spiral.[43] This spiral begins within the praxis situation where experiences become the objects of reflection on theological theories. These theological theories are themselves recognized as the product of past theory-praxis reflection. These theories are then found to be inadequate within the contemporary situation which leads to a critical questioning and analysis of the sources of these theories. Such critical engagement produces fresh insight and a revision of the theories. This revision also initiates a renewal of the praxis of faith so as to be faithful to the revised theories. Further questions will surface out of the renewed praxis situation which again forces a reconsideration of the theological theories. The process proceeds forward in this hermeneutical spiral resulting in an increase in theological understanding as well as the increased faithfulness of Christian praxis.

The dialectical theory-praxis relationship requires an openness within theology to question interpretations of the Bible that have been handed down and to challenge past theological formulations. Scripture and tradition have to be re-read and re-interpreted in the context of questions arising within contemporary praxis. Understanding that practical theological reflection proceeds forward along this hermeneutical spiral has led to the use of the pastoral cycle as a heuristic tool for "doing" practical theology.[44] Liberation theology has further influenced the pastoral cycle by incorporating a three-step "see-judge-act" approach within the cycle. Here "seeing" is defined as socio-analytical mediation, "judging" as hermeneutical mediation, and "acting" becomes practical mediation.[45] In contrast, Swinton and Mowat conceive of the pastoral cycle in four stages.[46] The first stage is pre-reflective and involves naming the current praxis requiring reflection and asking what initially appears to be going on. The second stage is cultural and contextual analysis which seeks to delve deeper into the complex dynamics of the situation for a fuller understanding. This may involve the use of other non-theological disciplines to study Christian praxis within the situation. Theological reflection forms the third stage where there is intentional reflection on the theological significance of information gleaned. Previous theological understanding may become challenged or transformed at this point. The last stage is where a revised form of praxis is formulated in response

---

43. Forrester, *Truthful Action*, 28–31; Heitink, *Practical Theology*, 151–54.

44. Ballard and Pritchard, *Practical Theology in Action*; Lartey, "Practical Theology as a Theological Form"; Swinton and Mowat, *Practical Theology and Qualitative Research*.

45. Boff and Boff, *Introducing Liberation Theology*, 24.

46. Swinton and Mowat, *Practical Theology and Qualitative Research*, 94–97.

to the dialectical conversation between theory and praxis in the previous stages. This revised praxis is again subjected to subsequent examination and reflection that will then yield further revision. Practical theology may thus be understood to proceed along this spiral of activity as a critically dialectic engagement between theory and praxis.

The second conclusion that may be drawn from the discussion is on the hermeneutical nature of practical theology. Scripture, tradition, and human experiences all serve as texts that need to be interpreted. In fact, it may be possible to say that all theology is essentially hermeneutical in nature. The paradigm of theory-to-praxis emphasized the interpretation of the pole of Scripture and tradition to formulate idealistic and timeless truths to be applied to all situations regardless of the context of time and culture. What is lacking is a critical, systematic, and disciplined interpretation of the pole of the present situation and praxis. The evolution of practical theology now demands a hermeneutic of situations be added to the theological reflection process. It must be recognized that Christian faith exists within situations and believers respond out of their interpretations of both the situation and their understanding of Scripture. Osmer notes this development has led to the recognition of humans as "hermeneutical beings" constantly interpreting and making sense of their daily experiences.[47] Boff adds to this consideration when he notes that all theology has been mediated by experience, culture, philosophy, and reason.[48] This implies that theology needs to interact with other disciplines, especially the disciplines of the social sciences so that better interpretations of contemporary and historical contexts may be made.

It is with this understanding of the necessity of studying contemporary situations and praxis that empirical research within theology makes a significant contribution. Empirical methods provide theology with the much-needed tools to describe, explain, and evaluate situations and religious experiences.[49] The issue arising will then be how exactly empirical methods are to be used in the service of theology. What ought to be the relationship between the disciplines of theology and the social sciences? This study will now proceed to consider an empirical approach to practical theology that fully embodies the dialectical relationship between theory and praxis as well as the hermeneutical nature of practical theology.

---

47. Osmer, *Practical Theology*, 20–23.
48. Boff and Boff, *Introducing Liberation Theology*, 24–25.
49. Van der Ven, *Practical Theology: An Empirical Approach*, 20.

2.3 THE EMPIRICAL THEOLOGY OF JOHANNES VAN DER VEN

Johannes van der Ven was the Professor of Empirical Theology at the University of Nijmegen in the Netherlands and previously served as the President of the International Academy of Practical Theology. Van der Ven has proposed an empirical approach to practical theology that has greatly impacted the field of practical theology and it is this approach that this study seeks to examine and adopt.[50]

Van der Ven notes the dialectical relationship between theory and praxis and likewise sees the relationship as a hermeneutical spiral.[51] This leads him to conclude that empirical-theological research is essential to investigate the praxis at hand. To this end, he argues that theology should embrace empirical tools and methods in much the same way that it has embraced literary methods in biblical studies, philosophy in systematic theology, and historical methods in historical theology.[52] Conceived in this way, practical theology uses empirical means to formulate, explore, analyze, and corroborate theological hypotheses formulated from human experiences and interpretations of religious texts. These experiences, interpretations, and religious practices are themselves examined empirically so that an accurate description and understanding may be reached of what is actually taking place.[53]

Van der Ven further notes the hermeneutical nature of practical theology, stressing that empirical research needs to be carried out within an empirical frame of reference. Drawing from Jürgen Habermas,[54] he maintains that all praxis is hermeneutic-communicative in nature and sees this in all functions of the church.[55] Van der Ven's empirical approach will be presented in detail in the following section.

2.4 HERMENEUTIC-COMMUNICATIVE PRAXIS

Van der Ven elaborates on the hermeneutic-communicative character of praxis in his work *Practical Theology: An Empirical Approach*.[56] He uses the

50. Van der Ven, *Practical Theology: An Empirical Approach*.
51. Van der Ven, "Practical Theology: From Applied to Empirical Theology," 13.
52. Ibid., 14.
53. Van der Ven, *Practical Theology: An Empirical Approach*, 20.
54. Habermas, *Theory of Communicative Action*.
55. Van der Ven, *Practical Theology: An Empirical Approach*, 41–44.
56. Van der Ven, *Practical Theology: An Empirical Approach*.

term "hermeneutic-communicative" to refer to the "verbal and non-verbal interpretation of written and spoken texts and their verbal and non-verbal communication."[57] As already mentioned, Van der Ven sees this occurring within all the basic functions of the church and so he concludes that this forms the basis for all praxis within practical theology.

Hermeneutic-communicative praxis may also be understood as linguistic praxis in the sense of Habermas's theory of communicative action. For Habermas, communicative action is mutually meaningful interaction by which people communicate their goals, negotiate their aims, and coordinate their actions. Habermas categorized this communication to include validity claims to truth (facts), rightness (norms), and authenticity (feelings). The aim of communicative action is to arrive at consensus whereby the hearer understands and tacitly accepts the speaker's validity claims resulting in coordination of action between speaker and hearer. However, if the hearer rejects the speaker's validity claims, the parties enter into discourse where the speaker's claims are subjected to discussion and critique so that the parties can negotiate a rationally motivated consensus. Communicative action takes place within the sphere of what Habermas has termed the lifeworld. This lifeworld forms the social background for daily encounters between people and includes shared assumptions and common knowledge. The lifeworld supports communicative action while communicative action feeds back into the repository of shared meanings in the lifeworld. Habermas further distinguishes action oriented towards success as instrumental and strategic action in contrast with communicative action that is oriented towards shared understanding. Strategic action takes place in the sphere of the system which represents structures within society and established patterns of instrumental action.

Van der Ven thus understands hermeneutic-communicative interaction to be the basis of all praxis within practical theology. Praxis is seen as religious communication which comprises the three validity claims as religious assertions, moral judgments, and intersubjective expressions.[58] He posits that it is within this hermeneutic-communicative action and discourse that humans formulate, reflect, and interpret their own discourse arriving at meaning and understanding.[59] Considered in this manner, theology becomes a critical theory of action and explains the reasons why people choose certain actions or courses instead of others.[60]

57. Ibid., 41.
58. Ibid., 16.
59. Ibid., 46.
60. Heitink, *Practical Theology*, 135–37.

Van der Ven builds on this concept of hermeneutic-communicative praxis to propose that it is characterized by a normative and eschatological aspect.[61] The normative aspect is defined by the principles of equality, freedom, universality, and solidarity. The eschatological aspect is conceived as praxis seeking to realize the possibility and potential of the future while possessing a critical memory of the past. He grounds his proposal theologically by turning to the *basileia* symbol in the praxis of Jesus described in the gospels.[62] He maintains that the normative principles of hermeneutic-communicative praxis are embodied within this eschatological symbol. This symbol bears multiple meanings and serves to evoke "an intense experience of God's being as king."[63] Hence, he understands the symbol to function as a source of inspiration to believers, stirring commitment, engagement, and participatory praxis. In this way, Van der Ven transforms the *basileia* symbol into a meta-ethical criterion to assess the success and failures of human communication.

2.4.1 Empiricism in Theology

After establishing the hermeneutic-communicative nature of praxis within practical theology, Van der Ven proceeds to present his empirical approach.[64] Firstly, he sees empirical theology attempting to describe and explain hermeneutic-communicative praxis. Description here involves identifying the characteristics of the praxis through categorizing concepts and tracing the relationships between these characteristics whereas explanation attempts to determine the cause and results of the relationship. In this way, empirical theology may be seen as analogous to the historical-critical approach in biblical studies.[65] Just as historical-critical exegesis is used as a tool to analyze Scripture, empirical-critical methods are used as a tool to analyze actual Christian praxis.

Van der Ven does not see empirical theology ending at mere description and explanation. Instead, he suggests that empirical theology further seeks to investigate and change praxis. This change is not of an incidental nature due to the effect of the investigation but rather he sees empirical theology seeking to intentionally initiate change within the framework of the investigation. Thus, Van der Ven sees empirical theology as a transforming

61. Van der Ven, *Practical Theology: An Empirical Approach*, 59–69.
62. Ibid., 69–76.
63. Ibid., 69.
64. Ibid., 77–87.
65. Ibid., 18.

activity which seeks to identify obstacles in hermeneutic-communicative praxis and transcend these limits toward the normative and eschatological perspectives he has posited.

Van der Ven defines the direct object of empirical theology as hermeneutic-communicative praxis. This is in contrast with others, like Tillich, who suggest the direct object of theology is God and therefore beyond analytical-empirical examination.[66] Van der Ven concedes that the transcendent God is indeed beyond empirical observation and therefore contends that God is only accessible through faith. He argues that God is the direct object of faith and faith is the direct object of theology. In this formulation, faith, and specifically hermeneutic-communicative praxis, may be studied through empirical means and hence an empirical approach to theology is justified.

The principle of falsification as opposed to verification is used by Van der Ven in his proposal.[67] This principle involves the formulation of research hypotheses and null hypotheses. A research hypothesis is corroborated when the null hypothesis is tested empirically and proved false. Conversely, a research hypothesis is weakened, though not necessarily disproved, if the null hypothesis is proved true. Such an approach avoids claiming that causal relationships are empirically observable; the hypothesis of a causal relationship is only corroborated and strengthened but never absolutely proved. Furthermore, Van der Ven's method uses data obtained inductively to formulate the theological theories and hypotheses that are then tested deductively through the falsification of the null hypotheses. The use of induction and deduction avoids the problematic claim to derive universal truth from specific cases.

2.4.2 Epistemological Concerns

Van der Ven discusses at length the way in which an empirical approach in theology should be epistemologically structured.[68] First, he considers the monodisciplinary model. He describes this model as applied theology where theories formulated from systematic and historical theology are applied within practical theology to concrete, present-day situations. In this sense, the monodisciplinary model is much the same as the theory-praxis paradigm discussed earlier where theory precedes praxis. This model may

---

66. Ibid., 81, 102–3.
67. Popper, *Logic of Scientific Discovery*.
68. Van der Ven, *Practical Theology: An Empirical Approach*, 89–112.

be suitable for simple social and church situations but is rejected in the complex, pluriform situations that are actually found in reality.

The multidisciplinary model is assessed next. This approach sees various disciplines studying a problem independently of each other and applying their own theories, concepts, and methods in investigation. Van der Ven sees this model as essentially a model with two phases. In the first phase, social scientists conduct empirical research to obtain data before the data is passed on to the second phase where theologians evaluate and critically reflect on the results within a theological framework. The weakness of such a model is that theology becomes overly dependent on research done by the social sciences and inadvertently becomes subordinate to social science. The relationship between theology and social science is also not well defined and so the transition in analysis and interpretation between the two phases is problematic. Furthermore, there is an issue on the criteria to be used for theological reflection on social science data and how this might actually take place.

Van der Ven moves on to consider the interdisciplinary model next. This model assumes and stresses mutual interaction and reciprocity between different disciplines. He likens the interdisciplinary model to be a parallel dialogue even as the previous multidisciplinary model may be likened to a series of monologues occurring in sequence. Interdisciplinary interaction may be understood as taking place either as an intrapersonal dialogue within the same person or as interpersonal dialogue between theologians and social scientists. Intrapersonal dialogue requires the researcher to adopt and be conversant in two sets of paradigms, methods, and techniques from two different disciplines so that the work produced could be equally accepted in two academic arenas. This, however, is a challenge for researchers who are traditionally equipped and adept in only one discipline. A further issue arises in deciding if research hypotheses should be evaluated by theological or social-scientific criteria, or perhaps even by both criteria. As an alternative, interpersonal dialogue seems promising but the challenge rests with the willingness of interlocutors to be open to mutual criticism. Van der Ven sees a lack of this openness in both theologians and social scientists alike.

Finally, Van der Ven arrives at the intradisciplinary model, which is the approach he advocates. This approach requires theology itself to become empirical and to embrace empirical methods and techniques. He defines the intradisciplinary approach as the "borrowing of concepts, methods, and techniques of one science by another and the integration of these elements into the other science."[69] Van der Ven justifies this approach by arguing

69. Ibid., 101.

that other sciences have used intradisciplinary approaches as exemplified in sciences such as biochemistry (biology and chemistry) and sociolinguistics (sociology and linguistics). He further notes that theology already displays this approach in integrating philosophy, psychology, linguistics, literary criticism, and historical criticism within itself. Thus, the adoption of empirical methods to the range of tools and techniques within theology should not be deemed unusual.

2.4.3 The Empirical-theological Cycle

The proposal by Van der Ven centers around an empirical-theological cycle developed from the four phases of the experience cycle.[70] The first phase of this experience cycle is perception where the person receives the influence of the environment through the human senses. The second phase is experimentation and describes the response of the person in testing various courses of action upon the environment. This is followed by the examination phase where the person investigates the extent these actions have on various effects. The last phase is assessment where value and meaning are ascribed to the experiments. These four phases may be categorically analyzed but are actually indivisible from one another. Together, they form a complete experience cycle that leads on to a spiral of further experience cycles bringing about the experience process.

Van der Ven builds an empirical-theological cycle based on the four phases of this experience cycle and adds a fifth phase at the beginning. This first phase is the development of the theological problem and goal. It is followed by induction, deduction, testing, and evaluation, which correspond respectively to perception, experimentation, description, and assessment within the experience cycle. The empirical-theological cycle likewise forms a spiral where evaluation may lead to the development of a further theological problem. The cycle corresponds with the hermeneutical spiral described earlier along which practical theology is understood to proceed along. It recognizes the dialectic between theory and praxis and holds them as mutually critical partners in the research process. The empirical-theological cycle has also been compared to the pastoral cycle as an action-reflection model beginning in the concrete reality of a situation.[71] Thus, the empirical-theological cycle serves to augment the pastoral cycle and provides a critical, disciplined, and systematic method of engaging in practical theology.

70. Ibid., 112–13.
71. Cartledge, *Practical Theology*, 20–22.

The five phases of the empirical-theological cycle will be briefly surveyed next. The first phase is the development of the theological problem and goal.[72] Theological problems under research should concern hermeneutic-communicative praxis since this was established as the direct object of empirical theology. To clarify again, faith is expressed within hermeneutic-communicative praxis and God is seen as the direct object of faith. Thus hermeneutic-communicative praxis of faith serves as the object, goal, and condition of empirical theology. It is considered a necessary condition since the researcher's participation in hermeneutic-communicative praxis is essential for proper understanding and testing.

The second phase of the cycle is induction. Van der Ven outlines this phase to consist of the dialectic between theological perception and reflection, and the formulation of the research question.[73] Theological perception recognizes that facts are always perceived within a framework of reference and never free from theory. Thus, the research needs to consider the distinctions between random and systematic perception, participatory and non-participatory observation, overt and covert assessment, and the researcher's perception of others and of self. Theological reflection interacts with perceptions acquired and requires the researcher to have a grasp of relevant theoretical literature as well as relevant empirical studies. This knowledge is essential in guiding the dialectic in perception and reflection. In formulation of the research question, the researcher uses the criterion of relevance in terms of scientific and practical value and considers how researchable the phenomenon is. This determines the form the research should take, ranging from descriptive to explorative to hypothesis-testing.

The third phase of the cycle is known as theological deduction.[74] Within this phase, the researcher moves from theological conceptualization to determination of the theological-conceptual model and finally theological operationalization. Proper conceptualization ensures that theories are logically consistent and that theory statements are mutually independent. It also requires theories to contain sufficient information yet not be superfluous. The theological-conceptual model contains concepts or variables, relationships between them, and the research unit. This model will then determine the subsequent operational method and analytical technique. It is important that the causal relationships proposed within the model are grounded in theological literature as it is these relationships that will be empirically tested. Operationalization is then necessary to transform the

---

72. Van der Ven, *Practical Theology: An Empirical Approach*, 119–20.
73. Ibid., 120–28.
74. Ibid., 128–39.

theological concepts into operations that can be observed and measured. Instruments and empirical-theological scales must be chosen or developed to measure these concepts.

The fourth phase of the cycle is empirical-theological testing.[75] This involves collection of data through various relevant means in accordance with the operationalization of the research. This is normally performed on a sample of the research population so consideration should be made on whether the sample is random, systematic, stratified, two-stage, or two-phase. Next, data obtained is entered, checked, and cleaned so that the data set is prepared for the empirical-theological analysis. This analysis includes describing the research population, constructing theological and attitudinal scales, determining the holders of these theological attitudes as well as the context, and finally explanation.

The last phase of the cycle is theological evaluation.[76] Theological interpretation, reflection, and methodological reflection make up this phase. Interpretation takes the research results and places them in a theological context in order to answer the research question. The meaning, significance, and relevance of these results must be reflected upon as well as the adequacy of executing the study. Theological-methodological reflection completes the phase and examines the methodological presuppositions and theological framework that was formulated in the earlier phases of research.

The proposal by Van der Ven for an empirical-theological cycle uses both induction and deduction and is careful in addressing the objections of objectivism, positivism, and empiricism.[77] Objectivism is avoided through the inclusion of an inductive phase where data is allowed to speak for itself and the researcher uses intuitive perception in the formulation of theological theories. Positivism asserts that data is collected without an interpretive framework. This does not apply to Van der Ven's proposal since the empirical-theological testing occurs within a framework of interpretation developed in the third phase. Lastly, the cycle concludes with theological evaluation where data are placed within a broader theoretical framework. This avoids giving exclusive power to empirical data and addresses the objection of empiricism.

---

75. Ibid., 140–51.
76. Ibid., 152–56.
77. Ibid., 114.

2.5 AN EVALUATION AND PROPOSAL

Van der Ven has made a significant contribution to theology through his proposal of empirical theology as practical theology. While this contribution is acknowledged, this study seeks to critically evaluate the approach and to make suggestions to enhance it. In particular, the intradisciplinary model of empirical theology and its hermeneutical approach will be discussed. The epistemology of empirical-theological research will also be considered.

2.5.1 Discussion on Intradisciplinary Model

The intradisciplinary model proposed by Van der Ven is both praised and criticized by Ruard Ganzevoort.[78] Ganzevoort acknowledges that Van der Ven's method presents a unique proposal for dialogue with the empirical methods of social science. The discussion above explained the rejection of the monodisciplinary model where practical theology amounted to nothing more than applied theology. The interdisciplinary model then seeks a proper integration of theology and social science but this is difficult to achieve in either the interpersonal or intrapersonal model. Van der Ven contends that the intradisciplinary model is the best option where theology becomes empirical and embraces the empirical methods of social science.

Ganzevoort notes that this innovative approach correctly identifies and insists on the use of appropriate non-theological disciplines to critically examine actual praxis. However, the approach also dramatically reduces theology's dialogue with social science and hence the complexity and issues inherent in such a dialogue. As Ganzevoort points out: "The obvious yet stunning effect of this [Van der Ven's] approach is that dialogue with social scientists becomes almost as absent as in monodisciplinarity."[79] As an example, Ganzevoort considers Van der Ven's work on suffering and theodicy and claims that the theoretical framework for his research is mainly based on systematic theology; little dialogue takes place with social science concepts such as religious coping. Thus, Ganzevoort sees Van der Ven's intradisciplinary model as another form of monodisciplinarity. Ganzevoort clarifies that he uses monodisciplinarity here to refer to a lack of integration of theology with social science. In his opinion, the mere use of social science methods does not constitute an adequate integration though their use is essential and important to theology. This differs from Van der Ven's defi-

---

78. Ganzevoort, "Van Der Ven's Empirical/Practical Theology and the Theological Encyclopaedia."

79. Ibid., 63.

nition of monodisciplinarity which is used to describe practical theology's subordination to systematic theology. Nevertheless, Ganzevoort calls for a clarification of Van der Ven's monodisciplinary model:

> On the level of a particular discipline, monodisciplinarity and intradisciplinarity are alike. It seems to me that Van der Ven's rejection of monodisciplinarity could gain strength when these two issues are distinguished: 1) practical theological discourse does not depend on systematic theological discourse, and 2) the appropriate methods for practical theology are empirical.[80]

Ganzevoort continues in his critique to acknowledge that Van der Ven does dialogue with social science at the level of meta-theory when he uses the theory of Jürgen Habermas. However, when the research moves into the phase of theological deduction, the discussion appears mainly centered within theological disciplines with little dialogue with the social sciences. Ganzevoort summarizes his view on the approach as follows:

> It seems then that Van der Ven employs a somewhat hidden four-level approach. On the level of metatheory, he follows social-scientific and philosophical theories. On the level of content, he is clearly involved in systematic theology. On the level of research, he employs empirical methods but makes less use of social scientific concepts or of the critical contribution social scientific theories might offer. On the level of praxis, Van der Ven merges social-scientific and theological categories.[81]

Thus, it may be said that while the research approach uses empirical methods, this does not represent an engagement with social science concepts.

Ganzevoort's criticism may be somewhat harsh since Van der Ven's intradisciplinary model does not claim to be a full integration of theology and social science. His critique of interdisciplinarity has highlighted his focus on seeing empirical theology accepted within theological circles rather than within the disciplines of the social sciences. The definition of Van der Ven's intradisciplinary model as earlier stated was the "borrowing of concepts, methods and techniques of one science by another and the integration of these elements into the other science."[82] It does not suggest that he seeks theology to fully adopt or adapt social science concepts into itself. Furthermore, Van der Ven does propose dialogue with social science theories in the

---

80. Ibid., 64.
81. Ibid., 65.
82. Van der Ven, *Practical Theology: An Empirical Approach*, 101.

phase of theological induction.[83] The requirements of theological reflection demand that the researcher be familiar with the theoretical and empirical literature of the relevant social sciences. This leads to the formulation of the theological question and thus further influences theological deduction.

Ganzevoort's criticism does, nevertheless, raise a pertinent issue on Van der Ven's approach. While Van der Ven makes a significant contribution in his proposal of empirical theology, he does not adequately discuss how theology and the social sciences should interact and relate to each other. He obviously sees value in social science research in the phase of theological induction and this was already described and noted. However, he does not address how concepts and empirical studies from the social sciences should influence the formulation of the research question. Would the social sciences be able to challenge accepted theological understanding? How should the fruit of disciplines such as sociology and psychology inform, influence, and challenge theology? Swinton and Mowat ask the question in this way: "How can a system of knowledge created by human beings challenge a system of knowledge that claims to be given by God?"[84] This issue will be considered in the next section.

2.5.1.1 *The Chalcedonian Pattern*

This study suggests that the Chalcedonian pattern, as used by Deborah van Deusen Hunsinger and James Loder, can enhance and augment the empirical approach of Van der Ven.[85] The approach applies the theological method of Karl Barth and is used for interdisciplinary discussions within pastoral counseling[86] and theological anthropology;[87] specifically, the relationship between theology and psychology. The approach may easily be extended to the relationship between theology and social sciences and hence to interdisciplinary discussions within the wider field of practical theology.[88] This study will first describe the Chalcedonian pattern then consider how D. Hunsinger and Loder have applied it in their respective fields of study.

The Chalcedonian definition describes the nature of Jesus Christ as completely God and completely human. It depicts Christ's divinity

---

83. Ibid., 124.
84. Swinton and Mowat, *Practical Theology and Qualitative Research*, 83.
85. Hunsinger, *Theology and Pastoral Counseling*; Loder, *Logic of the Spirit*.
86. Hunsinger, *Theology and Pastoral Counseling*.
87. Loder, *Logic of the Spirit*.
88. Mikoski, "Educating and Forming Disciples"; Osmer, *Practical Theology*; Swinton and Mowat, *Practical Theology and Qualitative Research*.

and humanity united together "inconfusedly, unchangeably, indivisibly, inseparably."[89] Divinity and humanity are found in hypostatic union within Christ, both natures fully engaged with each other yet maintaining their integrity without diminishing the other's nature. The Chalcedonian pattern has been noted to have greatly influenced the character of Karl Barth's Christology.[90] Barth expresses the relation of the two natures in Christ as "indissoluble differentiation," "inseparable unity," and "indestructible order."[91]

Indissoluble differentiation describes the two natures related without confusion or change. It stresses the necessity to clearly distinguish between these natures such that their integrity is maintained and neither one is subordinated to the other. Inseparable unity emphasizes that though the two natures are to be differentiated, they remain without separation or division from one another. Christ had two natures but only one hypostasis. Indestructible order underscores the asymmetry present in the relationship where Christ's divinity bears logical priority over His humanity. This does not suggest a hierarchical order since a hierarchy presupposes the two natures could be measured on some form of the same scale and would ignore the radical otherness of divinity.[92] G. Hunsinger provides an understanding of "logical priority" by turning to the definition of Susan Hurley:

> A conceptual account of X is an account of what we mean, understand, and intend ourselves to be talking about when we talk or think about X. If X is not correctly thus accounted for in terms of Y, then X is conceptually independent of Y; if Y is accounted for in terms of X, where X is not in turn accounted for in terms of Y, then X is both conceptually prior to and independent of Y.[93]

G. Hunsinger takes "X" to stand for the divine nature and "Y" to stand for the human nature, concluding that Christ's divinity takes logical priority and His humanity takes logical subsequence. The use of priority-subsequence again emphasizes their differentiated unity and does not subordinate the human nature to the divine.

Both D. Hunsinger and Loder have applied this understanding of the Chalcedonian pattern to their fields of study. Now that this pattern has been

---

89. Grudem, *Systematic Theology*, 1169.
90. Hunsinger, *How to Read Karl Barth*, 85; Hunsinger, *Disruptive Grace*, 131–47.
91. Barth, *Doctrine of Creation*, 437.
92. Hunsinger, *How to Read Karl Barth*, 286–97.
93. Hurley, *Natural Reasons*, 10.

described, interdisciplinary discussions such as the relationship between theology and psychology can be considered next.

2.5.1.2 The Approach of Deborah van Deusen Hunsinger

Deborah van Deusen Hunsinger is from the field of pastoral counseling and keenly feels the disjunction and disconnect between theology and psychology within her field. She may be said to exemplify a person operating within Van der Ven's category of an interpersonal model of interdisciplinarity where the researcher seeks to become conversant in two different academic disciplines. Due to the very nature of pastoral counseling, it is essential for practitioners to receive training and be competent in theology as well as in psychology.

D. Hunsinger speaks for her field in articulating the challenge of resolving conceptually how pastoral counseling can be both authentically theological as well as scientifically psychological as a discipline.[94] The importance and efficacy of both disciplines are appreciated yet their interpretive frameworks do not seem to allow for compatibility. Theology and psychology appear logically diverse yet necessarily connected within pastoral counseling. To resolve the disconnect, D. Hunsinger turns to Barth's theological method in applying the formal pattern of Chalcedon. She proposes the relationship between theology and psychology at the theoretical level to be "without separation or division, without confusion or change, and with the conceptual priority of theology over psychology."[95] To use Barth's terms, theology and psychology are related in indissoluble differentiation, inseparable unity, and indestructible order. It is important to point out that this approach uses the Chalcedonian pattern and not the Chalcedonian definition as a guide for interdisciplinary discussion. The pattern merely provides the form for characterizing the relationship and does not draw on the substantive definition of Chalcedon. Likewise, it is appropriate to say her approach draws from Barth's theological method rather than from Barth's theology itself.

D. Hunsinger uses Barth's discussion of the healing of a paralytic in Mark 2 as an illustration of the Chalcedonian pattern, particularly the concept of logical priority.[96] The paralytic in the Mark 2 narrative receives both physical healing as well as forgiveness of his sins. Barth sees that healing and forgiveness occur in differentiated unity in this case. They are in unity

---

94. Hunsinger, *Theology and Pastoral Counseling*, 2.
95. Ibid., 10.
96. Ibid., 65–67.

since healing serves as a sign to point to Jesus's authority to forgive sins. Yet, the two are also clearly distinguishable from each other.[97] The sign of healing points to the forgiveness of sins but forgiveness does not point to healing. From the perspective of faith, healing (the sign) finds its significance in the forgiveness of sins (the thing signified), but forgiveness does not find its significance in healing. Applying the definition of Hurley stated earlier, forgiveness of sins is understood to be logically prior and healing is logically subsequent. Thus, from a Barthian standpoint, this example shows that healing and salvation are in differentiated unity and asymmetrically ordered with salvation logically prior to healing.

In similar manner, the Chalcedonian pattern can be applied to theology and psychology or extended to other interdisciplinary discussions.[98] Theology and psychology are independent disciplines with concepts from each discipline existing within their own interpretive frameworks and bearing independent meaning. However, within pastoral counseling and from a Barthian perspective, the two disciplines exist in indissoluble differentiation, inseparable unity, and indestructible order with theology taking logical priority over psychology. Indissoluble differentiation emphasizes the importance of differentiating between concepts of different disciplines and not confusing them. Concepts cannot be simply translated back and forth without a loss of meaning and significance. A theological concept like "sin" cannot be understood psychologically as "neurosis" and "salvation" cannot be substituted with "health." Neurosis is located in an immanent order whereas sin is of the transcendent order.[99] Instead, the relationship between concepts of different disciplines is analogical and should not be confused with equivalence.

Inseparable unity implies that theological and psychological perspectives cannot be fully separated from each other though they are clearly distinguishable. Humans are psychological beings created to have a relationship with a divine God and so both theological and psychological perspectives are needed for completeness. For instance, the psychological concept of neurosis is ultimately grounded in the theological concept of sin and cannot be understood apart from it in matters of faith.

Indestructible order stresses their asymmetrical relationship with theology taking logical and ontological priority over psychology. This is

---

97. Barth comments on Mark 2: "The forgiveness of sins is manifestly the thing signified, while the healing is the sign, quite inseparable from, but very significantly related to, this thing signified, yet neither identical with it, nor a condition of it." Barth, *Doctrine of the Word of God*, 189.

98. Hunsinger, *Theology and Pastoral Counseling*, 68–75.

99. Ibid., 75–76.

because, from the perspective of faith, psychological concepts find their ultimate significance in theology but the reverse relationship is not true. The aspect of healing possesses meaning at the psychological level but points to and finds ultimate significance in salvation at the theological level. Hence, asymmetry implies that concepts in psychology must be properly placed in the overarching context of Christian theology.[100]

The proposal by D. Hunsinger provides a useful compass by which interdisciplinary discussions may be navigated.[101] It uses the explicit pattern of thought in Barth's theology and presents a means of thinking clearly about interdisciplinary endeavors. This proposal is used by Swinton and Mowat in applying the revised critical correlational method and in justifying the use of qualitative research methods in practical theology.[102] Osmer also notes the possibility of this approach in guiding interdisciplinary discussions within the wider field of practical theology.[103]

The proposal by D. Hunsinger echoes the third theory-praxis paradigm of the primacy of faith-love. The stress is on the non-identity between theology and human sciences which is seen in the characteristic of indissoluble differentiation. Thus, even when seeking to operate within the fourth paradigm of critical theoretical correlation, the relationship is limited to an analogous one so that concepts are not simply translated between the two disciplines, again emphasizing the radical otherness of divinity and theological concepts. Mutual interaction and critique between theology and the human sciences is permitted but the feature of indestructible order underscores that this exchange is asymmetrical within the perspective of faith as theology takes the position of logical priority.

A possible objection to the approach proposed by D. Hunsinger arises when the Barthian opposition to natural theology is considered.[104] Barth's objection apparently rules out all independent human means of knowing God apart from God's divine revelation within his theological framework. Such a position would apparently rule out the possibility of the human sciences contributing to theological endeavors due to their secular and independent framework. The disconnect between Barth and the human sciences are noted by D. Hunsinger.[105] Even though D. Hunsinger claims only to use

---

100. Hunsinger, "Interdisciplinary Map for Christian Counselors," 225.
101. Hunsinger, "Interdisciplinary Map for Christian Counselors."
102. Swinton and Mowat, *Practical Theology and Qualitative Research*, 83–91.
103. Osmer, *Practical Theology*, 168–69.
104. McGrath, *Scientific Theology: Nature*, 268–71.
105. D. Hunsinger describes the disconnect between Barth and psychology in this manner: "Barth took a rather dim view of what Jung valued so highly as 'immediate religious experience.' No way exists from our religious experiences to God, be they ever

Barth's theological method and not his theology, it would still seem at odds with Barth to apply his method to argue for the underlying unity of theology with human sciences. To resolve this issue, this study turns to the work of James Loder and his approach to interdisciplinarity.

2.5.1.3 The Approach of James Loder

James Loder presents another interdisciplinary approach, which turns to the theological method of Karl Barth but interpreted through Thomas Torrance.[106] The Barthian rejection of natural theology is fully recognized though it is also argued that the rejection appears grounded in Barth's linking of natural theology with human autonomy in wanting to know God on humanity's own terms. Barth's preeminent concern is that the only way to know God is in God's self-revelation in Jesus Christ. This point is noted by Torrance who counters that Barth does not actually reject the existence of natural knowledge of God, only the independence and self-sufficiency of such a discipline.[107] Hence, Torrance proposes that the relationship between natural theology and revealed theology be understood as analogous to the relationship between geometry and physics.

Three-dimensional geometry developed by Euclid serves as a foundational presupposition within the classical Newtonian world.[108] In this world, all physics is understood to operate and be bound by this well-defined space. However, Einstein's theory of relativity changed this understanding. Time and space are not separate entities in the Einsteinian universe but rather form a space-time continuum that is influenced by the attractive force of bodies of mass such as gravity. Within this Einsteinian universe, Euclidean geometry cannot be accepted as an uncritical presupposition like it is within the classical Newtonian world. Physical space is incorporated within physics and hence geometry "is transformed by being moved from an unexamined presupposition about where physics took place into being a sub-science of the inner rational structure of physics."[109] Geometry is thus

---

so sublime, Barth maintained, but only from God to us—in any of our life experiences, be they ever so ordinary or mundane . . . our knowledge of God is always somehow mediated through Jesus Christ as attested by Scripture." Hunsinger, *Theology and Pastoral Counseling*, ix.

106. Loder, *Logic of the Spirit*.

107. Torrance, "Problem of Natural Theology." Also see McGrath, *Scientific Theology: Nature*, 280–86.

108. O'Murchu, *Quantum Theology*, 26.

109. Loder, *Logic of the Spirit*, 32.

transformed from an independent discipline apart from physics into an integral sub-science within physics.

Torrance applies the geometry-physics analogy and substitutes natural theology for geometry and revealed theology for physics. He then argues that natural theology must move from being an independent discipline apart from God's self-revelation to be transformed into a sub-science of revealed theology, becoming part of its inner intelligibility. Barth apparently approved of Torrance's argument, which gives Torrance justification in claiming Barthian support for natural theology as an important and integral part of Christian theology.[110]

Loder follows after Torrance in applying this analogy to theology and human sciences.[111] Just as geometry becomes a sub-science within quantum physics, Loder sees the human sciences transformed into sub-sciences within theology. Loder makes three clarifications about his method. First, the transformation should seek to ensure the integrity of both disciplines but will involve the abandoning of presuppositions within human sciences that implicitly reject theological concerns and explanations. Second, the Chalcedonian pattern provides the method with its formal structure and credibility. Third, like D. Hunsinger, the relationship between theology and human science is characterized by indissoluble differentiation, inseparable unity, and indestructible order with the logical priority of theology.

Loder's proposal addresses the concern raised earlier in using Barth's theological method to relate theology and natural science in differentiated unity. It also contributes the concept of transforming human sciences into sub-sciences in the service of theology. In addition, Osmer describes the Chalcedonian approach as a transformational model of cross-disciplinary dialogue between the interlocutors of theology and human science.[112] Languages contain their own unique grammar and vocabulary and similarly, disciplines contain their own concepts, assumptions, and methods. The challenge in translating one language to another is apparent since the terms and concepts within one language often do not have an exact equivalent in another language. Since language functions as symbols of understand-

---

110. Torrance describes Barth's approval of his method in this account: "However, instead of rejecting natural theology *tout court*, Barth has transposed it into the material content of theology where in a changed form it constitutes the epistemological structure of our knowledge of God. . . . Karl Barth expressed full agreement with my interpretation of his thought, and said, rather characteristically, of the relation of geometry to physics, 'I must have been a blind hen not to have seen that analogy before.'" Torrance, *Space, Time and Resurrection*, x.

111. Loder, *Logic of the Spirit*, 36–37.

112. Osmer, *Practical Theology*, 167–70.

ing within a culture and worldview, translation includes the difficulty of navigating between different worldviews. Care should then be taken in interdisciplinary dialogue to avoid reductionism by taking terms and concepts from one field and simply translating them to another field. Instead, the understanding gleaned from one academic discipline needs to be transformed when placing it in the context of a different discipline. Researchers must then be "bilingual" so that they may appropriately draw from the perspectives of both theology and the human sciences.

This study suggests that the Chalcedonian pattern enhances and augments the empirical theology of Van der Ven in at least two ways. First, it provides clarity for conducting the second phase of the empirical-theological cycle. Van der Ven describes the need for the researcher to have a good grasp of relevant academic and empirical literature within theology and the social sciences. The Chalcedonian pattern justifies this need to be well versed with the human and social sciences like psychology and sociology as their underlying unity with theology must be recognized. Nevertheless, the Chalcedonian pattern also assists the researcher to think of this unity as a necessarily differentiated unity and so prevents reductionist translations of concepts from one discipline into the other. At the same time, the Chalcedonian pattern demands a transformation of social science, negating its limitations and rejection of the divine, and placing it within the overarching context of theology. Practical theology holds a commitment to faith and so within this context, theology takes logical priority over social sciences and the asymmetrical relationship must be respected.

The Chalcedonian pattern further guides the researcher in the final phase of theological evaluation. Van der Ven stresses the need for theological interpretation within this phase since the analytical data obtained from empirical-theological testing do not themselves answer the theological question or resolve the theological problem.[113] The Chalcedonian pattern may usefully guide this interpretation and guard against faulty translation. Indeed, the influence of the Chalcedonian pattern should pervade all phases of the empirical-theological cycle though its influence may be more pronounced within the second and final phases. To paraphrase D. Hunsinger, the practical significance of the Chalcedonian pattern is that it requires practical theologians to distinguish among the modes of academic discourse, neither to confuse them with one another, nor to separate them from one another, and yet also to understand the spiritual reality as the overarching context into which other perspectives are finally placed.[114]

---

113. Van der Ven, *Practical Theology: An Empirical Approach*, 152.

114. Hunsinger, *Theology and Pastoral Counseling*, 96.

The use of the Chalcedonian pattern also avoids the problems of the model of mutual critical correlation between theology and social science where both disciplines are granted equal importance in the research process. Such a model would lead to the concern expressed earlier of theology being challenged at the fundamental level by a system of knowledge created by humans.[115] This study asserts that the relationship is asymmetrical with theology occupying logical priority over other academic discourse especially at the fundamental level of, say, the reality of God or the divine revelation of Scripture. Some may see this approach as "Christological imperialism" but it would be necessary within practical theology which adopts a commitment to Christian faith.[116] The desire is to accord theology some level of primacy within matters of faith without trumping other disciplines. The more pertinent issue with this position is that practical theologians must remain open and self-aware of their theological commitments drawn from human interpretations limited by humanity's fallen state, cultural context, and human agendas.[117] This is where the research enables critical reflection, dialogue, correction, and growth within the body of theological knowledge.

Second, the Chalcedonian pattern enhances Van der Ven's intradisciplinary proposal where theology embraces empirical methods and techniques. From Loder's perspective, these empirical methods and techniques may now be said to be transformed into sub-sciences within the discipline of theology. Empirical methods become part of the inner structure and intelligibility of theology. The concern that surfaces is that empirical methods of qualitative and quantitative analysis are recognized as research tools of social science and therefore embody secular assumptions and presuppositions which are at best methodologically agnostic and at worst methodologically atheistic.[118] This concern in embracing such methods within theology is then addressed through Loder's concept of transformation. Implicit rejection of divine causes or theological realities must be negated so that these empirical methods may serve the concerns and goals of theology.

This study appreciates the use of the metaphor of conversion in employing social science methods to aid theology.[119] Conversion suggests the laying aside of autonomy and freedom and so these empirical methods lay aside their methodological presuppositions to accept a theistic reality and to serve the missional goals of theology within this world. However, it must

---

115. Swinton and Mowat, *Practical Theology and Qualitative Research*, 83.
116. Loder, *Logic of the Spirit*, 37.
117. Swinton and Mowat, *Practical Theology and Qualitative Research*, 89.
118. Furseth and Repstad, *Introduction to the Sociology of Religion*, 198.
119. Swinton and Mowat, *Practical Theology and Qualitative Research*, 92–93.

also be recognized that the conversion is not merely one-sided but rather occurs in both conversational partners. Van der Ven's empirical approach is a call for the conversion of practical theology so that it is transformed into empirical theology. Hence, practical theologians are likewise transformed as they learn empirical methods of research and dialogue with social science disciplines. The integration provided for in the Chalcedonian pattern is then not limited to theoretical integration between academic disciplines but also in integrating diverse disciplinary perspectives and methods within researchers themselves as they become "bilingual" in the "languages" of two disciplines. This is not to claim that empirical theology follows an interdisciplinary model since the concerns of Van der Ven towards this were already articulated. The intradisciplinary model still seems the best as it captures the transformation and conversion taking place in the application of the Chalcedonian pattern.

The concept of transformation and the embracing of empirical sub-sciences further prevent the issue of a two-phase multidisciplinary model. As mentioned earlier, such a model sees social scientists conducting empirical research then passing this data on to theologians for critical reflection within a theological framework. This model would result in theology becoming overly dependent on research done by social science and further throws up issues on how theological issues may be researched within the presuppositions of a social science framework. Van der Ven's proposal augmented with the Chalcedonian pattern transforms social science and its methods into sub-sciences within theology. Hence, the entire research project takes place within a theological framework while allowing for mutual critical exchange between theology and its dialogue partner.

2.5.2 Discussion on Hermeneutical Approach

2.5.2.1 *The Hermeneutical Framework of Van der Ven*

The description of the empirical-theological cycle earlier did not fully examine the means of evaluating empirical research in relation to a theological framework. Van der Ven has elsewhere discussed his approach for this task.[120] He sees two aspects of evaluation in relation to theological statements and evaluation in relation to faith statements. He borrows from Pannenberg in differentiating between theological and faith statements by viewing theological statements as always hypothetical and testable in principle.[121] The

---

120. Van der Ven, "Empirical or a Normative Approach."
121. Ibid., 120.

evaluation of research results in relation to theological statements involves a mutual critical interaction, both interlocutors serving to "enrich, augment, purify, or even correct" one another.[122] This aspect of evaluation occurs in the last phase of theological evaluation as the researcher attempts to answer the research question.

Van der Ven describes a further evaluation needed that is the evaluation of the research results in relation to faith statements. This involves establishing the relationship between people's beliefs revealed in the research and the Christian *sensus fidei* within the community. Such an evaluation necessitates a hermeneutical model in treating Scripture, which serves as the foundation for Christian beliefs.

Van der Ven follows after Boff in examining and rejecting the hermeneutic of the "text/application model" and "correspondence of terms model" in favor of a "correspondence of relations model."[123] The latter model involves a "relationship of relationships" where the relationship between Scriptural texts and their contexts is related to the relationship between current texts and their contexts. This may be schematized with the equation "Scripture : its context = ourselves : our contexts" where the equation may be read forward or backward, stressing the dialectical hermeneutic. Thus, Boff does not reduce Scripture to mere formulas and techniques that can be copied and applied in the present context. Instead, he advocates the view that believers ought to develop a hermeneutic competency from Scripture and so obtain a Christian manner or style for Christian living. Boff explains:

> We need not, then, look for formulas to "copy," or techniques to "apply," from scripture. What scripture will offer us are something like orientations, models, types, directives, principles, inspirations—elements permitting us to acquire, on our own initiative, a "hermeneutic competency," and thus the capacity to judge—on our own initiative, in our own right—"according to the mind of Christ," or "according to the Spirit," the new, unpredictable situations with which we are continually confronted. The Christian writings offer us not a *what*, but a *how*—a manner, a style, a spirit.[124]

Building on this understanding, the emphasis is placed on the formation of a hermeneutic *habitus* rather than the immediate practical application of Scripture. Boff further makes a qualification in his approach stressing that

---

122. Ibid.
123. Ibid., 121–24; Boff and Boff, *Introducing Liberation Theology*, 142–50.
124. Boff and Boff, *Introducing Liberation Theology*, 149. Italics in original.

Scripture remains the "norming norm" in the dialectical hermeneutic so that relativism is avoided.[125]

Van der Ven obviously draws much from liberation theology, which includes the work of Boff. This may explain his openness to methods drawn from the social sciences even as liberation theology draws from sociology, economics, and politics for its agenda.[126] This approach also accounts for his stress on the concrete situation as the context for theological reflection and the emphasis on praxis as the methodological starting point. However, praxis within liberation theology is primarily oriented to a Marxist analysis of society that seeks the transformation of communities as its goal.[127] Praxis is understood as social class struggle against oppression via economic and political systems. Within liberation theology, praxis forms the first act or "mediation" whereas theology occupies the second act.[128] A Marxist pre-understanding undergirds the first act and this ideological commitment may not be adequately critiqued from the Christian viewpoint.

Boff's hermeneutic model must also be understood in the context of the hermeneutical mediation that forms the second act. The overall theological commitment is to God's preferential option for the poor and Scripture is generally read and interpreted in the light of an emancipatory social ethic.[129] While appreciating the value of liberation theology to Pentecostal praxis, Peterson summarizes its negative implications as follows:

> Such [unacceptable implications] include the poor being the initial and often the only point of involvement; the use of social scientific analysis that adopts a Marxist ideology, a situational hermeneutic that can so easily result in a "fast and loose application" of the scripture to context; and a pastoral action that can resort to violence as its attempts to make structural change in "*la realidad.*"[130]

The criticisms raised are neither to deny nor negate the significant contribution that liberation theology has made to illuminate the "blind-spots" of evangelical theology. However, evangelicals remain largely critical of the hermeneutical style of liberation theology.[131]

---

125. Ibid., 136, 150.
126. Ibid., 24–32, 51–62; Conn, "Theologies of Liberation," 398–400.
127. Grenz and Olson, *20th Century Theology*, 220–21.
128. Ibid., 219.
129. Ibid., 218; Pixley and Boff, *Bible, the Church and the Poor*.
130. Peterson, "Kingdom of God," 55–56.
131. Henry, "Liberation Theology and the Scriptures."

2.5.2.2 An Evangelical Proposal

Due to the issues raised regarding Van der Ven's hermeneutic framework, it seems best to propose a different framework for empirical theology. One such proposal is put forward by Cartledge in his research on Charismatic *glossolalia*.[132] In particular, he criticizes Van der Ven for the manner in which *basileia* is used as an empowering symbol for liberating praxis, observing that this bears similarity to the style of liberation theology.[133] Cartledge's solution is to propose an alternative hermeneutical framework for empirical theology that he sees as evangelical-charismatic.[134] He develops his proposal from the thought of Anthony Thiselton and N. T. Wright.[135]

Thiselton follows after Habermas's model of linguistic and behavioral interaction in developing a socio-critical hermeneutic to pastoral theology.[136] He describes the concepts of lifeworld and system and their relationship as follows:

> The life-world belongs to the *hermeneutical level of interpersonal understanding and co-operative behavior*. . . . But the hermeneutical dimension cannot operate at the level of *psychosocial critique*: for this, a standpoint is demanded in which *contextual-behavioral features are transcended in a larger system*. System provides a frame or *dimension for ideological and social critique*.[137]

The lifeworld and system are not to be confused and also not to be de-coupled from each other. The system provides the necessary critique of the lifeworld so that constraints and distortions may be identified and transcended.

Thiselton sees the love of God expressed in the cross and resurrection of Jesus Christ as the system that provides the socio-critical criterion.[138] He explains:

---

132. Cartledge, *Charismatic Glossolalia*.

133. Cotterell describes liberation theology's hermeneutic in this manner: "According to liberation theology the approach to the word must take second place to a consideration of the human context . . . . Thus the environment sets the agenda for any theology, and the theology will produce the symbolism which may in turn supply the power to the people to transform the environment." Cotterell, *Mission and Meaninglessness*, 251.

134. Cartledge, *Charismatic Glossolalia*, 17–22.

135. Thiselton, *New Horizons in Hermeneutics*; Wright, "How Can the Bible Be Authoritative?"; Wright, *New Testament and the People of God*.

136. Thiselton, *New Horizons in Hermeneutics*, 604–11.

137. Ibid., 388. Italics in original.

138. Ibid., 611–19.

> In this sense, the cross and resurrection stand not only as a critique of human self-affirmation and power, but also a *meta-critique which assesses other criteria, and which transforms the very concept of power*. The power of the cross lies *precisely not in rhetorical self-assertion or manipulation* (I Cor. 2:1–5). . . . The power of the cross does *not lie in what merely overwhelms us as impressive* (II Cor. 8 through to 13). It is *power in weakness* (I Cor. 1:23–25) because it is derived from "a Christ crucified" (I Cor. 1:23). *It revaluates self-affirming, manipulative, dominating power as self-destructive.*[139]

The context for this criterion is found in the meta-narrative of Scripture. While the cross and resurrection remain the focus, the rest of Scripture cannot be ignored as they speak of all that God wants to do in and through Jesus Christ. Thus, Cartledge contends that Scripture takes the position of the transcontextual system that mutually critiques and interacts with the lifeworld which is the present context of Christian praxis.[140] Empirical methods and techniques serve as tools to research, analyze, and describe praxis within the lifeworld. In this sense, Scripture, as the transcontextual system, provides the understanding of what praxis should be. Empirical theology then focuses on the dialectical relation between what praxis is and what it should be.[141]

This study finds Cartledge's proposal to be useful as a framework for empirical research. In addition, it notes that Kevin Vanhoozer develops a similar hermeneutical approach but to a much greater depth and extent.[142] This study will develop its framework from Vanhoozer while integrating the insights of Cartledge.

2.5.2.2.1 Vanhoozer's Proposal

Vanhoozer assesses the current state of theology and perceives it as captive "to a debilitating dichotomy between theory and practice."[143] He diagnoses an "ugly ditch" between theory and practice and likewise an "ugly ditch" between exegesis and theology. His proposal seeks to restore the practical na-

---

139. Ibid., 615. Italics in original.
140. Cartledge, *Charismatic Glossolalia*, 19.
141. Van der Ven, "Practical Theology: From Applied to Empirical Theology," 18.
142. Vanhoozer, *Drama of Doctrine*. Vanhoozer's work has already influenced the development of Pentecostal theology. See Archer, *Pentecostal Hermeneutic*; Clifton, "Spirit and Doctrinal Development"; Yong, *Hospitality and the Other*.
143. Vanhoozer, *Drama of Doctrine*, 3.

ture of theology and to establish an understanding of doctrine as "direction for the fitting participation of individuals and communities in the drama of redemption."[144] This is accomplished through a reorientation of theology away from mere theoretical knowledge and towards practical wisdom. His basis is the description in John 14:6 of Jesus as "the way and the truth and the life" and suggests that this speaks of theology's basic orientation.[145] A preoccupation with "the truth" has led the church to perceive theology as mere theory. On the other hand, an over-emphasis on "the way" and "the life" breeds pragmatism. Therefore, a proper focus on all three is needed so that theology fosters "truthful ways of living." Theology at work in the church should then produce reflexive practitioners who embody Jesus today—"the way, the truth, and the life in new situations."[146] It is this emphasis on the practical nature of theology that makes his proposal particularly constructive for practical theology. Vanhoozer engages both theology as *scientia* as well as *sapientia* to create a conducive foundation for an empirical approach to practical theology.

Vanhoozer applies the metaphor of drama to theology and makes this the central perspective along which his proposal develops. The use of drama as a metaphor within theology is not new and has been variously explored.[147] Applying this metaphor to Christian life, the world is seen as a theatre and all humanity is caught up in a divine theo-drama that is not of their creation. God the Father is analogous to the playwright and producer, Jesus to the lead actor, and the Holy Spirit to the director, thus emphasizing the Trinitarian nature of the proposal.[148] Scripture constitutes the first four acts of the play and the church lives today within the fifth act, performing the faith till the consummation of history.

The use of drama and narrative emphasizes the continuity of both divine and human action within Scripture and throughout history, and the church's role in the dramatic realization of the future. This role is definitely real and divinely accorded and Christian life becomes a living performance that embodies theological truth even as it faithfully continues from canonical truth. The stress is on the practical nature of theology with its goal oriented around truthful living. As a result, this perspective attempts to bridge the "ugly ditches" described earlier. This proposal is much in line with

144. Ibid., 102.
145. Ibid., 12–15.
146. Ibid., 105.
147. For example, see Balthasar, *Theo-Drama*; Bartholomew, *Drama of Scripture*; Wells, *Improvisation*; Wright, "How Can the Bible Be Authoritative?"
148. Vanhoozer, *Drama of Doctrine*, 106.

2.5.2.2.2 ROLE OF SCRIPTURE: CANONICAL SCRIPT

Vanhoozer spends much effort in discussing the nature of Scripture and its role to his theo-dramatic proposal. One important issue he raises is the rejection of a hermeneutical model that reduces Scripture to a set of propositions.[150] Boff's hermeneutic described earlier had likewise discarded the "text/application model," which is basically a propositionalist model. This propositionalist approach discounts figurative language and mines narratives for propositional nuggets, thus reducing the entire genre of Scripture into cognitive assertions.[151] The unfortunate result of this approach is to effectively de-dramatize Scripture and to emphasize doctrine as cognitive assertions that are to be affirmed. This approach fails to recognize the full significance of God's creative communication through Scripture's various genres and, in some sense, contributes to the divide between theory and praxis.

Vanhoozer's solution is to propose a post-propositionalist theology where "post" is not taken as "against" but rather beyond.[152] To be clear, Vanhoozer affirms that Scripture contains propositions as well as propositional revelation. However, he further notes that all speech-acts have propositional content as well as intent that cannot be divorced or reduced from its context. This proposal takes seriously the wide variety of literary forms in Scripture and understands that God is seeking to creatively and fully communicate through these forms. Vanhoozer elaborates: "It is precisely [Scripture's] form and setting, however, that provide the clue to a speech-act's illocutionary force—to what a communicative agent is actually doing in his discourse (e.g., asserting, commanding, promising)."[153] Accordingly, his approach acknowledges and appreciates the propositional matter and illocutionary effect of speech-acts in general and Scripture in particular. This recognizes

---

149. Land, *Pentecostal Spirituality*, 66–67; Martin, "Introduction to Pentecostal Hermeneutics," 5–7; Menzies, *Pentecost*, 21–23.

150. Vanhoozer, *Drama of Doctrine*, 86–91, 268–72.

151. Vanhoozer elsewhere refers to this paradigm as the Hodge-Henry hypothesis after Charles Hodge and Carl Henry who were prime proponents of this paradigm. Vanhoozer, "Lost in Interpretation?"

152. Vanhoozer, *Drama of Doctrine*, 266–91.

153. Ibid., 279.

the hermeneutic-communicative nature of Scripture and echoes the truth claims within the theory of Habermas. Speech-acts possess claims to truth, rightness, and authenticity, which encompass illocutionary effects. Significantly, Vanhoozer sees Scripture as divine "communicative action" though his use of this term differs from Habermas.[154]

The interpretative framework to understand and participate in the divine drama is found in the authoritative script of the whole canon. Wright has elsewhere discussed this aspect on the authority of the Bible.[155] Wright uses the analogy of a five-act Shakespearean play where the final act is now "lost." Actors are able to perform an improvisation of the final act from the "authority" gained in the first four acts. They are able to immerse themselves in these acts to work out the identity and characterization necessary for their improvisation. The performance should then be consistent with the extant story yet innovative in its improvisation for the new situation. This analogy is applied to the Bible where the canon of Scripture forms the first four acts of the play. The church now lives in the final "lost" act and is called to live out a performance of the faith that is both consistent with Scripture yet innovative in responding to contemporary life. The church is thus living under the authority of the biblical story.

Vanhoozer further appreciates the primary role that the canonical script plays in the identity formation of the church.[156] He makes a distinction here between *idem*-identity and *ipse*-identity. *Idem*-identity stresses a "hard" identity of unchanging similarity and would lead to the uncritical and unimaginative repetition of what is perceived from the script. This is not the kind of identity that he sees Scripture forming. Instead, he argues that Scripture seeks to produce *ipse*-identity, which is a "softer" form emphasizing continuity of character and permitting improvisation. Improvisation on the part of the church's performance is necessary as it encounters contemporary contexts which have no precedence or equivalence within Scripture. Thus, the identity that Scripture forms allows "creative fidelity" and "ruled spontaneity."

Vanhoozer reinforces the need for the church to derive its identity from the full canon and not select passages or to favor certain genre. What is formed in the believer is ultimately a *habitus*—"dispositions to see, judge,

---

154. Vanhoozer uses communicative action to refer to "all the things that agents do with words (and not with words)." This includes more than the mere transmitting of cognitive knowledge. Ibid., 177 note 114. For more discussion of the text as communicative act, see Vanhoozer, *Is There a Meaning in This Text?* 201–65.

155. Wright, *New Testament and the People of God*, 139–43.

156. Vanhoozer, *Drama of Doctrine*, 126–28.

and act according to canonical patterns and practices."[157] It is "not simply a hermeneutic, a way of dealing with the text, but a way of life: a scripted and spirited performance, a way of wisdom generated and sustained by word and Spirit . . . to replace distorted patterns of thinking with patterns that correspond to canonical practices, to theo-dramatic reality, and, ultimately to the mind of Christ."[158] Vanhoozer's proposal appears similar with what Boff described as "hermeneutic competency" and "hermeneutic *habitus*."[159] Both approaches stress the purpose of Scripture forming "the mind of Christ"—a character, identity, competency, *habitus*—within the church and thus moves beyond the paradigm of mere "text/application."

The contemporary performance of the church living out this Scripture-shaped identity can be judged according to its consistency and correspondence with the canonical script. To modify Boff's description, there must be a theo-dramatic correspondence in relations between the biblical actors and their context and the church today with its context. Of course, the main actor and model is Jesus Christ, who remains the central focus of, and the lead actor within the theo-drama. It is ultimately to Christ that the praxis of the church must correspond to.

2.5.2.2.3 Role of the Holy Spirit: Director

Vanhoozer includes a pneumatological perspective to his model in describing the role of the Holy Spirit as the director of the ensemble.[160] He identifies the Holy Spirit at work in the book of Acts, directing the biblical cast in what to say, what to do, and even granting the power and ability to perform the part. This same Holy Spirit inspired the authoring of the canonical script, illuminates readers today, and dynamically works within the community of faith, guiding the performance for a fitting rendition. Vanhoozer sees this activity representative of what John 16:13 meant in saying that the Holy Spirit would "guide you into all truth."

Cartledge posits that the Holy Spirit enables the community of faith to live out its performance with innovation and consistency.[161] He substantiates this by examining the five *paraclete* sayings in the gospel of John on the role of the Holy Spirit and finds the concepts of innovation and consistency present in some measure (John 14:16–17; 14:26; 15:26–27; 16:7–11;

---

157. Ibid., 376.
158. Ibid., 255.
159. Boff and Boff, *Introducing Liberation Theology*, 149.
160. Vanhoozer, *Drama of Doctrine*, 102, 105–7.
161. Cartledge, *Charismatic Glossolalia*.

16:12–15). Vanhoozer's model may easily incorporate this insight to the Holy Spirit's directorial role in ensuring consistency and innovation.

The Holy Spirit serves then to mediate between the written word and the enacted word in the life of the church. Vanhoozer extends his metaphor even further by asserting that the Holy Spirit is firstly the costume designer and make-up artist who clothes the church with Christ's righteousness; secondly the prompter who reminds the church of the lines in the divine script; thirdly the prop master who accessorizes the church with spiritual gifts so that the church is equipped to fulfill its part.[162] Surely, the role of the Holy Spirit is not to be ignored or downplayed.

2.5.2.2.4 Role of the Theologian: Dramaturge

The role of dramaturge is accorded the theologian within the proposal of Vanhoozer.[163] The dramaturge in theatre functions as an advisor to the production who engages in research of the script as well as the audience so as to enable meaningful and truthful performances. While some may see this as over-stretching the overall drama metaphor, the points raised by Vanhoozer find significant resonance within practical theology.

The key point raised in this proposal is the engagement with theology as both *scientia* and *sapientia* for the role of dramaturge. Theology is portrayed as *scientia* in this discussion as it involves the activity of exegesis from the canonical script so that the church may understand it better and thus be able to live out ever more faithful performances. The object of this activity is the communicative action (Vanhoozer's sense) of God in Scripture and the theologian uses all the various tools and methods in order to best determine the meaning within the text. Again, the emphasis is on understanding the canonical script as a whole and not just the parts so the church may appreciate its full identity as the people of God.

The other aspect of theology is that it is also *sapientia*. If *scientia* concerns getting meaning out of the text, *sapientia* concerns how to continue the meaning with theo-dramatic consistency, coherence, and correspondence. Vanhoozer elaborates: "The *sapiential* task of theology is that of knowing how to transpose the drama of redemption into the present. Better: theo-dramatic transposition means playing the same drama of redemption in a different cultural key."[164] Central to this claim is the concept of "transposing

---

162. Vanhoozer, *Drama of Doctrine*, 448.
163. Ibid., 246–56.
164. Ibid., 254.

praxis."[165] This involves understanding the message of the canonical text and embodying this message in performance within the contemporary cultural context. The activity is not simply copying or translating Scripture into contemporary praxis since this would ignore the difference in cultural context. Hence, Vanhoozer prefers to see this as "transposition" in the same way that a musical piece may be transposed to a different key.

Vanhoozer's concept of theology involving *scientia* and *sapientia* serves well the overall framework of practical theology. The need to transpose praxis requires tools and methods of studying contemporary praxis so that it may be critically compared and correlated to Scripture. It is suggested that this need may be filled by empirical theology as described within this study. Empirical theology presents empirical tools and interacts with methods from the social sciences so that a systematic and disciplined interrogation of contemporary praxis is possible. It is unfortunate that while Vanhoozer mentions the historical-exegetical tools that permit research on the script which forms one pole of the performance, he lacks mention of empirical tools that would investigate the other pole—the actual performance itself. Empirical theology provides the hermeneutic of situations so that the manner in which humans make sense of their situation is incorporated in the theo-dramatic proposal.[166] Furthermore, research in the cultural context is needed as this is the setting in which the drama of redemption must now be performed. Thus, insights from the social sciences, which study the cultural context, must be incorporated into theology. Again, it is asserted that this dialogue with the social sciences may be guided through the framework of practical theology described in this study.

The model by Vanhoozer lacks a substantive discussion on the dialectic that necessarily takes place in interpreting the script and performing it. It is noted that he does speak of the dramaturgical circle as "we understand in order to perform and we perform in order to understand"[167] in addition to the *sapiential* circle as "I believe in order to understand; I understand in order to put into practice; I put into practice in order to grow in knowledge and belief."[168] However, he fails to elaborate on how this process actually takes place. It was already established that there exists a hermeneutical spiral of dialectic engagement between theory and praxis. It is suggested that Van der Ven's empirical-theological cycle serves this function in facilitating this dialectic between canonical script and transposed praxis.

165. Ibid., 252–56.
166. Farley, "Interpreting Situations."
167. Vanhoozer, *Drama of Doctrine*, 248.
168. Ibid., 256.

2.5.2.2.5 Summary

This chapter has examined the hermeneutical model of Vanhoozer and found it to be similar in some respects to the approach by Boff and adopted by Van der Ven. However, Vanhoozer's model is set within an evangelical framework and overcomes the issues raised earlier with Van der Ven's approach. In addition, Vanhoozer's model acknowledges the need to take seriously the various genres found within Scripture and all God is communicating through the Bible's divine discourse. It upholds the authority of Scripture and understands its key role in the identity formation of the church. Therefore, this study seeks to use this model as the hermeneutical framework for empirical theological research.

2.5.3 Discussion on Epistemology

Research strategies within empirical studies are commonly understood to be guided by certain philosophical paradigms. These paradigms prescribe a set of beliefs that define the nature of reality, the world, the researcher, and the relationships possible.[169] Vanhoozer has elsewhere described his hermeneutical model to be set within the paradigm of critical realism.[170] This paradigm has also been espoused by other biblical scholars, most notably by Wright and Osborne.[171] Wright describes critical realism in this manner:

> This is a way of describing the process of "knowing" that acknowledges the *reality of the thing known, as something other than the knower* (hence "realism"), while also fully acknowledging that the only access we have to this reality lies along the spiraling path of *appropriate dialogue or conversation between the knower and the thing known* (hence "critical").[172]

While it upholds the claim of a reality independent of the observer, it also takes seriously that reality can only be perceived through human perceptions that are influenced by presuppositions and pre-judgments. Furthermore, the Christian worldview must consider that human perception is both fallen and faulty. Thus, knowledge proceeds along a dialectical interaction between the observer and the object; between observation and critical

---

169. Creswell, *Research Design*, 6.
170. Vanhoozer, *Is There a Meaning in This Text?* 299–303.
171. Wright, *New Testament and the People of God*, 32–44. Also see Osborne, *Hermeneutical Spiral*, 398–399.
172. Wright, *New Testament and the People of God*, 35. Italics in original.

reflection; between hypothesis and testing. Osborne points out that this leaves a degree of tentativeness in all theological assertions and results in a tension between theological construction and the final authority they have on the faith community.[173] The dialectic interaction between theory and praxis was already discussed in the nature of practical theology. Thus, the model of empirical theology adopted in this present study may be considered to operate within this paradigm of critical realism.

The paradigm of critical realism is acknowledged within social science research to be a postpositivist approach that seeks to mediate between the naïve realism of positivism and the relativism of constructivism.[174] This approach is a common framework for conducting empirical investigation and applies to both qualitative and quantitative methods. Within qualitative studies, it stresses the collection of emic viewpoints to determine meaning and purpose that people ascribe to their actions. For quantitative studies, it uses the falsification of hypotheses rather than verification so that theories are strengthened in a continuous process of formulation and testing. The goal is to discern reality as closely as possible while recognizing that knowledge will never be perfect. Van der Ven's model acknowledges this paradigm in his discussion of critical rationalism and hence is coherent with Vanhoozer's hermeneutic.[175] The paradigm of critical realism is also noted to inform other empirical-theological investigations.[176]

2.6 CONCLUSION

This chapter has sought to provide a framework for empirical theology within which this present study might operate. It examined the field of practical theology and noted its hermeneutic nature as well as the dialectic relationship between theory and praxis. The empirical theology of Johannes van der Ven was presented and its considerations on empiricism and epistemology. Van der Ven's proposal was critiqued on two aspects in terms of its intradisciplinary model and hermeneutical framework. The Chalcedonian pattern was identified as a useful concept to guide dialogue between disciplines and to augment the intradisciplinary model. The hermeneutical

---

173. Osborne, *Hermeneutical Spiral*, 397.

174. Clark, "Critical Realism"; Guba and Lincoln, "Competing Paradigms in Qualitative Research," 110.

175. Van der Ven, *Practical Theology: An Empirical Approach*, 81–82, 105.

176. Alexander, "Missional Leadership"; Armstrong, "Lay Christian Views"; Cartledge, *Charismatic Glossolalia*. For a discussion of critical realism in science and theology, see McGrath, *Scientific Theology: Realism*; Polkinghorne, *Belief in God*.

framework used by Van der Ven was found to be problematic and hence an evangelical framework was proposed as a basis for empirical theology. This is the framework that will be applied to this study.

3

A Qualitative Study on Prophecy

3.1 INTRODUCTION

THE PREVIOUS CHAPTER PRESENTED a framework for empirical theology that consists of a cycle of five phases: the development of the theological goal, theological induction, theological deduction, empirical-theological testing, and theological evaluation. The first phase of theological goal development was presented in the first chapter. This chapter begins the second phase of theological induction consisting of a qualitative study on the practice of prophecy amongst ministers in the Assemblies of God of Singapore (AGS). It will then present an analysis of this data to provide a description of the phenomenon and themes that arise from the investigation.

3.2 CASE STUDY METHOD

The second phase of Van der Ven's model of empirical theology is theological induction. This requires theological perception of the phenomenon in its context so as to engage in theological reflection. A firm grasp of the extant literature on the subject is also crucial. The challenge of theological induction is compounded in this study by the dearth of academic studies on prophecy within the Asian context. The literature review in the following chapters will reveal that there are no known empirical studies on prophecy in Singapore or Asia. Current theoretical literature and empirical studies are focused on the practice of prophecy within churches in the West. It would be presumptuous to assume that these works are characteristic of prophecy within Singapore. Thus, there is an obvious need for an initial phase of empirical examination of the phenomenon in Singapore before engaging in a review of the literature.

This initial phase aims to provide a thick description of prophecy among the AG churches in Singapore. A thick description offers a rich, detailed account of the phenomenon that moves beyond a report of surface observations so as to reveal meanings, emotions, and the significance of human actions and behaviors.[1] It is more than the accumulation of detailed descriptions but seeks to provide the context and setting so that the interpretation of human praxis is possible. Hence, the goal of a thick description of prophecy is in accord with the nature of practical theology. The approach recognizes human actions as value and theory-laden, which is important and relevant for this study. Subsequently, the qualitative data will be analyzed to identify patterns and themes that can be studied further in the next phase of empirical research. This will also enable the identification of categories and typologies for the development of instruments in the second phase of study.

Qualitative methods are commonly used in empirical research.[2] The characteristics of qualitative methods include collecting data in the natural setting of the phenomenon, the researcher as the key instrument for data collection, use of multiple sources for data collection, inductive data analysis, a focus on meaning from the participants rather than from theoretical literature, emergent research design, interpretive inquiry, and a holistic account of the phenomenon. The qualitative approach was adopted since it met the requirements for this phase of theological induction.

There are at least five common approaches for conducting qualitative research.[3] The case study approach was selected for use in this present study. This approach entails the study of an issue or a phenomenon through one or more cases within a bounded system. The phenomenon is examined within its real-life context through detailed, in-depth data collection.[4] According to Yin, case studies are most appropriate for asking "how" or "why" research questions, where the researcher has little control over the phenomenon, and

---

1. Dawson, "Thick Description"; Patton, *Qualitative Research and Evaluation Methods*, 60–62. Clifford Geertz introduced the term "thick description" in the use of ethnography within anthropology. See Geertz, "Thick Description."

2. Creswell, *Qualitative Inquiry & Research Design*, 37–39.

3. Ibid., 53–84. Creswell lists these approaches as narrative research, phenomenology, grounded theory, ethnography, and case study.

4. Ibid., 73; Yin, *Case Study Research*, 12–14.

where the contemporary context is the focus.⁵ These guidelines are true for the current study and so the case study method was deemed suitable.

The bounded system for this study consists of credentialed ministers within the AGS. Each interviewee is treated as a case representative of the other ministers within the AGS. Tentative generalizations from the data collected can be subsequently tested on the population of AGS ministers in the quantitative study. The study fits into Creswell's designation of a collective case study where multiple cases are selected to gather different perspectives on the phenomenon or issue.⁶ Furthermore, the use of multiple cases permits application of the logic of replication in analyzing the data across the different cases.⁷

3.2.1 Data Collection

The history of the AG movement in Singapore was reviewed through various published academic works so as to understand the background of the movement. In addition, the AGS celebrated its eightieth anniversary in 2008 and many of the recent AGS publications were focused on recollecting the history of the movement. The reports of various AGS meetings were also examined. These included the minutes of the annual general meeting and reports of the monthly prayer fellowship attended by AGS workers. The AGS also publishes a quarterly magazine named the *Singapore Evangel* that serves as the official channel informing the AGS community of events and developments within various churches. Issues from 2003 to 2010 were reviewed for this study.

The study collected data through a series of interviews with the AGS ministers. The phenomenon of prophecy can be better understood through the experiences of those participating in the phenomenon. Since only a limited number of people could be interviewed at this stage, it seemed best to focus on the senior pastors of the AGS congregations so as to obtain a general representation of what actually takes place.

The above data collection methods describe the use of systematic perception instead of random perception. Publications and reports were systematically reviewed while interviews were planned and arranged. The study utilizes overt perception rather than covert perception. Permission was obtained from the General Council of the AGS before embarking on this research project. Senior pastors were invited to participate in the interview

---

5. Yin, *Case Study Research*, 5–9.
6. Creswell, *Qualitative Inquiry & Research Design*, 74.
7. Yin, *Case Study Research*, 47–52.

and indeed some senior pastors rejected the invitation. The approach further utilized indirect perception of the phenomenon but direct perception of the interviewees' experiences and meanings through the interview.

3.2.1.1 Interview Questions and Pilot Study

An important part of the qualitative study concerns the formulation of interview questions and the conduct of the interview itself. The aim is to ask genuinely open-ended questions that allow the interviewees to respond in their own words and to express their personal perspectives. Patton lists three main types of interviews: the informal conversational interview, the general interview guide approach, and the standardized open-ended interview.[8] The desire for this study is to obtain a rich description of the phenomenon and to have a flexible interview strategy due to the inductive nature of the inquiry. However, the issue of reliability arises if each interview differs drastically from the other.

The study opted for the general interview guide approach to balance the contrasting concerns. This approach provides a list of questions to explore and probe selected subject areas. The sequence of these questions may be predetermined. However, the interviewer remains free to word questions flexibly and to establish a conversational style. There is also some flexibility to delve deeper into specific subject areas depending on the response of the interviewee. An open-ended question was used at the close of the interview that asked the interviewee if there was anything else they would like to share. This question permits the exploration of areas and issues that are important to the interviewee but were not pre-determined by the researcher.

A pilot study is recommended to assist the researcher in refining the data collection plans and procedures.[9] This study utilized the assistance of two volunteers for a pilot study. The pilot study followed the actual interview protocol and the interview was conducted as if it was an actual interview. The participants of the pilot study provided feedback after the interview regarding the clarity of the interview questions as well as the interview process. This led to the refining of the interview questions and helped the researcher gain familiarity with the overall process.

---

8. Patton, *Qualitative Research and Evaluation Methods*, 342.
9. Gillham, *Research Interviewing*, 73–74; Yin, *Case Study Research*, 78–80.

3.2.1.2 *Case Selection*

Case selection forms another significant consideration in case study research. Creswell highlights the challenge of determining the number of cases to select and how these cases should be selected.[10] He also admits that there is no adequate solution to address this issue besides the recommendation that cases should be selected so as to capture a wide perspective.

The senior pastors of selected AG churches in Singapore were interviewed for this study. It was felt that their views and opinions best represent the phenomenon of prophecy as it is actually occurring in the various churches. At this point in the research in 2009 to 2010, there were forty-nine AG churches in Singapore.[11] The size of these churches ranged from those having a weekly attendance of less than fifty people to larger churches reporting several thousand people in their services. The interviewees were selected to represent a broad range of church sizes, languages, ethnicity, and gender.

The study sent out interview requests to fifteen senior pastors. Of these, only ten acceded to being interviewed. The interviewees' age mostly reflected their senior position in leadership: one pastor was between thirty to forty years old, three pastors were between forty-one to fifty years old, and six pastors were between fifty-one to sixty years old. The interviewees came from churches of varying sizes: one pastor had a church of less than 200 people, four pastors had churches of 201 to 500 people, two pastors had churches with 501 to 800 people, and three pastors had churches with more than 800 people. The interviewees possessed a range of experience serving as a senior pastor: three pastors had served for less than five years, four pastors had served between six to ten years, and three pastors had served between sixteen to twenty years. The interviewees consisted of nine men and one woman. Repeated invitations were extended to three other senior pastors who were women but these invitations were not accepted. This study has refrained from presenting each interviewee's age, gender, and church size so as to ensure the anonymity of the interviewees and the confidentiality of the data.

The interviewees represented ten out of the forty-nine churches within the denomination. The represented churches have a combined weekly attendance of 10,960 people out of the total weekly attendance of 21,809 people for the entire AGS in 2009. The senior pastors interviewed represented 50.3 percent of the overall denomination and was deemed to be a good reflection

---

10. Creswell, *Qualitative Inquiry & Research Design*, 75–76.

11. The statistics used for church attendance are average figures for 2009. These appeared in the 2010 AGS Annual General Meeting report.

of the overall movement. In addition, the interviewees included a number of past and present members of the AGS executive council. They were selected so that data collected could be considered a more authoritative representation of the AGS churches.

3.2.1.3 *Conduct of Interviews*

Yin advocates the use of a case study protocol to increase the reliability of the research.[12] The protocol guides the researcher in carrying out the data collection, especially where multiple cases are involved. This study used a protocol which contained an overview of the case study project, field procedures, and the interview questions.

The interviews largely followed the five phases outlined by Gillham.[13] The preparation phase includes the recruitment of interviewees and making arrangements for the interviews. In this instance, interviews were conducted over a period of three months. Most of the interviews were arranged at the interviewees' church location. However, two of the interviews were conducted at a neutral venue due to certain challenges with the arrangements. The second phase is the initial social contact in which the researcher introduces himself to the interviewee. This is followed by the orientation phase where the purpose of the interview is explained. The researcher presented each interviewee with a copy of the research information sheet and explained the purpose of the overall study and the interview itself. He also highlighted the way in which data collected would be used. Interviewees were assured of anonymity and confidentiality. Interviewees were also informed that they could stop the interview at any time or withdraw from the study even after the interview. Consent for the interview was recorded though the signing of a consent form.

The next phase is the substantive phase where the main core of interviewing occurs. The researcher relied on the semi-structured questions prepared in the protocol. The interviews were recorded using two audio recorders. Some hand-written notes were taken during the interview but the focus remained on interacting with the interviewees and clarifying their responses. The closure phase comes at the end of the interview and is partly social but also included a review of the information collected. Immediately after the interview, the researcher recorded personal reflections and observations. These notes were important for analyzing the data subsequently.

---

12. Yin, *Case Study Research*, 67–77.
13. Gillham, *Research Interviewing*, 76–79.

3.2.2 Data Analysis

The interview recordings were transcribed for subsequent data analysis. Interviewees were each given a code from RESA to RESJ. The transcribed interviews were then entered into WeftQDA, an open-source tool for analyzing textual data. The analysis consisted of examining, coding, and categorizing the qualitative data to address the purpose of the study. Among the various strategies available for analysis, this study identified developing a case description as a suitable strategy.[14] This simple strategy is utilized when the research purpose is largely descriptive and exploratory. It provides a general framework for organizing and understanding the phenomenon. This study constructed a framework around the process of receiving, delivering, and judging prophecy. The purpose and significance of prophecy was also considered.

This study adopted a second strategy of content analysis to identify patterns and themes arising from the qualitative data.[15] Patton recommends this strategy for developing typologies or for constructing instruments to measure a phenomenon. Analysis may be done either inductively or deductively. This study utilized inductive analysis where the researcher becomes immersed or grounded in the data so as to discover embedded meanings and relationships. The process of thematic coding and categorizing results in the discovery of core consistencies which may be described as patterns or themes.[16] Patton defines a pattern as a descriptive finding whereas a theme concerns more categorical or topical forms. The results of this analysis will be presented later in this chapter.

3.2.3 Ethical Considerations

Ethical issues are an important consideration for all research studies that involve human participants.[17] Various codes of professional ethics and research ethics frameworks were consulted in designing the research strategy. This research was conducted within a doctoral program and so approval from the program's research ethics committee was sought and received. This approval covered the research design, research procedure, interview questions, and survey questionnaires.

---

14. Yin, *Case Study Research*, 114–15.
15. Patton, *Qualitative Research and Evaluation Methods*, 453–54.
16. Gibbs, *Analyzing Qualitative Data*, 38–55.
17. Creswell, *Research Design*, 87–92.

Various practices were adopted to ensure that the research abided by the ethical principles identified.[18] There was no coercion in recruiting research participants. All participants were invited to take part in this research study and in fact some chose not to participate. Participants were briefed on the purpose of the study, the research methods employed, and possible uses for the data collected. This was done verbally for the qualitative interview and also through a research information sheet that was given to the participants. Informed consent was obtained from all interviewees through the use of consent forms. Participants were told that the interviews would be audio recorded and that they could request for the recording to be stopped at any point. Furthermore, interviewees could choose to withdraw from the study altogether at a later point in time. Participants were guaranteed anonymity through the use of pseudonyms for people and churches.

3.3 THE RESEARCH CONTEXT

3.3.1 An Overview of Singapore

Singapore is an island located at the southern tip of Peninsula Malaysia. The island is approximately 42 kilometers in length, 23 kilometers in breadth, and has a land area of about 712 km2. In 2010, the country's population was a little over five million people.[19] This comprises 74.1 percent Chinese, 13.4 percent Malays, 9.2 percent Indians, and 3.3 percent from other ethnic groups. Buddhism and Taoism[20] (44.2 percent) is the most popular religion, followed by Christianity (18.3 percent), Islam (14.7 percent), Hinduism (5.1 percent), and other religions (0.7 percent). The remaining 17 percent of the population reported no religious affiliation. English serves as the language of administration and is the main medium of instruction in schools. However, the country recognizes Malay, Tamil, Chinese, and English as its official languages. These facts show that Singapore is a densely populated urban city which is multi-ethnic and multi-religious.

Modern Singapore was founded in 1819 with the arrival of the British East India Company represented by Sir Stamford Raffles.[21] Raffles signed an agreement with the local leaders to establish a trading outpost for Brit-

---

18. Gillham, *Research Interviewing*, 10–17.

19. Department of Statistics, *Census of Singapore 2010*.

20. The census chose to group Buddhism and Taoism together in its report. This may partly be due to the mix between these two beliefs in Singapore.

21. Singh and Arasu, *Singapore*, 9–13; Turnbull, *History of Modern Singapore*, 19–50.

ain along the Straits of Malacca. The Sultan of Johor subsequently signed a treaty in 1824 that gave the British possession of Singapore. The island remained a British colony until the Second World War when the Japanese occupied it from 1942 to 1945.[22] After the war, Singapore returned to British control until 1963. In that year, Singapore attained freedom by merging together with its northern neighbor, Malaya, which had already gained independence in 1957. This union was short-lived and Singapore separated from Malaya, achieving full independence in 1965.[23] The city-state of Singapore progressed rapidly and is now one of the most modern, metropolitan centers in the world.

3.3.2 The Assemblies of God of Singapore

The AG movement came to Singapore through the ministry of Cecil and Edith M. Jackson.[24] The Jacksons were originally missionaries in Canton, China when social unrest broke out and foreigners had to leave for their safety. The Jacksons boarded a boat thinking they were headed to Hong Kong but instead found themselves arriving in Singapore in 1928. Cecil Jackson took up a job to teach religious knowledge in a Methodist mission school. The Jacksons soon established a Cantonese congregation due to their fluency with this Chinese dialect. This congregation represented the first AG congregation in Singapore.

The Jacksons subsequently started an English congregation in 1932. The English and Chinese congregations ran separately for a time before they were brought together to form Elim Church.[25] This remained the only AG church in Singapore until the Japanese occupation.[26] One prominent AG missionary in this pioneering period was Rev. Lula Baird.[27] Her decision to serve in Singapore is cited as an example of supernatural direction common among the early pioneers. While still a student in the United States, Baird was praying when she fell onto the floor speaking in tongues. She testified that the word "Singapore" came out of her mouth three times.[28] She took this as prophetic direction from God to serve as a missionary to

22. Singh and Arasu, *Singapore*, 87; Turnbull, *History of Modern Singapore*, 195.

23. Singh and Arasu, *Singapore*, 293.

24. Abeysekera, *History of the Assemblies of God of Singapore*, 93–94; Ong, "Historical Analysis of the Factors of Growth," 12–23.

25. Ong, "Historical Analysis of the Factors of Growth," 21–22.

26. Tan, "Singapore," 224.

27. Tian, "Pioneering Days."

28. Ibid., 7.

this country. This account is even more amazing since she had never heard of Singapore at that point and had initially thought it was part of China. Baird's subsequent missionary efforts in Singapore saw her pioneering two AG churches and providing leadership at another church.[29]

After the war, several other AG churches were planted in Singapore and Malaya, many through the work of missionaries from the United States.[30] This led to the formation of the Assemblies of God of Malaya and Singapore in 1957.[31] With the separation and independence of Singapore from Malaysia, the AGS was formed in 1966.[32] In 1977, the denomination founded the Bible Institute of Singapore to provide theological and ministerial training for its church workers.[33] This school was later renamed as the Assemblies of God Bible College and recently renamed again as ACTS College. It continues to serve the needs of the denomination to this present time.

In 2009, the AGS denomination comprised of forty-nine churches with a combined weekly attendance of 21,809.[34] The mission statement of the AGS states that it is "committed to establish a Pentecostal fellowship, for the development of progressive local churches, ministries, and ministers, to fulfil the Great Commission."[35] In particular, the denomination seeks to emphasize the unique distinctive of the Baptism of the Holy Spirit and the Spirit-filled life. The core values of the AGS are the Tenets of Faith, prayer, unity, and excellence in ministry. The AGS is a member of the World Assemblies of God Fellowship and also a member of the Asia Pacific Assemblies of God Fellowship. The AGS is autonomous from the Assemblies of God in the United States of America (AGUSA) though there are historical links due to the pioneering work of AGUSA missionaries in establishing several AGS churches.

---

29. Ibid., 10.
30. Abeysekera, *History of the Assemblies of God of Singapore*, 165–71.
31. Ong, "Historical Analysis of the Factors of Growth," 31.
32. Ibid., 37.
33. Ibid.
34. Statistics taken from the 2010 AGS Annual General Meeting report.
35. This is stated in the AGS Credential Induction Exercise booklet.

3.4 DATA COLLECTED FROM INTERVIEWS

3.4.1 Understanding of Prophecy

The first concern was to obtain the interviewees' understanding of prophecy and their definition of this phenomenon. The data showed that prophecy was generally understood to involve receiving an inspired message from God that was then relayed to other people. RESB called it "an inspired word given by God to his people" whereas RESH saw it as the "verbal expression of the mind of God." RESC likened prophecy to being "a voice for God to the church." RESG was more detailed in describing prophecy as "hearing the voice of God and articulating, demonstrating, the very words of God, the very message that God has spoken to you. So it can be in terms of fore-telling as well as forth-telling." The concepts of forth-telling and fore-telling were also mentioned by RESD and RESF. When asked to elaborate, the interviewees described forth-telling as simply conveying a message from God whereas fore-telling concerned communicating information about the future. This distinction between forth-telling and fore-telling was important as it showed that the interviewees did not consider prophecy to be purely predictive in nature. Their responses showed a broader understanding of prophecy to be simply speaking on God's behalf.

Interviewees were careful to distinguish prophecy from preaching. RESJ was representative of the others in explaining that preaching was an activity which required preparation in terms of studying Scripture, formulating the homiletical thought, and crafting a sermon. In contrast, prophecy occurred spontaneously when a believer received an inspired message from God to proclaim to other believers. However, interviewees acknowledged occasions when pastors spontaneously received a prophetic message while they were preaching and this was woven into the sermon. RESF described it in this way: "There are times when somehow a message dawns in our heart while preaching and it burns in us and you find that you must speak that, and share that, and you can't just keep it, and you know this is for the church." Many of the interviewees described prophecy as a spiritual gift, emphasizing that it was a supernatural occurrence rather than mere human ability (RESA, RESC, RESJ, RESI). In contrast, preaching was classified as an acquired skill.

The data showed that all the interviewees thought of prophecy as a verbal activity though some mentioned writing down the message first for others to evaluate (RESG, RESJ). Even in this case, the written message would be read out to the congregation rather than published in print. Interestingly, the interviewees kept referring to a prophetic message as a "word." This was used almost as a technical term to refer to the message of a prophecy. For example, RESE described prophecy as "a *word* that is given or a *word* that is released to build someone up, to encourage someone or to even bring confirmation to certain things."[36] Similarly, RESI spoke of how "the Holy Spirit supernaturally gives a *word* to somebody to speak on behalf of God."[37] The term "revelation" was also used synonymously with the word "prophecy" (RESB, RESG, RESJ). This was evident in descriptions of prophecy such as this one provided by RESJ: "Sometimes when you are talking to people, the Lord will just give you a *revelation* and you speak that word and the person begins to realize that the word of God can be so real."[38]

Several interviewees introduced the terms "word of knowledge" and "word of wisdom" during the interviews even though these terms were not part of the interview protocol. In these instances, interviewees were asked to explain what these terms meant to them. The common perception shared was that the word of knowledge concerns facts or information which God reveals to a believer and which was not naturally known by the believer. The word of wisdom concerned what to do with this information or how to make a decision. Both RESD and RESF felt that the word of wisdom was a spiritual gift used primarily in counseling situations.

The interviewees were pressed further to explain how the word of knowledge and the word of wisdom compared with prophecy. Some interviewees insisted that there was a distinction between these phenomena (RESA, RESB, RESD, RESF, RESI). However, they were not able to articulate clearly the differences between them. While maintaining they were distinct and different, RESI added an important clarification that God is the source of these phenomena and that God was communicating with people through these phenomena. In contrast, other interviewees felt there was little to differentiate between these phenomena (RESC, RESD, RESG, RESJ). The terms "overlap" and "complementary" were used to describe the relationship between these phenomena. RESG went further to say: "In every prophetic word there is a measure of the gift of knowledge and a measure of the word of wisdom. I think they are manifested very much collectively in a prophetic utterance." RESE even suggested that the various terms were synonymous in describing the same phenomenon of spontaneous divine communication. Interestingly, none of the interviewees referred to the Bible or cited biblical examples when attempting to distinguish between the phenomena.

36. Emphasis added.
37. Emphasis added.
38. Emphasis added.

Interviewees were further asked to compare and contrast Christian prophecy with comparable practices amongst Asian religions in Singapore.[39] Most interviewees expressed surprise at this question and commented that they had never engaged in a comparison before. Interviewees identified divination, fortune-telling, geomancy, and the activity of temple mediums as possible parallels with Christian prophecy (RESA, RESC, RESD, RESE, RESG, RESI, RESJ). Both Christian and non-Christian prophecy involve divine communication relayed through a human intermediary. However, an analysis of their responses revealed two perceived differences. The first difference was that Christian prophecy was attributed to the "Holy Spirit" or to "God" whereas the non-Christian phenomenon was not. This concurs strongly with the monotheistic worldview in Christianity. RESD even suggested that non-Christian prophecy was a "counterfeit" of "genuine" Christian practice. The second difference concerned the content of the prophetic message. Non-Christian phenomena focused on issues of material blessings, health, and prosperity. These were described as "personal," "self-centered," or "me-centered" (RESA, RESE, RESI, RESJ). In contrast, Christian prophecy focused on spiritual edification of the community and sought to strengthen the spiritual relationship between believers and God. This would ultimately bring "glory to Christ" rather than bring personal benefit to people (RESD, RESH).

3.4.2 The Purpose of Prophecy

The data showed that the overall function of prophecy is to communicate a message to people on behalf of God. Interviewees described various examples of prophecies that they had experienced and content analysis was employed to identify themes describing the purpose of prophecy. In the themes discussed below, specific examples are presented to illustrate prophecy in Singapore and its purpose. This is necessary since prophecy within the Singapore context has not been rigorously documented before.

3.4.2.1 *Spiritual Edification*

The first purpose of prophecy is to spiritually edify the recipients of the prophecy. This purpose was one of the first cited by the interviewees and

---

39. Divination, fortune-telling and geomancy are common among popular folk religions in Singapore. See Choong, "Chinese Divination"; Corduan, *Neighboring Faiths*, 282–83, 298–301; Ju, "Chinese Spirit-Mediums in Singapore"; Osman, *Malay Folk Beliefs*; Sinha, "'Hinduism' and 'Taoism' in Singapore."

mentioned by almost all. Several interviewees (RESE, RESF, RESG, RESH) quoted or paraphrased 1 Corinthians 14:3 in describing this aspect of prophecy as for "strengthening, encouragement, and comfort." RESE's description of prophecy below may be considered a typical example of the descriptions shared by other interviewees:

> In a service setting, like a Sunday morning service setting, in the midst of worship, I often feel that God drops a word in my heart. And when that happens I normally take a couple of moments to pray and seek clarity about what God is speaking about; get a sense of what is happening in that service. And I will just go up and say [to the congregation] that I sense God is speaking to us here this morning. So that will be generally how I would normally operate in a service setting or different ones will do that in a service. An example would be something along the line of God calling people not to look at the problems that they are in, or the situations that they are in. That God is anointing people or raising them up to be his sons and daughters in this generation, to make an impact where they are, something like that. Sometimes it could be in the context—I'm just trying to recall—God is calling us to be servants, to be bold in terms of preaching, evangelizing, reaching the lost. It could be themes along those lines.

When asked about the purpose of prophecy, RESE responded: "To strengthen, to comfort. I mean it is also to build them up. I think that is one of the key things. I think prophecy is there to edify the body at large. I always think that one of the key things in prophecy is to edify or to build up the body." The descriptions and responses provided by the interviewees showed that prophecy typically occurred during a service setting and resulted in the corporate edification of the congregation that was present.

An important clarification is that prophecy did not always literally call people to be encouraged or to take comfort. Instead the prophecy evoked a response of encouragement or comfort in the recipients. For instance, RESA provided the example of prophecy in a church service where the content demonstrated that God knew the personal struggles of congregation members. This aroused a sense of God's care and concern for the believers resulting in the members feeling loved, encouraged, and edified. The label of "spiritual edification" was chosen for this category as it is sufficiently broad to include these nuanced responses.

3.4.2.2 *Confirmation and Direction*

A second purpose of prophecy is to provide confirmation for a decision or to set a direction (RESB, RESE, RESF, RESH, RESI). Depending on whom the prophecy is intended for, this purpose may apply to either the general congregation or to specific individuals. The interviewees made an important qualification that believers should never initiate a decision solely from a prophecy but should also seek to know God's direction through their own prayer and discernment. They believed that God communicates with believers through Scripture, through prayer, through the counsel of spiritual leaders, and through circumstances. Prophecy was seen as bringing confirmation to a message God was communicating through these other means. RESE explains:

> When God gives you a prophecy it is not for directional purposes. It is to confirm what God has already spoken to you. And even if it is something that you are hearing for the first time, take that prophecy and continue to wait until God speaks to you. So, it is never meant for you to make a life-altering decision that alters your life unless there has been a confirmation.

Likewise, RESI cautioned against believers treating prophecy as a form of Christian fortune-telling or divination. Instead, RESI called it an "affirmation and confirmation to the person of what God is already speaking."

RESH provided a lengthy but significant example of prophecy providing confirmation of RESH's local church direction. RESH shared an instance when a leader from another church approached RESH to purchase a plot of land to build a church building. This leader had apparently heard from God in prayer to approach RESH specifically. However, RESH struggled greatly with this suggestion as the proposed location was far from ideal. RESH came together with the church board and prayed to seek God's direction. They sensed that God was leading the church to become a "multi-center church" and to accept the proposal to build a new worship center in addition to their present location. The board members were impressed specifically with the words "multi-center church" and this was to prove significant. The new direction was a bold move and there was great uncertainty over it. The very next day, the church had an overseas guest preacher who was completely unaware of the situation. The guest preacher prophesied over the church during the service that they were to become a "multi-center church." The mention of those specific words convinced RESH and the church board that this was a confirmation of God's will for the church. They subsequently proceeded to purchase the property and established themselves as a multi-center church. Crucially, the prophetic confirmation of God's direction resulted in the congregation supporting the bold move despite their small size. It helped them to persevere in the face of various challenges and led the church to grow significantly, both numerically and spiritually.

In discussing the role of prophecy in confirmation and direction, the interviewees were unanimous in warning of possible abuse and manipulation. Some examples were shared of supposed prophecies which called for inappropriate decisions or which pointed individuals in a questionable direction. In all these cases, the interviewees cited how the church leadership intervened to correct the misguided "prophecies." The criteria for evaluating prophecies will be discussed later.

3.4.2.3 *Warning and Correction*

A third purpose of prophecy observed from the data is to provide warning or correction to the congregation or to specific individuals. This category may alternatively be considered a sub-category of spiritual edification that was discussed above. However, the examples cited seemed distinct enough to present this as a category on its own. An example of prophecy fulfilling this purpose was recounted by RESJ:

> I remember there was one case where this married man was living with another person. And I didn't know anything but just went over to him because he was standing there, to pray for him. I just told him, "Brother, the Lord loves you. he loves you with all that he is and the Lord has a word for you. Turn away from your sin. Go back to your wife." And I was shocked when I said this because it is like, suddenly, a word came out from my mouth without me knowing it.

In this case, the prophecy led to the man confessing his wrongdoing and seeking counseling for his marriage. RESJ was careful to stress that RESJ had no prior knowledge of the man's background and that the confrontation was totally out of character with the way RESJ operated in ministry.

Prophecy can also provide warning and correction to the general church congregation. RESI gave examples of prophecies that addressed spiritual apathy or disunity within the congregation and warned of negative consequences if the issues were not addressed. These prophecies would exhort the congregation to return back to God and to heal strained relationships amongst members. RESF added that prophecies that brought correction were not meant to bring condemnation on believers but rather to seek repentance and transformation of the parties concerned.

3.4.2.4 Healing

A fourth purpose of prophecy was in relation to the physical healing of individuals. Interviewees tended to see prophecy as complementing a "gift of healing" drawn from 1 Corinthians 12:9.[40] RESC and RESJ provided general examples of a corporate setting where the pastor receives a prophetic message from God during a congregational service. The prophecy would be that God wanted to heal people of a particular illness and to call people suffering from this illness to the front of the service hall to receive prayer. The interviewees testified of several occurrences of people who were healed in this manner.

RESD provided a personal example of prophecy occurring in conjunction with healing though this instance was somewhat unusual in that it involved praying for a person in proxy. RESD was at a Christian meeting overseas when there was a prophecy calling for people suffering from Crohn's disease to come to the altar for prayer and healing. RESD expressed great surprise since Crohn's disease is a fairly uncommon illness and yet the prophecy specifically mentioned it. Furthermore, RESD's wife was suffering from Crohn's disease for seven years up to that point. RESD expressed skepticism over the prophecy since his wife was not responding to any medical treatment and the doctors had given her only two more years to live. RESD also specifically mentioned he did not believe in praying for a person in proxy but, in this instance, he went to receive prayer on behalf of his wife who was back in Singapore. When RESD returned back to Singapore, he prayed for his wife at a church prayer meeting and she had a vision where she saw Jesus "washing her intestines." RESD shared the positive result of this episode: "I brought her to the doctor to confirm. They found no trace of the Crohn's. She was restored back." The incident brought firm conviction to RESD's family that God had the ability bring physical healing and that God could communicate this intention through prophecy.

3.4.2.5 Evangelism

Evangelism was identified as a fifth purpose of prophecy. While the interviewees did not specifically list evangelism as one of the purposes, an analysis of the data showed that RESB, RESC, RESD, and RESF described instances of people converting to Christianity as a result of a prophetic

---

40. 1 Corinthians 12:9 actually uses the plural χαρίσματα and is more appropriately translated "gifts of healings." However, Fee suggests that each occurrence of healing is a "gift" in itself. See Fee, *First Epistle to the Corinthians*, 594.

message. RESB provided a general description of non-Christians attending a church service when a prophecy was delivered. The prophecy brought a conviction of the reality of God that resulted in their faith conversion. RESF further elaborated on other instances where a prophecy was delivered calling for people who were sick to come forward and receive physical healing. The manifestation of both healing and prophecy in the service served to convince non-Christians of the reality and love of Christ resulting in conversions occurring. Thus, evangelism might be considered an indirect result of the manifestation of prophecy.

RESC provided a specific example of how evangelism took place through prophecy. A woman who was not a Christian visited RESC's church service for the first time. Even though RESC had never met the woman before, RESC felt a strong prompting that God wanted to speak to her. RESC thus began to prophesy to the woman midway through the service. In the prophecy, RESC described that the woman was going through a divorce and was very worried about her two children. RESC communicated God's love and concern for the woman and an impression that the marriage would be restored within the next two weeks. The woman was shocked by the prophecy because she was indeed undergoing a divorce and her troubles had brought her to church that day. The woman's marriage was subsequently restored and the woman decided to convert to Christianity as she was convinced of the reality of Jesus and Jesus's love for her.

3.4.3 The Practice of Prophecy

3.4.3.1 The Reception of Prophecy

The interviewees all reported prior experience in delivering a prophecy. This study requested that they describe these experiences in detail. It was found that prophecy was initiated by a spiritual experience in which the interviewees felt that God was trying to use them to communicate a message to others. The interviewees listed several ways in which they received this message from God.

The most common experience reported was receiving an impression that was believed to originate from God. All interviewees had encountered such an experience and described it in similar terms. RESG, RESI, and RESJ all spoke of receiving a general "impression" of what God wanted to say; RESH called it a "prompting"; RESA described it as something "you just sense in your heart"; and RESG termed it a "knowing." The impression was clear and distinct, and brought a general idea of what message should be communicated in the prophecy.

The second most commonly reported experience was seeing a "picture," a "mental image," or a "vision" of some sort (RESA, RESB, RESF, RESG, RESI, RESJ). RESB described it as God "downloading" pictures into the mind. The interviewees clarified that the "picture" or "mental image" appeared within their mind rather than as something that they actually saw with their physical eyes. Though they had never experienced it, they did not rule out the possibility of receiving a vision while in a trance. Interestingly, RESE reported never experiencing a "picture" or "mental image" which initiated prophecy.

A third experience, similar to an "impression," but more detailed was reported as receiving a "word," "statement," or "phrase." RESE described how "God drops a word in your heart" while RESF expressed it as a "word or statement just comes to my mind." These words or phrases would subsequently be used in the delivery of the prophecy. In some instances, the interviewees reported that the words just appeared spontaneously in their mind as a thought. In others, the interviewees reported hearing a voice speak to them (RESC, RESI, RESJ). RESJ called this the "inner voice of the Holy Spirit" but seemed a little uncertain if it was an actual voice when probed further by the researcher. In contrast, RESC seemed sure that it was an audible voice but could not explain if the voice was "internal" or "external." The congregation did not hear the voice and so it seemed moot to attempt any distinction between "internal" or "external" voices.

RESF and RESJ described a fourth experience where prophecy was initiated by a verse or passage of Scripture coming forcefully to their mind. RESF shared that the Scripture verse would suddenly "keep flashing back and forth" in RESF's mind. RESJ likewise spoke of Bible verses "appearing" in RESJ's mind. These Scripture passages contained the message that was to be communicated to the congregation.

A fifth spiritual experience initiating prophecy was shared by RESG. RESG described it as a "physical sensation" which resulted in an awareness of what the prophetic message was. This was distinguished from a simple cognitive "impression" in that it involved a physical touch or a physical weight pressing on RESG. However, this spiritual experience seemed to be unique to RESG and was not reported by any other interviewee.

A sixth possibility observed from the data is where a believer speaks a message in an unknown tongue (*glossolalia*) which is then followed by an interpretation into a known language. The interpretation may be provided by the same believer who gave the message in tongues, by another congregational member, or by the pastor. There was some uncertainty about whether this phenomenon should be considered a prophecy. RESA and RESB were more inclined to think that this phenomenon should not be confused with prophecy. RESF claimed that "tongues is more in the area of exalting God" and so the interpretation should likewise be praise that is directed at exalting God. Likewise, RESI felt that tongues with interpretation should describe "the wonders of God, how great God is, how wonderful God is, and how glorious God is." In this way, tongues with interpretation would be directed towards God whereas prophecy was directed towards people. In contrast, RESD, RESH, and RESG all viewed a message in tongues with interpretation to be the functional equivalent of prophecy. They viewed both phenomena as God communicating with people and saw no reason for insisting that tongues with interpretation should not be directed towards people.

The spiritual experiences listed above usually occur spontaneously though some interviewees spoke of "waiting on God" (RESA, RESE) prior to receiving a prophetic message. Some interviewees reported occasions where they received the entire prophetic message before actually speaking and delivering it to others (RESA, RESI). However, other accounts indicate the prophetic message is revealed progressively as they speak and prophesy (RESD, RESE, RESF, RESG, RESJ). RESG describes both these instances:

> I think prophecy, if you study the nature of prophecy, prophecy can come one word at a time or it can come like a torrential rain. So, in a sense, sometimes you only have an impression and you start out with that impression and as you speak on that impression, more words come, as you are being led. And then there are times as you are sitting in a service or, you know, you may be standing up, you are sitting in a service and before you stand up you just sense this whole message.

RESD provided another description of how the prophetic message was progressively revealed while prophesying:

> Sometimes when it [the prophecy] comes I will just speak to the person. But the more I speak, the words just continue and follows. It is not like I get one whole paragraph. I would just say, "I believe that the Lord is saying this to you," and I will just say to the person. The more I say, the more the flow continues and continues.

These descriptions indicate that the spiritual experiences by which God communicates a prophetic message may continue as a person speaks and prophesies. Even though this study considers the reception and delivery of prophecy in separate phases, it must be acknowledged that these phases overlap.

3.4.3.2 *The Delivery of Prophecy*

After experiencing a spiritual impetus to prophesy, the interviewees described the actual process of delivering the prophecy to other people. This delivery was always communicated to the congregation in a verbal manner in all the examples recorded in the interviews. The first area of analysis concerned the psychological state of the person prophesying. The interviewees reported an internal pressure which prompted them to speak out and proclaim the prophetic message they had received. RESD described the feeling as "like a certain push from within that it [the prophecy] must come out." RESF felt a sense of nervousness mixed with some fear, and yet "the excitement of the message that is inside and you feel that you must speak and you just can't hold on." RESG expressed a feeling of "exhilaration" which was followed by a "sense of release" once the prophecy was delivered. RESH described it as a "very charged up atmosphere" which was followed by a "prompting to say something."

None of the interviewees reported falling into a trance or losing consciousness while prophesying. They acknowledged that it was possible for a person to be overwhelmed by a vision from God but none of them had ever had such an experience. This seems to suggest that such experiences are rare in practice. All the interviewees reported that they could choose when to start speaking out the prophecy and when to stop. RESB's view may be considered typical of the other interviewees:

> I can shut up, I can keep quiet, and I can choose not to say anything. We are never in a trance. We are still in control but yet at the same time not in control. But when I say "not in control," I am not saying out of control. I am saying that you are under the guidance of the Holy Spirit.

RESA quoted 1 Corinthians 14:32 to say that the phenomenon is always under the control of the one prophesying. RESA clarified that this did not mean a person could prophesy at will but felt that it had to be divinely initiated by God.

A second area of analysis focused on the choice of words used to express the prophecy. Several interviewees shared of instances where they spoke out words that surprised even themselves (RESA, RESD, RESG, RESH, RESJ). RESA and RESJ described incidents in which they expressed a message that was completely out of character with what they would normally say. For RESH, it was like "a torrent of words that tumbles out and a lot of it is not premeditated." Similarly, RESG called it a "torrential rain" of words coming out of RESG's mouth. In these instances, the interviewees felt that the words and sentences came from God. However, the interviewees described more common instances of using their own words to express the prophecy. RESB felt that God chooses to use a person's vocabulary and personality to express the message that God wanted to deliver. Likewise, RESD was conscious that RESD was phrasing the prophecy in RESD's own words. RESD further noted that the prophecy was often expressed in sentences that were grammatically poor. This was attributed to RESD's poor command of the language and was not to be attributed to divine inspiration. One view was that the thoughts and impressions prompting the prophecy came from God but the actual phrasing of the spoken message was left to the one prophesying (RESF, RESG, RESJ). RESG explains: "It's not as if God orchestrates the sentences for you. He gives you the main thought. He gives you the main thrust and then you begin to speak. You put it into your own sentences." RESG added an opinion that prophecies should be introduced with phrases like "I sense," "I feel," or "I think God is leading me to say." This would make it clear that the ones prophesying were expressing the message in their own words.

The descriptions provided by the interviewees further indicated that some human interpretation was taking place while delivering the prophecy. RESJ explained that God may initiate a prophecy by bringing a mental picture to mind. The prophecy would then involve describing the mental picture and this might include an interpretation of what the picture signifies or symbolizes. This was also true of impressions or Bible verses which RESJ received. While RESJ felt that the Holy Spirit was guiding the entire process, RESJ was conscious of human reasoning and interpretation occurring while delivering the prophecy. RESC likewise described this as the addition of "human flavorings" while expressing the prophecy. RESD spoke of the "human element" influencing the delivery of a prophecy, especially with regard to the interpretation and application of the message. This "human element" was largely seen as negative and the source of mistakes.

3.4.4 The Judging of Prophecy

All interviewees in the study believed in the necessity of judging and evaluating prophecies. Various criteria were used to do this. The first and most common criterion cited was whether the content of the prophecy was in agreement with Scripture. Interviewees stressed the importance for prophecies to be "in line with Scripture," "in line with the word of God," or "biblical" (RESA, RESC, RESD, RESE, RESF, RESG, RESH, RESI, RESJ). Prophecies that were found to contradict established biblical truths or Christian doctrine were rejected in the congregations represented by these interviewees. Likewise, prophecies containing teaching that could not be substantiated from Scripture were also rejected.

A second criterion, related to the content of the prophecy, was whether the message served to edify its recipients. The teaching in 1 Corinthians 14:3 was cited as a biblical basis for this criterion (RESD, RESF, RESH, RESJ). RESF explains: "I always believe that it [prophecies] cannot be something that is going to bring condemnation to the whole body because Paul says very clearly that the gift of prophecy is for edifying, for building up, for comfort, and for encouragement." In particular, RESH and RESJ cautioned against people who prophesy from a "negative spirit" or a "negative mindset." They felt that such prophecies would be judgmental and leave the congregation with a sense of condemnation. However, RESH qualified that in some cases, the content of the message was "correct" but the one prophesying had chosen to express it in a negative manner. This emphasized the "human element" (RESD) in prophesying which was mentioned previously. RESF also qualified that prophecies may sometimes bring correction to the congregation by highlighting unhealthy spiritual issues. These prophecies exhort the congregation to repent and turn back to God and so they would be considered as edifying the community of faith.

The character of the person prophesying was identified as a third criterion from the data. Interviewees felt that the person prophesying should demonstrate a godly lifestyle and exhibit the "fruit of the Spirit" (RESA, RESD, RESE, RESG, RESH, RESI). RESH explained that this criterion did not immediately cause a prophecy to be dismissed since it was accepted that God could manifest spiritual gifts in any believer, regardless of character. However, prophecies from people with questionable character would be closely scrutinized in terms of the other criteria. The character of the person prophesying was also evident in their attitude towards the local church leadership. Respect and submission to the pastoral team overseeing the congregation was expected and even demanded (RESD, RESI). This criterion seemed to imply that believers who were unfamiliar to the local congregation would not be allowed to prophesy.

The fourth criterion found from this study is the manner in which the prophecy is delivered. Interviewees stressed the importance of order during congregational meetings and that prophecies should not disrupt the meeting (RESG, RESH, RESI, RESJ). RESG shared the opinion that 1 Corinthians

14:26–33 sought to correct prophecies which were disrupting the peace and order of the assembly. Hence, the guidelines given by Paul were felt to be highly relevant for the practice of prophecy today.

Beyond the criteria for evaluating prophecy, interviewees were also asked who was involved in the evaluation process and how this was practically carried out. All interviewees agreed that the pastor and the pastoral team played the key role in evaluating a prophecy. After the evaluation, the pastor in charge of the meeting would address the congregation from the pulpit. This would either be to direct the congregation to respond to the prophecy or to dismiss a prophecy that was not felt to come from God. The latter occasions would inevitably cause some uneasiness and discomfort amongst the congregation. RESH described the challenge resulting from a "false" prophecy:

> You have people blurting out [prophesying] when you don't know them or worse, you know them and you know that they are in no position to make that prophecy because their lives are in a mess. Of course, you can judge after that but the damage has been done. They have already said all those words. You may pull them aside and tell them next time don't do it. But that word has already gone forth.

This challenge led to RESG, RESH, and RESJ requesting people wanting to prophesy in their congregational meetings to approach a pastor for permission. The pastor would then quickly evaluate the main thrust of the prophetic message and determine if it should be shared with the congregation. This protocol was also partly due to the size of the meetings and the practical challenge of delivering a prophecy which everyone in the meeting would be able to hear. In some instances, RESG and RESJ shared that the pastor may even ask for the prophecy to be written down and then the pastor would read out the message rather than let the person address the congregation.

The judging and evaluating of personal prophecies raised a different issue for the interviewees. All the interviewees acknowledged that prophecies directed at specific individuals had occurred in their congregation. The criteria for evaluation listed above would still apply and the process for evaluation would remain the same if the prophecy were delivered in a congregational setting. However, some interviewees expressed reservations about prophesying in one-to-one settings (RESB, RESF, RESH, RESI). RESF commented:

> If it [prophecy] is one to one, the accountability aspect is a question. Who is this person who prophesies one to one? The one who gives the prophecy must be accountable either to the Senior

Pastor or a pastor should be standing there to hear what they have to say. Just in case someone who prophesies over another person, and the person has no one to turn to or does not seek advice from someone or talk to a leader and ask, "What do you think about this prophecy?"

Likewise, RESI felt that nobody would be able to evaluate the prophecy except the recipient of the prophecy. RESI explains:

> But that [one-to-one prophecy] is pretty dangerous. Because, like in 1 Corinthians 14, if God has a word then let the others test the prophecy. So, in a one-to-one encounter, who is going to test that word? I would say it can happen and the person who receive that word must really test the word.

This would imply that recipients should be sufficiently mature to evaluate a prophetic message for themselves (RESG). RESC shared that RESC's congregation were all taught to evaluate personal prophecies in such situations. However, RESH felt that personal prophecy was at odds with 1 Corinthians 14:29 which suggests a corporate accountability. RESH also raised other issues with this practice:

> I have concerns. I am not skeptical but I have concerns that it may lead to the people of God being too overly dependent on personal words of prophecy when God has already given His Word for us to read and for us to live by. You can get into this rut where you won't move until somebody comes and goes into a trance and says something over you, then you move. I feel it creates a dependency problem.

Furthermore, the interviewees related unfortunate stories of people who were hurt or manipulated through the practice of one-to-one prophecies. Still, the interviewees did not wish to ban the practice but rather emphasized the enforcement of a protocol for prophesying. RESG suggested that believers should refrain from proclaiming a prophecy in a one-to-one situation but should instead verbally pray with the person in accordance with what they felt God was saying. This facilitated ministry to the person without introducing the issues related to personal prophecy.

3.4.5 Themes Which Enhance the Practice of Prophecy

The discussion above has sought to present a case description of the practice of prophecy. In addition, the data was analyzed to identify themes that are related to the practice of prophecy. In particular, this study identified compassion, courage, and intimacy with God as themes that served to enhance the practice of prophecy.

3.4.5.1 Compassion

The first theme of compassion was apparent from the many responses that emphasized the importance of having a love for people when practicing prophecy. This was expressed as "compassion" (RESA, RESH, RESJ), a "love for people" (RESB, RESG), and a "desire for the good of the body" (RESD). RESB states this emphatically when describing the most important requirement for operating in spiritual gifts: "Love. Number one is love for people. That is the greatest. All gifts function most effectively when it comes out of love. And when [we] have that love and burden for them, it [prophecy] flows." Other interviewees explained that God sought to use believers who had strong compassion for others. RESD felt that compassion motivated believers to be more "open" to the Holy Spirit so that they might be a "blessing to the body of believers." This "openness" to the Holy Spirit allowed prophecy to be manifested through them. RESB associated compassion with 1 Corinthians 13 which describes the importance of ministering spiritual gifts in love. In this sense, compassion enables the manifestation of all spiritual gifts and not just prophecy alone.

The emphasis on compassion in enhancing the practice of prophecy must be balanced with cases of abuse and manipulation described by the interviewees. This seemed to suggest that certain individuals were prophesying out of personal motivation rather than a compassion for others. An obvious explanation is that these individuals were not delivering authentic prophecies but rather false prophecies so as to manipulate believers. Interviewees were clearly aware of this since they all spoke of the need to evaluate the content of prophecies and the character of the one prophesying. These cases were also an exception within the congregations rather than a common occurrence.

3.4.5.2 Courage

A second theme observed from the data was courage. Courage was identified as necessary for a believer to exercise the gift of prophecy. For example, RESH shared of the need to be "bold in spirit to make utterances." RESJ called this the "courage and faith to allow the Holy Spirit to use them" through prophecy. RESG felt "everyone who wants to prophesy will just have to step out and be bold enough to speak." RESG continued to describe this attitude as "courage to step out [and prophesy] even though there are unknowns, even though you don't know everything." RESC likewise described prophecy as "a gift activated by faith." This theme of courage was also apparent when interviewees listed "fear" as a hindrance to prophesying (RESA, RESD, RESE). This was explained as a "fear of rejection" (RESA) or looking silly in front of others (RESD).

The theme of courage was also found in the characteristic response of recipients of prophecies. RESI saw prophecy encouraging "faith to believe for something impossible" whereas RESG described how "faith can be stirred up" through a prophecy. One specific example described earlier concerned a prophecy to RESH's church to become a "multi-center church." This prophecy enabled the church to take courage and purchase a second property despite their initial unwillingness. Prophecies concerning physical healing also called recipients to take courage and trust God for the divine healing of their bodies.

3.4.5.3 Intimacy with God

The analysis of the data suggests that intimacy with God is a third theme which enhances believers' ability to prophesy. RESB spoke of the need for "an on-going vital relationship with God"; RESE alluded to "an inner life of consistency with God"; RESH called it "intimacy and sensitivity to the Holy Spirit"; and RESI shared the importance of "how open you are to the Holy Spirit." This theme was similarly evident when RESA and RESF related the importance of holiness and godliness for being "in tune with God" so that believers could discern what God wanted to say to others through prophecy. The reverse relationship was also cited when RESG observed that "sin has tremendous hindrances to hearing God's voice accurately." This is not to suggest that believers must be free from sin to minister through prophecy. Prophecy and all spiritual gifts were not seen as indications of spiritual maturity by the interviewees. Rather, RESI explained that spiritual gifts were expressions of God's grace and God could sovereignly choose whomever God wanted to use.

The manifestation of prophecy was also observed to evoke a sense of intimacy within the congregation. As RESC describes it, prophecy "shows that our God is a living God who sees and speaks and knows everything you are going through." Others testified that prophecy resulted in the feeling that "God is so close" (RESA) and serves as a "strong testimony that God is real" (RESD). RESE described how believers "sense a tangible presence of

God" through prophecy. Prophecies that occur in conjunction with physical healing bring a deep sense of God's care and concern. For example, the healing of RESD's wife from Crohn's disease brought an immense sense of God's love for the family. This increased sense of intimacy brought through prophecy stirs excitement amongst congregation members and creates an expectation to encounter and hear from God through prophecy when they attended church services. This study already noted that this sense of intimacy and the reality of God resulted in the faith conversion of some non-Christians. Furthermore, the interviewees noted that prophecy had a positive influence with the congregation participating more enthusiastically in singing and prayer immediately after a prophecy is delivered.

3.5 SUMMARY AND DISCUSSION

This chapter has presented a qualitative study of prophecy in the AG churches in Singapore. As previously mentioned, the objectives are to present a thick description of prophecy in Singapore, to identify theological themes related to prophecy, and to detect categories for the development of instruments for use in empirical-theological testing. The study's survey of the history of the AGS showed a theme of supernatural guidance in bringing the Jacksons to Singapore. Even though the Jacksons arrived in Singapore by mistake, it appears to be divine providence since they established the AG movement in the country. Supernatural guidance was also evident in Rev. Baird's missions call to Singapore when she exclaimed aloud the country's name during her prayer. Current AGS meetings and publications continue to show an active expectation of the supernatural in practical ministry. Believers and ministers are encouraged to exercise spiritual gifts such as prophecy for the healthy functioning of the church. The interviews likewise showed that local congregations actively practice prophecy, speaking in tongues, and divine healing.

Interviews were conducted with ten AGS senior pastors and then analyzed to produce a case description around the process of receiving, delivering, and judging prophecy. The study identified the purpose of prophecy as spiritual edification, confirmation and direction, warning and correction, healing, and evangelism. The spiritual experiences initiating prophecy were categorized as receiving an impression, a mental image, a word or statement, a Scripture verse or passage, a physical sensation, and an unknown tongue (*glossolalia*) followed by an interpretation. The prophetic message may sometimes be fully revealed to the one prophesying before the actual delivery. In other cases, the prophetic message comes progressively as the believer starts to prophesy. The one prophesying remains in psychological control of oneself and usually chooses the words to express the prophetic message. Prophecies are judged based on their biblical fidelity, edification of others, the character of the person prophesying, and the manner in which the prophecy is delivered. Content analysis further showed that compassion, courage, and intimacy with God were themes related to the practice of prophecy. This study is now able to reflect on the data collected and make two comments.

First, data obtained from this qualitative study demonstrates a strong supernatural worldview within the AGS denomination. Supernatural activity was evident in the AGS history and is encouraged and expected in present-day church life. This worldview of the AGS accords well with Vanhoozer's hermeneutical model adopted by this study. As previously mentioned, Vanhoozer envisions the Holy Spirit as the director in his theodramatic proposal. The Holy Spirit mediates between the written word and the lived reality of the church enabling believers to perform in critical faithfulness with the divine script. Likewise, the qualitative data shows that the Holy Spirit assumes a central role in the AGS, leading, guiding, encouraging, correcting, and healing the community. Furthermore, the Holy Spirit's provision of spiritual gifts like prophecy within the AGS fits in well with Vanhoozer's analogy of the Holy Spirit as the prop master who equips and empowers the church.

Scripture maintains an authoritative position within the AGS as they evaluate all prophetic messages based on its agreement with accepted biblical truth. As in Vanhoozer's model, Scripture maintains the role of canonical script within the AGS, guiding the practice of prophecy and permitting contemporary improvisation in living out biblical truth but restricting unfaithful performances. Vanhoozer's model places an emphasis on the development of the believer's *habitus*. This shaping of the *habitus* can also be seen in the dispositions of compassion, courage, and intimacy with God which enhance prophecy and are in turn cultivated in the congregation as a result of prophecy.

Second, the various themes and categories identified enables further exploration in the following phases of this study. The spiritual experiences identified as initiating prophecy provide useful data for developing an instrument to measure prophetic activity. There is also the possibility of determining the frequency of these experiences amongst a larger sample of AGS ministers. This chapter associated the purpose of prophecy with various themes found in the interviews. There is potential for further investigation of these themes and how common they are in relation to prophecy. The criteria for judging prophecy can also be tested to see how they are utilized in congregational and personal prophecy. The themes of compassion, courage, and intimacy with God should also be further researched in the literature survey and in the quantitative phase of this empirical study. These themes seem to play a key role in stimulating prophecy within the church and in turn the themes are themselves stirred up in the congregation through the practice of prophecy.

The next two chapters will continue the phase of theological induction by surveying the literature of the Pentecostal movement in relation to prophecy. The literature survey will then be combined with the results from this qualitative study in the phase of theological deduction and operationalization.

4

The Nature and Purpose of Prophecy

4.1 INTRODUCTION

THIS CHAPTER SEEKS TO present a survey of the literature on the nature and purpose of prophecy in the New Testament.[1] Due to the vast number of studies in this area, the survey will mainly focus on the Classical Pentecostal position and practice. Furthermore, attention is paid to resources that are significant and influential to the Singapore church since this is the locus of the overall study. The topic of prophecy has been of great interest to the Pentecostal movement from its earliest developments. Discussions on prophecy may be found in books on spiritual gifts written by some of the early Pentecostal pioneers like Howard Carter, Donald Gee, Harold Horton, and Stanley Horton.[2] Extended scholarly treatment on prophecy can be found in works by Pentecostal scholars such as William Kay, Anthony Palma, Cecil Robeck Jr., and Roger Stronstad.[3] In Singapore, theologian Simon Chan has examined prophecy while David Lim has discussed proph-

---

1. Works cited should be understood as representative rather than exhaustive.

2. Carter, *Spiritual Gifts*; Gee, *Spiritual Gifts in the Work of the Ministry Today*; Gee, *Concerning Spiritual Gifts*; Horton, *Gifts of the Spirit*; Horton, *What the Bible Says about the Holy Spirit*.

3. Kay, *Prophecy!*; Palma, "Prophecy: Nature and Scope"; Palma, "Prophecy: Regulation and Purpose"; Robeck, "Gift of Prophecy in Acts and Paul Part 1"; Robeck, "Gift of Prophecy in Acts and Paul Part 2"; Robeck, "Prophetic Authority"; Robeck, "Role and Function of Prophetic Gifts"; Robeck, "Prophecy, Gift of"; Stronstad, *Prophethood of All Believers*. Also see The Assemblies of God USA, "Apostles and Prophets."

ecy within a larger work on spiritual gifts.[4] There is a general paucity of scholarly research done by Pentecostals themselves due partly to the movement's beginnings among the lower social classes and partly to the preferred practical orientation of its leaders.[5]

One of the more significant and influential scholars in the area of prophecy is Wayne Grudem.[6] Though Grudem is not directly associated with Classical Pentecostals and is critical of their doctrine,[7] Pentecostals have welcomed his work on prophecy and generally accepted his conclusions on this gift.[8] Other works, which have typified prophecy as the reception and communication of a revelatory message from God, include David Aune, Christopher Forbes, Elim Hiu, and Max Turner.[9] Their views are generally supportive of the Pentecostal position and practice of prophecy while also providing some critique.

There are numerous other studies on the phenomena with some suggesting that prophecy is equivalent to preaching,[10] charismatic exegesis,[11]

---

4. Chan, "Prophecy and Discernment"; Lim, *Spiritual Gifts*.

5. Russell Spittler accurately characterizes scholarship within the Pentecostal movement when he writes, "Pentecostals have made better missionaries than theologians. They write pamphlets, not books—tracts, not treatises. When a Pentecostal book is published, it will reflect more likely personal testimony than reasoned argument." Spittler, "Suggested Areas for Further Research in Pentecostal Studies," 39. Also note the comments by Hollenweger on the challenges of global academic research on Pentecostalism. See Hollenweger, *Pentecostalism*, 288–306.

6. Grudem, *Gift of Prophecy in 1 Corinthians*; Grudem, *Gift of Prophecy in the New Testament and Today*. The former represents his PhD dissertation at Cambridge University and the latter is a popular version of his work. This popular version is widely distributed in Singapore.

7. Grudem specifically discusses and rejects the Classical Pentecostal doctrine of the Baptism of the Holy Spirit and the initial evidence of speaking in tongues. See Grudem, *Systematic Theology*, 763–84.

8. Lim bases his discussion of prophecy on Grudem's work while Fee is generally appreciative of Grudem. See Lim, *Spiritual Gifts*; Fee, *First Epistle to the Corinthians*; Fee, *God's Empowering Presence*. Also see Menzies, "Review of *The Gift of Prophecy in 1 Corinthians*"; Horton, "Review of *The Gift of Prophecy in the New Testament and Today*." It is significant that in a booklet on spiritual gifts by the AG, Grudem's work is cited as a recommended resource. Grudem appears to be the only scholar listed who is not a Classical Pentecostal. See Horton, *Gifts and Fruit of the Spirit*.

9. Aune, *Prophecy in Early Christianity*; Forbes, *Prophecy and Inspired Speech*; Hiu, *Regulations Concerning Tongues and Prophecy*; Turner, *Holy Spirit and Spiritual Gifts*.

10. Gillespie, *First Theologians*; Hill, *New Testament Prophecy*; Thiselton, *First Epistle to the Corinthians*.

11. Boring, *Continuing Voice of Jesus*; Ellis, "Role of the Christian Prophet"; Ellis, *Prophecy and Hermeneutic*.

or a gift which has ceased.[12] There are also books written by Charismatic and Third Wave authors which are scholarly yet targeted at the popular level. Some notable examples are by Jack Deere, Ernest Gentile, and David Pytches.[13] The perspective on prophecy from the Roman Catholic tradition is discussed by Niels Hvidt but this tradition has significantly less influence with Classical Pentecostals.[14]

4.2 THE NATURE OF PROPHECY

4.2.1 The "Prophethood" of Believers

Classical Pentecostals generally understand prophecy to be a divine enablement from God. However, before discussing this view, there is a more general sense in which Pentecostals see all believers in the New Testament functioning as prophets for God. Petts describes this as the first level of prophecy in the New Testament where all Christians are able to speak for God and represent God to the world.[15] This broad understanding holds that a prophet functions primarily as a spokesperson for a deity.[16] With the outpouring of the Holy Spirit in Acts 2, all believers are specifically described as able to prophesy, regardless of their age and gender (Acts 2:16–18). The Acts 2 account is interpreted in light of Acts 1:8 where all believers are declared to be empowered witnesses of the gospel to the world. Believers thus function as a representative of God and continue to speak for God to the world (2 Cor 5:20).

Stronstad similarly articulates this general understanding in terms of the "prophethood" of all believers. Stronstad argues for this in his detailed studies of the Luke-Acts narrative.[17] He identifies a parallel structure between the two volumes authored by Luke and asserts that the author's intention is to convey the transfer of the Spirit of prophecy from Jesus to

---

12. Farnell, "The Current Debate about New Testament Prophecy"; Farnell, "The Gift of Prophecy in the Old and New Testaments"; Farnell, "Does the New Testament Teach Two Prophetic Gifts?"; Farnell, "When Will the Gift of Prophecy Cease?"; Gentry, *Charismatic Gift of Prophecy*.

13. Deere, *Surprised by the Voice of God*; Deere, *Beginner's Guide to the Gift of Prophecy*; Gentile, *Your Sons and Daughters Shall Prophesy*; Pytches, *Prophecy in the Local Church*.

14. Hvidt, *Christian Prophecy*.

15. Petts, *Body Builders*, 44.

16. Robeck, "Prophecy, Gift of," 1002.

17. Stronstad, *Charismatic Theology of St. Luke*; Stronstad, *Prophethood of All Believers*.

the disciples in Acts and thus to the church at large. Luke is seen to portray Jesus as the eschatological, anointed, and charismatic prophet whose inauguration (Luke 4:16–30) is marked by the descent of the Spirit (Luke 3:21–22). Likewise, the early disciples are inaugurated as a prophetic community (Acts 2:17–21) through the outpouring of the Spirit (Acts 2:1–4). The church is now a prophetic community, empowered in both word and deed, to be witnesses of Christ to the world.

The concept of the "prophethood" of believers can also be seen in extensive studies on Luke-Acts by R. P. Menzies and Turner.[18] These studies recognize Luke's depiction of the Holy Spirit as the Spirit of prophecy, empowering both Jesus and the early church. For R. P. Menzies, the Lukan narratives do not assign any soteriological function to the Spirit and instead portray the Spirit as empowering the church for service through a prophetic endowment of special insight and prophetic speech. Turner, on the other hand, asserts that the Spirit in Luke-Acts fulfills both soteriological and missiological functions as the Spirit of prophecy. In particular, Turner sees charismatic revelation, wisdom, invasive prophecy, and praise (including tongues) as prototypical gifts of the "Spirit of prophecy." This charismatic dimension should then characterize all of the Christian life. In both these works, the church becomes a prophetic community, empowered by the Spirit of prophecy, to witness for Christ to the world.

The positions of Petts, Stronstad, and R. P. Menzies stress the Pentecostal understanding that the primary function of the gift of the Spirit is vocational or missiological, rather than soteriological. Even Turner acknowledges this vocational empowerment though he also stresses the soteriological dimension. All believers become empowered "prophets" as they represent and speak for God to the world.[19]

---

18. See Menzies, *Development of Early Christian Pneumatology*; Menzies, *Empowered for Witness*; Turner, *Power from on High*; Turner, *Holy Spirit and Spiritual Gifts*. While Menzies and Turner share much in common in noting the prophetic/charismatic dimension of the faith community within Luke-Acts, they differ in a crucial aspect. Menzies argues strongly for the Classical Pentecostal doctrine of subsequence and initial evidence whereas Turner rejects this. An Asian perspective from a Classical Pentecostal scholar is provided by Joshua Iap. See Iap, 聖靈的洗 *[Baptism in the Spirit]*.

19. Gaffin, a noted cessationist, also acknowledges the "prophethood" of all believers in a sense similar to what was described in this section. Gaffin, *Perspectives on Pentecost*, 59.

4.2.2 Prophecy as a Spiritual Gift

The second level of prophecy described by Petts is the understanding of prophecy as a spiritual gift.[20] This view is widely acknowledged and accepted within the Pentecostal tradition. In fact, prophecy is the most widely mentioned of all the gifts in the New Testament canon.[21] Some might even say that Paul considers prophecy to be the preeminent gift above the rest of the gifts.[22] In attempting to define prophecy, most scholars have focused on the book of Acts and the letters of Paul, especially 1 Corinthians 12–14. It is well recognized that the Pauline letters are occasional documents addressing a specific historical context and so caution must be exercised in drawing inferences from these texts. Paul does not seek to provide a structured and comprehensive explanation of spiritual gifts in any of his letters.

While the term "spiritual gift" is extremely common within the Pentecostal movement, the actual term appears only once in Scripture and does not refer to prophecy in that instance.[23] Instead, Paul uses either πνευματικά (*pneumatika*) or χαρίσματα (*charismata*) to separately refer to what interpreters have termed "spiritual gifts."[24] These terms appear to be used interchangeably by Paul though each carries a different emphasis on the nature of the gifts.[25] This concept of spiritual gifts will be discussed below since prophecy is clearly considered to be one of the gifts.

---

20. Petts, *Body Builders*, 45–47.

21. See, for example, Acts 2:17–18; 11:27–30; 13:1–3; 15:32; 19:6; 21:8–14; 1 Thessalonians 5:20; 2 Thessalonians 2:2; 1 Corinthians 11:4–5; 1 Corinthians 12; 1 Corinthians 14; Romans 12:6; Ephesians 2:20, 3:5, 4:11; 1 Timothy 1:18, 4:14. Some of these passages refer to a "prophet" rather than the gift of "prophecy" but it may be reasonably assumed that the "prophet" exercised the gift.

22. Friedrich, "προφήτης." In *TDNT* 6: 850.

23. Romans 1:11 contains the phrase "πνευματικὸν χάρισμα" which may be translated as "spiritual gift." Both Moo and Mounce feel that Paul is not referring to the gifts in 1 Corinthians 12 but is rather wanting to share some spiritual insight to strengthen the church. See Moo, *Romans*, 676; Mounce, *Romans*, 59–60.

24. Prophecy is described as among the χαρίσματα in 1 Corinthians 12 and is listed as one of the πνευματικά in 1 Corinthians 14.

25. For the view that the terms are interchangeable, see Conzelmann, *1 Corinthians*, 207; Dunn, *Theology of Paul*, 554–55; Fee, *First Epistle to the Corinthians*, 654–55; Palma, *Holy Spirit*, 185–86. In contrast, Ellis argues that χαρίσματα is a more general term that refers to all the gifts whereas πνευματικά refers only to gifts of inspired speech. R. P. Menzies and W. Menzies agree with Ellis on this point though their intent is to assert that Spirit-baptism serves as the "gateway" (their term) to the πνευματικά which they see as prophetic-type gifts. Bruce and Blomberg interpret πνευματικῶν in 1 Corinthians 12:1 to refer to "spiritual people" rather than "spiritual gifts." Another possibility suggested by Schatzmann is that πνευματικά is the term favored by the Corinthian church whereas Paul is seeking to replace it with the term χαρίσματα. Fee stands with Grudem

The first term, πνευματικά (*pneumatika*), may literally be translated as "spiritual things" or "spiritual matters."[26] The term does not connote "gift" on its own but acquires this connotation since Paul uses it as the introduction to 1 Corinthians 12 and 14 where "gifts" are discussed. The use of the term πνευματικά places the stress on the source of the gifts being the activity of the Spirit (πνεῦμα) within the community of faith.[27] Indeed, Paul even refers to gifts as the manifestations of the Spirit in 1 Corinthians 12:7 such that the gifts serve as the evidence of the Spirit's activity. To experience the gifts is to experience the dynamic activity of the Holy Spirit. It is for this reason that the phenomena are also sometimes referred to as "gifts of the Spirit" though this term is never explicitly used in Scripture. Spiritual gifts are thus primarily the evidence of divine activity within the faith community and should only be thought of secondarily as human activity.

The second and more prominent term used by Paul to refer to prophecy and the rest of the gifts is χάρισμα/χαρίσματα (*charisma/charismata*). This term is acknowledged as specifically Pauline, appearing almost exclusively within his writings in the biblical documents.[28] A survey of Scripture will show the term χάρισμα possessing a wide range of meanings in Paul's writings though it seems best to understand it as a concrete expression of God's χάρις (*charis*).[29] Turner provides a different perspective in asserting that χάρισμα is not primarily related to Paul's concept of grace but more correctly associated with the verb χαρίζομαι (*charizomai*), thus emphasizing God's generosity rather than the underlying phenomenon.[30] In the context of the most prominent passage in 1 Corinthians 12, χαρίσματα is often translated as "gifts" with some even suggesting that Paul uses this term in a technical or semi-technical sense to refer to spiritual gifts.[31] Paul's emphasis in using

---

in rejecting the other various interpretations of πνευματικά. For all the views above, see Blomberg, *1 Corinthians*, 243; Bruce, *1 and 2 Corinthians*, 116; Ellis, *Prophecy and Hermeneutic*, 24; Grudem, *Gift of Prophecy in 1 Corinthians*, 157–62; Menzies and Menzies, *Spirit and Power*, 195–96; Schatzmann, *Pauline Theology of Charismata*, 31–21.

26. BDAG 837.

27. Fee, *First Epistle to the Corinthians*, 576; Palma, *Holy Spirit*, 185.

28. Thiselton, *First Epistle to the Corinthians*, 930.

29. See Fee, *God's Empowering Presence*, 32–35; Schatzmann, *Pauline Theology of Charismata*, 8. Schatzmann provides an extensive discussion of χάρισμα/χαρίσματα in his book.

30. Turner, *Holy Spirit and Spiritual Gifts*, 256–61. This point is acknowledged by Palma. See Palma, *Holy Spirit*, 184. Also see BDAG 1081.

31. Dunn, *Theology of Paul*, 553; Williams, *Renewal Theology*, 323. In contrast, Berding and Aker have argued that there is little evidence to support a technical meaning for the term χάρισμα. Berding instead suggests that χάρισμα should be interpreted as "spiritual ministries" in most contexts where it appears. See Aker, "Charismata";

this term is to stress that the phenomena listed in 1 Corinthians 12:8–10 are concrete expressions of God's χάρις in word and deed. The χαρίσματα are thus "gifts of grace" or "gracious bestowments" within the community of faith so that believers might edify one another allowing the entire body of believers to be built up.[32] This is important so that gifts are seen as demonstrations of God's generosity and not as an indicator of spiritual maturity or human merit. The accent on God's grace has even led some within the Pentecostal-Charismatic movement to coin the term "gracelets" (as in "droplets of grace") when referring to spiritual gifts.[33]

The association of χαρίσματα with the Holy Spirit is seen in 1 Corinthians 12:4 where it is explicitly described as the activity of the πνεῦμα. This has led to χαρίσματα being translated as "spiritual gifts" even though the adjective is not present in the Greek text. In 1 Corinthians 12:5–6, the terms διακονιῶν (*diakonion*) and ἐνεργημάτων (*energematon*) are also used in parallel with χαρίσματα. Fee considers these parallel expressions to be different ways of looking at the φανέρωσις (*phanerosis*) of the Spirit with the primary emphasis on the variety of gifts, service, and workings through one Spirit/Lord/God.[34] Schatzmann goes further to suggest that χαρίσματα emphasizes the concept of grace, διακονιῶν denotes the purpose of the gifts as service to the body, and ἐνεργημάτων describes the concrete results of the activities.[35] Keener simply sees these terms as rhetorical variation and rejects any assertion that they may be used to classify the gifts.[36]

From the discussion above, prophecy in the New Testament should be understood as part of the πνευματικά and χαρίσματα. Prophecy is a manifestation of the Holy Spirit's activity among believers and should not be confused with human activity. Prophecy is also a concrete expression of God's grace that results in the strengthening and edification of the body of believers.

Berding, *What Are Spiritual Gifts?* Interestingly, Turner makes the same point that χάρισμα is not a technical term but still interprets it as "gracious gift." Turner, *Holy Spirit and Spiritual Gifts*, 256–61.

32. Fee, *God's Empowering Presence*, 33.

33. The term is widely attributed to Russell Spittler. See Wagner, *Your Spiritual Gifts*, 40; Wimber and Springer, *Power Points*, 147–48..

34. Fee, *First Epistle to the Corinthians*, 586–87. Fee also discusses Paul's striking association of the gifts with the Persons of the Trinity.

35. Schatzmann, *Pauline Theology of Charismata*, 34.

36. Keener, *1–2 Corinthians*, 100.

4.2.3 Prophecy as Spontaneous Revelation

There is broad consensus among Pentecostals that prophecy is the reception and communication of a spontaneous revelation.[37] This understanding can be found from the beginnings of the Pentecostal movement. For example, Pentecostal statesman Donald Gee describes prophecy as "divinely inspired utterances" which come from the impulse of an immediate revelation.[38] Palma declares more explicitly, "The essential nature of prophecy is that of a divine revelation given to the prophet which he in turn communicates to others."[39] Robeck concurs with this view when he highlights the role of the Holy Spirit in bringing revelation to believers that are then proclaimed as prophecy.[40] Likewise, Lim describes prophecy as instances where the Holy Spirit illuminates a message to the believer that is then communicated to the larger body.[41] This view on prophecy finds strong scholarly support from the work of Grudem.[42] One of Grudem's principal arguments is for understanding prophecy as the reception and proclamation of a spontaneous revelation from God. In fact, he goes so far as to declare "if there is no ἀποκάλυψις, there is no prophecy."[43] Practically, he suggests that prophecy in the New Testament should be recognized as simply "telling something that God has brought spontaneously to mind."[44] The concept of revelation and the biblical evidence for it serving as an impetus for prophecy will be discussed below.

---

37. There are many outside the Pentecostal movement who also hold this view. For example, Dunn writes, "For Paul prophecy is a word of revelation. It does not denote the delivery of a previously prepared sermon; it is not a word that can be summoned up to order, or a skill that can be learned; it is a spontaneous utterance, a revelation given in words to the prophet to be delivered as it is given." Dunn, *Jesus and the Spirit*, 228. See also Carson, *Showing the Spirit*; Forbes, *Prophecy and Inspired Speech*; Turner, *Holy Spirit and Spiritual Gifts*; Hiu, *Regulations Concerning Tongues and Prophecy*.

38. Gee, *Concerning Spiritual Gifts*, 57. In contrast, Howard Carter, another early Pentecostal leader, notes the content of revelation within prophecy but asserts that this revelation is the result of the message of wisdom or the message of knowledge. Carter thus proposes multiple gifts in operation. This view will be discussed later. Carter, *Spiritual Gifts*, 71.

39. Palma, "Prophecy: Nature and Scope," 11.

40. Robeck, "Gift of Prophecy in Acts and Paul Part 2," 42.

41. Lim, *Spiritual Gifts*, 79.

42. Grudem, *Gift of Prophecy in 1 Corinthians*; Grudem, *Gift of Prophecy in the New Testament and Today*.

43. Grudem, *Gift of Prophecy in 1 Corinthians*, 143.

44. Grudem, *Systematic Theology*, 1049.

4.2.3.1 The Concept of Revelation

The word ἀποκαλύπτω/ἀποκαλυφθῇ normally translated "to reveal/revelation" carries the meaning of disclosing or unveiling something which was previously secret or unknown.[45] Within Scripture, it describes the disclosure of some transcendent knowledge from God to people. The word often connotes an eschatological aspect to the information revealed and so is often related with the *parousia*.[46] The "revelation" received can be understood as a glimpse of things in the age to come. Grudem suggests that the knowledge represents "kingdom-knowledge" or "kingdom-perspective" rather than knowledge which is acquired through human means.[47] This distinguishes revelation and prophecy from pagan fortune-telling and divination as was found in the Greco-Roman world, most notably at Delphi.[48] Carson's examination of the words ἀποκαλύπτω/ἀποκαλυφθῇ likewise lead him to conclude that it is simply the means through which supernatural knowledge is made known.[49] He makes an important appeal not to confuse the biblical terminology of revelation with the modern terminology of theology to avoid thinking that revelation adds to the canon of Scripture. Interestingly, he also points out that revelation can take place even without the person realizing it.

Petts has attempted to differentiate between revelation as simply communicating "what God wants to say to the church or an individual" from supernatural revelation which is "supernatural insight into events, past, present, or future."[50] His motivation appears to be out of deference to those within the Classical Pentecostal movement who see prophecy as simply verbal proclamation while the message of wisdom and knowledge provides the means of supernatural revelation.[51] The discussion will later show that "prophecy" and "revelation" are used almost synonymously by Paul and so Petts's attempted distinction cannot be sustained.[52]

---

45. BDAG 112.
46. For example, see 1 Corinthians 1:7 and 2 Thessalonians 1:7.
47. Grudem, *Gift of Prophecy in 1 Corinthians*, 129–31.
48. Witherington, *Conflict and Community in Corinth*, 276–79.
49. Carson, *Showing the Spirit*, 176–82.
50. Petts, *Body Builders*, 139.
51. H. Horton writes, "The Word of Knowledge is the revelation of *past* happenings or of things existing or events taking place in the *present*. The Word of Wisdom is the revelation of the Purpose of God concerning people, things or events in the *future* or looking to the future." Horton emphasizes that these gifts are unspoken flashes of revelation. See Horton, *Gifts of the Spirit*, 57.
52. Petts acknowledges this point but yet seems reluctant to modify his

4.2.3.2 Evidence from 1 Corinthians

The evidence for the relationship between revelation and prophecy can mainly be found in 1 Corinthians 14. In 1 Corinthians 14:6, Paul provides a list containing "revelation," "knowledge," "prophecy," and "word of instruction." This list may be interpreted as an "a-b-a-b" parallelism between the reception of information (revelation and knowledge) and the means of communicating it to others (prophecy and instruction).[53] This parallelism implies that prophecy communicates revelation whereas instruction communicates knowledge. Fee, however, differs in his interpretation of this verse.[54] He feels that Paul uses terms for speech activities without much precision and that the list is somewhat *ad hoc*. Thus, Fee suggests that these terms refer to various Spirit-inspired utterances with considerable overlap between them. Such an approach still maintains a relationship between prophecy and revelation though less distinct than what is asserted by Palma and Grudem. However, further consideration of the other verses and especially 1 Corinthians 14:30 suggests that Palma's and Grudem's position is more likely.

In 1 Corinthians 14:24–25, a hypothetical scenario is painted where an unbeliever enters a Christian gathering and hears a prophecy that discloses the unbeliever's personal secrets. This results in the conviction and conversion of the unbeliever, with the unbeliever acknowledging the presence of God in the meeting. This leads Grudem to conclude that the one delivering the prophecy received the information through a revelation from God.[55] Fee likewise appreciates the emphasis of this account on the revelatory nature of prophecy and recognizes that prophecy could result in the conviction of sin and the conversion of unbelievers.[56]

Next, in 1 Corinthians 14:26, Paul provides another list describing "a hymn, or a word of instruction, a revelation, a tongue, or an interpretation." The surprising aspect of this list is that it omits reference to prophecy even though the following passage in 1 Corinthians 14:29–32 explicitly discusses this gift.[57] This causes Palma to assert that "revelation" is used as a synonym

---

understanding of prophecy. Petts, *Body Builders*, 140–41.

53. Grudem, *Gift of Prophecy in 1 Corinthians*, 138–39; Palma, *Holy Spirit*, 211. Likewise, Gaffin agrees that "revelation" is a variant reference to "prophecy." See Gaffin, *Perspectives on Pentecost*, 60.

54. Fee, *First Epistle to the Corinthians*, 662–63.

55. Grudem, *Gift of Prophecy in 1 Corinthians*, 140.

56. Fee, *First Epistle to the Corinthians*, 686–87.

57. Note that the gift of tongues appears in the list and is also featured in Paul's discussion.

for "prophecy" in the list.[58] In contrast, Fee again suggests that Paul's list in this verse is not exhaustive and only meant to be representative of various speech activities. He does note the surprising explicit omission of prophecy from the list and accepts that Paul could have used the term "revelation" to refer to "prophecy."[59]

The strongest evidence for consideration can be found in 1 Corinthians 14:30.[60] Here, Paul describes a situation where someone is speaking to the gathered believers when someone else receives a revelation (ἀποκαλυφθῇ). Paul's instruction is that the first speaker should stop so that the second speaker can prophesy. Grudem adds that it is the reception of a revelation that in fact qualifies the second speaker to prophesy and interrupt the first speaker.[61] Indeed it seems strange if Paul, who argues for order in the assembly, permits an interruption for any reason less than a divine impetus. Grudem continues to opine that none of the Corinthian believers could argue that they regularly prophesied without receiving a revelation and so reject Paul's instruction here. Furthermore, Paul explicitly states in Ephesians 3:5 that the Holy Spirit grants revelation to the apostles and prophets. The evidence from the discussion above indicates that Paul understood prophecy to begin with the reception of a revelation from God.

4.2.3.3 Evidence from Acts

The book of Acts presents several accounts of prophecies in the early church as recorded by Luke.[62] These accounts include inspired speech which ac-

---

58. Palma, *Holy Spirit*, 211.

59. Fee, *First Epistle to the Corinthians*, 691. Thiselton critiques Fee, among others, for assuming the nature of the Corinthian meetings were "charismatic" or "spontaneous." Thiselton feels this assumption has influenced Fee's exegesis such that Fee sees the gifts, including prophecy, in 1 Corinthians 12 and 14 as essentially spontaneous. Thiselton is much more inclined to see the gifts as reflective and argues against prophecy as merely spontaneous utterance. However, it is difficult to see how Thiselton's own assumptions have not influenced his exegesis. He at least acknowledges some spontaneity at 1 Corinthians 14:30 but does not feel this is the norm. Thiselton's focus is, of course, on 1 Corinthians and he does not appear to consider the spontaneous nature of prophecy in the Acts narrative such as in Acts 19:6. Thiselton, *First Epistle to the Corinthians*, 1134–35.

60. Robeck, "Gift of Prophecy in Acts and Paul Part 2," 42.

61. Grudem, *Gift of Prophecy in 1 Corinthians*, 140.

62. See Acts 2:14–21; 11:27–30; 13:1–3; 15:32–35; 19:6 and 21:10–11. The account in Acts 15:32–35 does not specifically mention prophecy but Robeck sees this possibly indicated in the description of the believers being encouraged and strengthened. Cf. 1 Corinthians 14:3. Robeck, "Gift of Prophecy in Acts and Paul Part 1," 32–33.

company the infilling of the Holy Spirit, predictions of the future, instructions on ministry appointments, and exhortations which encourage and strengthen believers. Grudem highlights the account in Acts 19:6 in particular, where the Ephesian disciples spoke in tongues and prophesied.[63] The spontaneity and spiritual immaturity of these disciples rules out any possibility of intelligent preaching of any form and instead suggests an extraordinary work by the Holy Spirit. This quite possibly was the utterance of an intelligible message received by divine revelation. From these accounts, Robeck observes that prophecies occur spontaneously, do not require the speaker to undergo any preparation, and communicates information that originates from God.[64] The spontaneous nature of prophecy in Acts and the prediction of future events cause Robeck to conclude that prophecy is initiated by a divine revelation from God.[65]

Forbes's study of Acts arrives at conclusions similar to Robeck though he highlights that Luke differs from Paul in having a wider understanding of prophecy.[66] He maintains that Luke does not distinguish between tongues and prophecy as distinctly as Paul does in 1 Corinthians. He even feels the Acts 2 account presents tongues as prophecy. Forbes then goes on to cite various passages in Luke's gospel to suggest Luke includes inspired prayer and praise as part of prophecy.[67] However, Forbes fails to acknowledge the intelligibility of the tongues to the crowd that was present in the Acts 2 account. This contrasts with the unintelligible tongues mentioned by Paul in 1 Corinthians 14. In this sense, the tongues in Acts 2 seem closer to interpreted tongues (1 Cor 14:5) that could then be considered the functional equivalent of prophecy. Also, Luke mentions both tongues and prophecy in Acts 19:6 indicating that he did not confuse the two forms of inspired utterances.[68] As for the accounts in Luke's gospel, the inspired utterances demonstrate revelatory knowledge that the people could not have obtained unless God had revealed it to them. The spontaneity with which the utterances occur further suggests these were not prepared speeches. This fits well with an understanding of prophecy as the proclamation of a God-given

63. Grudem, *Gift of Prophecy in 1 Corinthians*, 141.

64. Robeck, "Gift of Prophecy in Acts and Paul Part 1," 36.

65. Grudem's own examination of the Acts accounts leads him to similar conclusions. See Grudem, *Gift of Prophecy in 1 Corinthians*, 141.

66. Forbes, *Prophecy and Inspired Speech*, 219–21.

67. See Luke 1:42; 1:67; 2:28 and 2:36.

68. Palma asserts that tongues and prophecy in this verse are two distinct phenomena rather than one phenomenon referenced by different terms. Palma, *Holy Spirit*, 154–55.

revelation. In any case, care should be made to distinguish between prophecy before and after Pentecost.[69]

4.2.3.4 Evidence from the Rest of the New Testament

Grudem provides other instances in the gospels that demonstrate the abilities the biblical authors expected of prophets.[70] The incidents in Luke 7:39, Luke 22:63–64, John 4:17–19 and John 11:51 clearly reveal an expectation of prophets to possesses information through divine revelation.[71] The incident in John 4:17–19 is particularly revealing. The fact that Jesus knew information about a woman's background causes her to recognize him as a prophet. The account almost parallels Paul's description in 1 Corinthians 14:24–25 and again emphasizes that prophecy communicates information which only God could reveal.

The instruction on testing prophets/prophecies in 1 John 4:1–6 further explains the nature of prophecy. These instructions parallel those by Moses (Deut 18:20–22) that were meant for prophets in the Old Testament.[72] The point is that true prophets in both the New and Old Testaments were only supposed to proclaim what God revealed to them. Prophecy only occurs with a revelation from God. Grudem highlights the negative consideration as well in that Scripture does not present an example of prophecy that originates from anything other than a divine revelation from God.[73]

The book of Revelation is unique among the New Testament writings in its genre as well as in its self-claim to be prophecy.[74] The book is a written account of the divine revelation that the apostle John received. John is specifically instructed to write down the revelation and to communicate it to the rest of the church body for their strengthening. However, his work is a blend of apocalyptic and prophetic elements which demands caution in assuming it represents the defining stereotype of New Testament prophecy.[75]

---

69. Kay astutely makes this important distinction. Kay, *Prophecy!*, 11–15.

70. Grudem qualifies that these are examples of pre-Pentecost prophecy and so may not accurately reflect the phenomenon post-Pentecost. Grudem, *Gift of Prophecy in 1 Corinthians*, 141.

71. Kruse, *John*, 134.

72. Akin, *1, 2, 3 John*, 171.

73. Grudem, *Gift of Prophecy in 1 Corinthians*, 141–42.

74. See Revelation 1:3; 22:7, 10, 18–19.

75. Aune, *Prophecy in Early Christianity*, 274–75. Also see ibid., 112–14; Hill, "Prophecy and Prophets." In contrast, Newton has called for greater recognition of the book of Revelation as paradigmatic of New Testament prophecy. Newton, "Scope of Christian Prophecy."

It was also prophecy recorded by an apostle that was meant to be canonized as Scripture. It is therefore difficult to imagine that this is the form of prophecy that took place in Corinth or Thessalonica or the type of prophecy that Paul encouraged all believers to seek after (1 Cor 14:1). At most it may be said to represent only one form of prophecy within the New Testament. Still, the book of Revelation agrees with the understanding of prophecy as the communication of a spontaneous revelation.[76]

4.2.3.5 Summary

The discussion above shows ample evidence for the Pentecostal understanding of prophecy as the reception and communication of a revelation from God.[77] The revelation is spontaneous and initiated purely by God rather than from human activity. Furthermore, prophecy is not simply the reception of a revelation but also involves communicating it to others. This is almost an unspoken assumption in most discussions on prophecy though Grudem does well to emphasize it.[78] Scripture records instances of the reception of a revelation but does not term it as prophecy.[79] Often, these revelations of knowledge concern the mystery of the gospel and are meant for the recipient's personal benefit. Robeck has emphasized that prophecy is meant to build up the church and to be exercised when believers are gathered together.[80] It seems logical then for prophecy to be the communication of revelation and not merely the reception of it. This is much in line with the concept of the prophet as a spokesperson for God.

4.2.4 Comparison with the Old Testament

Various biblical studies have discussed prophecy in the Old Testament.[81] These studies note the main role of the prophet was to receive and an-

---

76. Grudem, *Gift of Prophecy in 1 Corinthians*, 106–9.

77. It is interesting that cessationists who believe that miraculous spiritual gifts have ceased also describe prophecy as the direct reception and communication of revelatory information from God. However, cessationists associate this mode of revelation almost exclusively with the writing of Scripture. See Farnell, "When Will the Gift of Prophecy Cease?"

78. Grudem, *Gift of Prophecy in 1 Corinthians*, 139–40.

79. See, for example, Matthew 11:25, 27; John 12:38; Romans 1:17–18; Philippians 3:15; 1 Peter 1:12; Galatians 2:2; Ephesians 1:17.

80. Robeck, "Gift of Prophecy in Acts and Paul Part 2," 43.

81. Blenkinsopp, *History of Prophecy in Israel*; Grabbe, *Priests, Prophets, Diviners,*

nounce messages believed to originate from Israel's God. The contents of the message were usually religious, expressing God's immediate will for the people in terms of worship or activities which should be encouraged or discouraged.

Pentecostals generally see some level of continuity between prophecy in the Old and New Testament. Robeck considers the passage in Exodus 4:10–16 to provide a paradigmatic understanding of prophecy.[82] Just as Aaron served as a spokesperson for Moses, a prophet would serve as the spokesperson for God. This role as spokesperson extended beyond simply being a divinely appointed leader to include receiving and delivering revelatory messages which communicated God's will. These communications took the form of exhortations, warnings, judgments, instructions, and even commands. Thus, prophecy in the Old Testament largely coheres with the nature of prophecy seen in the New Testament as the reception and communication of a revelation from God.[83]

There are, however, certain distinctions between prophecy in the Old and New Testament. More precisely, the Pentecost event in Acts 2 divides and distinguishes prophecy in the Old Testament and the gospels in comparison with prophecy in the rest of the New Testament.[84] This is because the framework and covenant setting of prophecy in each time period differs. Prophecy in the Old Testament functioned in accordance with the Mosaic covenant. Prophets served as spiritual leaders of the nation alongside the priests and king. With the rise of the monarchy, prophets served as advisors to the king, exhorting the king and Israel towards covenant faithfulness. Much of the prophecy in the Old Testament pointed towards the future arrival of the Messiah. Prophets in the Old Testament were uniquely endowed with the Spirit of God and this was the source of their prophetic utterances.[85] After Pentecost, the Holy Spirit was poured out upon all believers leading to the "prophethood" of believers as discussed earlier. Believers were encouraged to prophesy so that the local congregation could be encouraged and

---

Sages; Lindblom, *Prophecy in Ancient Israel*; Petersen, *Prophecy in Israel*; Wilson, *Prophecy and Society*.

82. Robeck, "Prophecy, Gift of," 1002.

83. Petts, *Body Builders*, 40–42; Turner, *Holy Spirit and Spiritual Gifts*, 187–92. Tyra argues that prophetic utterance in the Old Testament was often simply an indication of the coming of the Holy Spirit upon an individual. Tyra, *Holy Spirit in Mission*, 41–46.

84. Fee, *God's Empowering Presence*, 892; Gentile, *Your Sons and Daughters Shall Prophesy*, 143–56; Kay, "Perspectives on Prophecy"; Soh, "Biblical Perspectives on Prophecy." Also note the discussion in Friedrich, "προφήτης." In *TDNT* 6: 849–50.

85. Numbers 11:25; 1 Samuel 10:6, 10, 19:20.

edified.[86] The social and political framework had changed such that New Testament prophets no longer functioned in relation to civil authorities. The New Testament church is an entity totally different from the sovereign nation of ancient Israel. Hence, the death penalty demanded for false prophecy (Deut 13:1–5; 18:20) is not mentioned in instructions to test prophecy (1 Cor 14:29; 1 Thess 5:19–21; 1 John 4:1–3).[87]

Grudem's extensive study of New Testament prophecy has made significant contributions to an understanding of this phenomenon. However, Grudem's earlier work suggested there were two types of prophecy in the New Testament.[88] One type was apostolic prophecy which claimed divine authority of the actual words of the prophecy. The second, "weaker" type was congregational prophecy where authority extended to the general content of the message but not the actual words used. The New Testament apostles are thus portrayed as the counterparts to the Old Testament prophets in prophesying the actual words of God whereas congregational prophecy lacks this exactness.[89] This proposition has received severe criticism as it assumes the canonical prophets were the stereotype for all Old Testament prophets.[90] It suggests a level of uniformity for Old Testament prophecy and neglects its wide diversity.[91] Grudem's later work addresses some of this criticism by clarifying that he has been largely misunderstood.[92] He does not wish to describe two "types" of prophecy but rather different levels of authority accorded to prophecy. Perhaps it would be more helpful for Grudem to acknowledge the wide range of prophecy in both the Old and New Testament and that not all prophecies were inscripturated into the canon in both time periods.

---

86. 1 Corinthians 14:1–3.

87. Those who insist that the death penalty for false prophecy applies to the New Testament church should consider that Deuteronomy 13 prescribes the same penalty on false teachers. In contrast, the death penalty is not demanded for false teaching in the New Testament church or today.

88. Grudem, *Gift of Prophecy in 1 Corinthians*, 110–11. Lim follows after Grudem in describing two types/levels of prophecy. Lim, *Spiritual Gifts*, 104–5.

89. Grudem, *Gift of Prophecy in 1 Corinthians*, 43–54.

90. Carson, *Showing the Spirit*, 176–77; Turner, *Holy Spirit and Spiritual Gifts*, 191, 210–12. Cessationist Farnell has also criticized Grudem on this point but seeks to assert that all prophecy in the New Testament functioned at the level of canonical authority. Farnell, "Does the New Testament Teach Two Prophetic Gifts?"

91. Hilber, "Diversity of OT Prophetic Phenomena"; Penney, "Testing of New Testament Prophecy," 38–46.

92. Grudem, *Gift of Prophecy in the New Testament and Today*, 47–49.

4.2.5 Prophecy and the Prediction of Future Events

There is clear consensus amongst scholars that prophecy in Scripture is not simply the prediction of future events. While prophecies may contain such an element, this is not the defining characteristic of either prophecy in the Old Testament or in the New Testament.[93] Prophecy is usually described as consisting of either fore-telling of future events (Acts 11:27–28; 21:11) or forth-telling in terms of speaking on behalf of another (Acts 13:1–3; 15:32).[94] There are also other Bible passages that highlight what might constitute prophecy in the New Testament.[95] These instances suggest an expectation for prophecy to provide specific knowledge that could not be known through human abilities but do not suggest knowledge of future events. This nature is also apparent in the Greco-Roman understanding of prophecy.[96]

4.2.6 Prophecy, Charismatic Exegesis, and Preaching

Classical Pentecostals generally define prophecy as distinct from preaching and teaching.[97] Preaching and teaching are based on the exposition of Scripture whereas prophecy is based on direct revelation from God. There may be occasional instances of prophetic revelation during the preparation or delivery of preaching and teaching but care is taken not to equate preaching and teaching with prophecy. Hence, Robeck represents Pentecostals when he asserts, "prophecy is based upon revelation (*apokalupsei*), preaching and teaching are built upon *logos*, *sophias*, and *gnoseos*."[98]

Contrary to the position above, some have argued for prophecy to be equated with charismatic exegesis—the inspired exposition of Scripture. Boring makes this claim when he describes the New Testament prophet as an immediately inspired spokesperson for Jesus to the community of believers.[99] He acknowledges Dunn's position that revelation serves as the impe-

---

93. Grudem, *Gift of Prophecy in 1 Corinthians*, 183–84; Petts, *Body Builders*, 138–39; Robeck, "Prophecy, Gift of," 1002.

94. Carlson, *Spiritual Dynamics*, 107; Petts, *Body Builders*, 40.

95. See Luke 7:39; John 4:17–19; Luke 22:63–64. These instances are examples of pre-Pentecost prophecy but should not differ markedly from post-Pentecost expectations. Grudem, *Gift of Prophecy in 1 Corinthians*, 141.

96. For a detailed discussion of Greco–Roman prophecy, see Aune, *Prophecy in Early Christianity*, Chapters 2 and 3; Forbes, *Prophecy and Inspired Speech*, Chapter 8.

97. See, for example, Chan, "Prophecy and Discernment," 119; Warrington, *Pentecostal Theology*, 83.

98. Robeck, "Gift of Prophecy in Acts and Paul Part 2," 42.

99. Boring, *Continuing Voice of Jesus*.

tus for prophecy and makes some distinction between prophecy and "simple preaching." However, Boring also asserts that New Testament prophets served mainly to interpret Scripture in the light of immediate events and to interpret eschatologically the events in the light of Scripture.[100] He cites Paul as the prime example for this activity while also conceding that Luke does not explicitly describe prophets as interpreters of Scripture. Boring then continues to claim that prophetic speech in the New Testament included quoting, modifying, and elaborating on the traditional sayings of Jesus, in the style of a prophetic *pesher*. A similar view is propagated by Ellis, though he goes further in asserting that New Testament prophecy be fully equated with the inspired exegesis of the Old Testament.[101] He sees evidence for this in the parallels between New Testament documents and the Qumran scrolls which contained rabbinic interpretation and commentary of the Old Testament. He proposes that the phrase λέγει κύριος (*legei kurios*) served as an introductory formula in the New Testament to indicate an eschatological re-application of the Old Testament in the tradition of the midrashic *pesher*. In fact, Ellis comments that since both prophets and teachers exposited Scripture, their roles were virtually indistinguishable.

The position represented by Boring and Ellis is strongly criticized by Aune and Forbes.[102] Aune points out that there is no evidence for the use of λέγει κύριος as an introductory formula in early Christian prophecy and even cites instances where the church fathers used the phrase while clearly not prophesying. He accepts that the New Testament authors modified the Old Testament when quoting from it but finds no evidence to connect this with prophecy. In fact, while Ellis cites the speeches in Acts to support his position, Forbes notes that Scripture never claims these speeches are prophecy. In contrast, the most evident cases of prophecy involving Agabus do not include any form of charismatic exegesis. Furthermore, there is insufficient explanation on the difference between charismatic exegesis and non-charismatic exegesis. Forbes highlights that apostles, prophets, teachers, and even ordinary believers in the New Testament engaged in interpreting the Old Testament so a distinction is essential in asserting one form of interpretation as the distinctive activity of prophecy.

Aside from charismatic exegesis, some others have proposed that New Testament prophecy is the equivalent of preaching.[103] Hill's important and

100. Ibid., 138ff.

101. Ellis, *Prophecy and Hermeneutic*.

102. Aune, *Prophecy in Early Christianity*, 339–46; Forbes, *Prophecy and Inspired Speech*, 229–36.

103. See, for example, Packer who essentially equates contemporary preaching with prophecy. Packer, *Keep in Step with the Spirit*, 217. Also note Calvin's view on

significant study of New Testament prophecy arrives at this proposal though he qualifies his conclusion as he feels there are too few examples of New Testament prophecy to arrive at a stereotype.[104] Hill bases his conclusions on the function of prophecy in bringing encouragement, comfort, conviction, and conversion. Hill specifically terms prophecy as "pastoral preaching" which is primarily directed to those within the church as opposed to "evangelistic preaching" which is primarily directed to those outside the church. Gillespie's study of early Christian prophecy leads him to a similar conclusion as Hill.[105] He sees Scriptural evidence for prophecy to be an extended discourse that interpreted theologically the implications of the gospel. From 1 Thessalonians 5:20, Gillespie notes that prophecy was subject to critical evaluation by the community of the church. This evaluation was done, as Gillespie interprets it, according to Romans 12:6 where prophecy is linked with the traditioned faith of the gospel. Finally, he notes from 1 Corinthians 14 that prophecy resulted in the edification, exhortation, and comfort of believers and also the conviction and conversion of unbelievers. From this, Gillespie concludes that prophecy was a form of gospel proclamation that explicated the theological and ethical implications for the local congregation. Thiselton agrees with Hill and Gillespie in equating prophecy with preaching.[106] He appreciates the relationship between prophecy and revelation but sees no reason why revelation obtained through sustained prayer, meditation, and contemplation which is then fashioned into a sermon should be rejected as prophecy simply because the revelation was not "instantaneous."

Several criticisms have been raised against equating prophecy with preaching. Turner questions the assumption that prophecy consists of an extended discourse since Paul compares it with tongues and interpretation that were relatively short utterances.[107] He also disagrees with Gillespie's interpretation of Romans 12:6 that prophecy necessarily consists of the preaching of the gospel. Instead, Turner feels the verse is better understood as an amplification of Romans 12:3. Fee also differs in his interpretation of this verse, preferring to see prophecy as an expression of the faith of those who prophesy, just as all the Christian ministries listed in Romans

---

1 Thessalonians 5:20 and 1 Corinthians 12:28. See Calvin, *Epistles to the Philippians, Colossians and Thessalonians*, 299; Calvin, *Epistles to the Corinthians*, 1:415.

104. Hill, *New Testament Prophecy*.
105. Gillespie, *First Theologians*.
106. Thiselton, *First Epistle to the Corinthians*, 960–63.
107. Turner, *Holy Spirit and Spiritual Gifts*, 205–6.

12:7–8 are an expression of the believer's faith.¹⁰⁸ Furthermore, it is hard to see how the prophetic predictions by Agabus (Acts 11:28; 21:11) and the spontaneous prophesying by immature believers (Acts 19:6) fit in with the conception of prophecy as preaching. While Gillespie seeks only to present a Pauline perspective in his work, a wider consideration of information would be better.

Elsewhere, Ahn criticizes the approach for mistaking the intended result of prophecy and turning it into its characteristic activity.¹⁰⁹ The intended result of edification, exhortation, and comfort (1 Cor 14:3) would apply to all forms of Christian ministry but this does not make these ministries equivalent to preaching. Consistency would then wrongly demand equating tongues and interpretation with preaching (1 Cor 14:5). Forbes adds support to distinguishing between prophecy and preaching by emphasizing that the Greek verbs "to preach" (κηρύσσω, καταγγέλλω) and "to teach" (διδάσκω) are used in Scripture when describing the communication of revelation received in the past.¹¹⁰ In contrast, prophecy describes communication of an immediate revelation which is directed to the community of believers—a point discussed in the earlier sections. Thiselton's point that revelation need not be immediate or spontaneous is noted here but some spontaneity should at least be conceded in the case of 1 Corinthians 14:30 where the second speaker receives an immediate revelation which spurs him to stand and interrupt the first speaker.¹¹¹ It seems highly unlikely that the second speaker was prompted to deliver a prepared sermon. In addition, the prediction of future events is solely attributed to prophecy. Though prophecy is not limited to foretelling the future, this function should highlight at least one difference between preaching and some forms of prophecy.

In summary, it seems best to differentiate between New Testament prophecy on the one hand and charismatic exegesis and preaching on the other. Some prophetic element might be present in the exposition of Scripture or even during the delivery of a sermon.¹¹² Prophecy, teaching, and preaching may even produce the same results in terms of building up the community of believers. However, the discussion reveals sufficient grounds to make a distinction between the delivery of a message based on Scripture

---

108. Fee, *God's Empowering Presence*, 607–8.

109. Ahn, "Prophecy in the Pauline Communities," 81.

110. Forbes, *Prophecy and Inspired Speech*, 225–28.

111. Thiselton accepts some spontaneity in this instance but suggests that the revelation received by the second speaker is meant to bring correction to the excesses of the first speaker. Thiselton, *First Epistle to the Corinthians*, 1141–42.

112. Sheppard calls this "anointed preaching" but highlights the spontaneous nature of the received revelation. Sheppard, "Prophecy," 64.

and the delivery of a prophetic message based on an immediate revelation. Clarity on this matter is essential as it presently influences how a popular Chinese version of the Bible is translated.[113]

4.2.7 Prophecy and Tongues with Interpretation

One of the more unique practices within the Pentecostal movement is the verbal delivery of a message in an unintelligible tongue followed by a verbal interpretation into a known language.[114] The same individual may give the message in tongues and the interpretation but it is more common for them to be delivered by different individuals. This practice has led to a debate on whether tongues with interpretation should be considered the equivalent of prophecy and, if so, in what way it is equivalent. At the heart of this debate is the proper interpretation of the short description of the phenomenon provided in 1 Corinthians 14.

There are several Classical Pentecostals who view tongues with interpretation as the equivalent of prophecy.[115] These scholars often stress the equivalence is in the value of the gift in bringing an intelligible message to the congregation. In this sense, both phenomena bring the communication of a revelation which serves to edify the community of believers (1 Cor 14:5). Thus, it is common to hear Pentecostals speak of God communicating through a "message in tongues" which is then interpreted. Opponents to this view usually highlight the difference between the intended audience of the uttered speech and the contents of the speech itself.[116] Various Scripture passages suggest that tongues are directed towards God and consists of prayer or praise.[117] This implies that tongues should be understood as primarily personal and devotional in nature resulting only in the edification of the one speaking (1 Cor 14:4). In contrast, prophecy is directed towards the congregation and results in the edification of the body of believers. An interpreted tongue should then be an expression of prayer or praise toward God and sound quite different from a prophecy.

113. Menzies, "Anti-Charismatic Bias."

114. Spittler, "Interpretation of Tongues, Gift of."

115. For example, see Aker, "Gift of Tongues"; Gee, *Spiritual Gifts in the Work of the Ministry Today*, 52–53; Horton, *Gifts of the Spirit*, 172; Horton, *What the Bible Says about the Holy Spirit*, 226; Robeck, "Gift of Prophecy in Acts and Paul Part 2," 44–45; Spittler, "Interpretation of Tongues, Gift of." Also note the empirical observations of Muindi. See Muindi, "Nature and Significance of Prophecy," 97–101.

116. Fee, *First Epistle to the Corinthians*, 656; Lim, *Spiritual Gifts*, 140; MacDonald, "Biblical Glossolalia."

117. See Acts 2:11; Acts 10:46 and 1 Corinthians 14:2.

Those who claim equivalence between tongues with interpretation and prophecy have addressed the concerns above in a variety of ways. Gee notes that tongues and prophecy are usually directed at a different audience but proposes that the interpretation elevates the gift of tongues such that it becomes equivalent to prophecy.[118] Petts emphasizes that the equivalence is only in the value of the gifts for edification rather than an absolute equivalence.[119] Nevertheless, he notes that while Scripture may describe a tongue without interpretation as directed towards God, it does not claim that a tongue with interpretation must likewise be directed towards God. Aker brings a similar perspective by contending that 1 Corinthians 14:1–5 does not describe direction but rather the one who understands the language that is spoken.[120] The interpretation is clearly meant for the understanding of believers so there seems little reason to insist that it must be directed towards God. H. Horton provides a different perspective by stressing that the interpretation of a tongue is not the same as a verbatim translation and hence the direction of an interpreted message may differ from the original message.[121] Similarly, Spittler maintains any insistence for the interpretation to correspond to the uttered tongue in length, intonation, and direction is unnecessarily restrictive.[122] Instead, there should be greater recognition that the Holy Spirit may inspire various forms of utterances that result in the edification of the church. Beyond this discussion, there are also practical instances in contemporary gatherings where the interpretation of a tongue is markedly different in length and quality from the uttered tongue.[123] In such instances, Gee suggests that a prophecy has actually been delivered rather than an interpretation. The uttered tongue has merely increased the faith of the congregation resulting in the delivery of a prophecy.

Finally, it may be wise to heed Gee's comments on the limited discussion of tongues with interpretation within Scripture.[124] There are no practical examples described in the book of Acts and it is only briefly alluded to in 1 Corinthians 14. The church may need to concede that Scripture does not present sufficient information to form a conclusive understanding of the practice. The meagre Scriptural discussion strongly indicates that the

---

118. Gee, *Spiritual Gifts in the Work of the Ministry Today*, 52–53.
119. Petts, *Body Builders*, 127.
120. Aker, "Gift of Tongues," 19–20.
121. Horton, *Gifts of the Spirit*, 149.
122. Spittler, "Interpretation of Tongues, Gift of," 802.
123. Ibid.; Gee, *Spiritual Gifts in the Work of the Ministry Today*, 53.
124. Gee, *Spiritual Gifts in the Work of the Ministry Today*, 52–53.

practice was relatively uncommon and suggests that it should not be encouraged in contemporary practice.

4.2.8 Prophecy, the Message of Wisdom, and the Message of Knowledge

In examining prophecy, it is also essential to discuss the message of wisdom and the message of knowledge which are mentioned among other gifts of grace in 1 Corinthians 12:8. These gifts are commonly asserted to be revelatory in nature and hence they overlap somewhat with prophecy. However, there is little discussion of these specific gifts within Scripture resulting in some ambiguity over what Paul is exactly alluding to.

Warrington provides a survey of the various views on these gifts among Pentecostals.[125] The message of wisdom is commonly accepted as inspired revelation given by God for guidance in a particular situation. Warrington notes that various ones relate the gift with preaching, teaching, and interpreting Scripture. However, it seems more appropriate to interpret Paul's use of the term σοφίας in the context of Paul's letter to the Corinthians.[126] In this sense, the gift should be associated with the proclamation of the mission and purpose of Christ (1 Cor 2:6–16). Still, there are many such as Lim, who accept a broader definition of the gift as communicating "God's plans, purposes, and ways of accomplishing things."[127]

The message of knowledge is typically accepted as a parallel to the message of wisdom. Warrington observes that most Pentecostals see it as the awareness of divinely communicated facts or information that the recipient would not otherwise have known.[128] This information is normally related to spiritual knowledge or the spiritual health of the church, leading some to associate the gift with the teaching ministry in the church.[129] A popular view is that the message of knowledge concerns mere factual information while the message of wisdom guides the application of those facts in specific situations.[130] While this understanding seems attractive, it does not concur

---

125. Warrington, *Pentecostal Theology*, 77–78.
126. Fee, *First Epistle to the Corinthians*, 591–92.
127. Lim, *Spiritual Gifts*, 71.
128. Warrington, *Pentecostal Theology*, 78.
129. Gee argues for this while acknowledging criticisms of his view. See Gee, *Concerning Spiritual Gifts*, 133–43. Similarly Horton, *What the Bible Says about the Holy Spirit*, 271–73.
130. See, for example, Wagner, *Your Spiritual Gifts*, 190–93.

with Paul's use of these terms and stems more from modern distinctions between wisdom and knowledge.

In discussing these gifts, the concern for the present study is their relationship with prophecy. One possibility is to assert that the message of wisdom concerns the revelation of information about the future while the message of knowledge is the revelation of information about the past.[131] Information provided by both these gifts is then communicated to others through the gift of prophecy. A second possibility is to associate the message of wisdom and knowledge with supernatural insight in preaching and teaching and so distinguish it from prophecy.[132] A third possibility is to view the message of wisdom and knowledge as "non-miraculous" so that they simply refer to the ability to speak and convey wisdom and knowledge.[133] Petts examines these three views and finds each to be less than convincing.[134] Petts's own conclusion suggests that these gifts convey some form of revelatory information, which would mean a degree of overlap with prophecy. Indeed, Fee admits that Scripture does not provide sufficient evidence to distinguish between the gifts and that Paul might not be seeking to make such a distinction in the first place.[135]

Pentecostal praxis does not generally distinguish between prophecy, the message of wisdom, and the message of knowledge. While scholars may debate about the differences and nuances of the various terms, Pentecostals tend to use the terms synonymously.[136] Thus, Pentecostals may refer to a prophetic utterance as conveying a "message of wisdom" or a "message of knowledge." This point is significant in understanding the exact phenomenon that Pentecostals are referring to despite the use of different labels.[137]

---

131. Horton, *Gifts of the Spirit*, 57.
132. Gee, *Concerning Spiritual Gifts*, 33–48.
133. Grudem, *Gift of Prophecy in the New Testament and Today*, 293–302.
134. Petts, *Body Builders*, 229–42.
135. Fee, *First Epistle to the Corinthians*, 591–93.
136. This point is noted by Cartledge in his survey of Pentecostal and Charismatic literature. See Cartledge, "Charismatic Prophecy," *JPT*, 88–94. Also see Keener, *Gift & Giver*, 115–16; Stibbe, *Know Your Spiritual Gifts*, 48–49.
137. Grudem specifically calls on Pentecostals and Charismatics to use the "correct" label of "prophecy" in referring to spontaneous revelatory utterances and to avoid using the labels "word of wisdom" or "word of knowledge." Of course, this is only true if there is no overlap between the gifts. See Grudem, *Gift of Prophecy in the New Testament and Today*, 300–301.

4.2.9 Prophecy and the Cessation of Spiritual Gifts

All Pentecostals may be called continuationists in that they believe in the continuing activity of spiritual gifts and miraculous phenomena in the church today.[138] In contrast, cessationists are those who claim that the "miraculous" spiritual gifts such as prophecy, tongues, gifts of healings, and miraculous powers ceased at some point in the past. This point in time is variously suggested as the closing of the canon of Scripture, the maturing of the early church, or the passing away of the last apostle. The arguments and counter-arguments between continuationists and cessationists are well documented within literature and are largely a repetition of the same points.[139] A full examination is beyond the scope of this study but this brief discussion is included for completeness.

Of the various works on cessationism, the argument presented by Farnell is particularly relevant to the present study.[140] His points are not unique but they are directed specifically at the continuation of prophecy today. Farnell provides three main arguments in support for the cessation of prophecy.[141] First, Farnell appeals to the miraculous nature of New Testament prophecy and fully equates prophecy with the communication of direct revelatory information from God. The purpose of prophecy is asserted to be the writing of the canon of Scripture and for guiding the church while this process was taking place. Second, Farnell appeals to Ephesians 2:20 in highlighting the foundational purpose of apostles and prophets in receiving and transmitting revelation. The implication is then drawn that the gifts of apostleship and prophecy have ceased with the establishment of the church and the closing of the canon of Scripture. Farnell acknowledges here that

---

138. See, for example, Palma, *Holy Spirit*, 198–200; Warrington, *Pentecostal Theology*, 70–71.

139. Works which articulate the cessationist position include Edgar, *Satisfied by the Promise of the Spirit*; Gaffin, *Perspectives on Pentecost*; MacArthur, *Charismatic Chaos*; MacArthur, *Strange Fire*; Walvoord, "Holy Spirit and Spiritual Gifts"; Warfield, *Counterfeit Miracles*. An example of the cessationist position in Singapore is articulated by Khoo, *Charismatism Q&A*.

The definitive work on the continuation of spiritual gifts is Ruthven, *On the Cessation of the Charismata*. Other notable works include Deere, *Surprised by the Power of the Spirit*; Greig and Springer, *Kingdom and the Power*; Turner, *Holy Spirit and Spiritual Gifts*, 278–93; Williams, "Biblical Truth and Experience." A good summary of the various positions is provided in Grudem, *Are Miraculous Gifts for Today?*

140. Farnell, "The Current Debate about New Testament Prophecy"; Farnell, "The Gift of Prophecy in the Old and New Testaments"; Farnell, "Does the New Testament Teach Two Prophetic Gifts?"; Farnell, "When Will the Gift of Prophecy Cease?"

141. The points which follow are summarized from Farnell, "When Will the Gift of Prophecy Cease?"

this assertion is not explicitly stated in the text but considers it a reasonable theological deduction. Third, Farnell identifies 1 Corinthians 13:8–13 as the crucial passage which describes the temporary nature of prophecy and tongues. In particular, he interprets τὸ τέλειον (*to teleion*) in verse ten to refer to the maturity of the church. To be clear, Farnell argues for the "relative" maturity of the first century church and the completed canon that permitted the withdrawal of prophecy as a means of guidance and revelation. He recognizes that the ultimate maturity of the church will only occur at Christ's *parousia*.

The following responses may be made to the points raised by Farnell above. First, the discussion earlier shows Pentecostals agree that prophecy is the communication of revelatory information given directly by God. One main distinction between continuationists and cessationists concerns the purpose of prophecy. Farnell and other cessationists associate prophecy and revelation primarily with the writing of Scripture. Thus, they reject the possibility of contemporary prophecy because they see this as a challenge to the finality of the canon. While the writing of Scripture is acknowledged to be one of the purposes of prophecy (2 Pet 1:20–21), the wide diversity of prophecy apparent in both the Old Testament as well as the New Testament cannot be ignored.[142] Cessationists seem to assume that the Old Testament writing prophets set the biblical norm for the practice of prophecy—even though many of the prophets did not write Scripture. The previous discussion shows that ἀποκαλύπτω/ἀποκαλυφθῇ simply means the divine communication of spiritual truth and should not be confused with the terminology of systematic theology.[143] Turner also underscores the limited role of prophecy in the development of theology within the New Testament; a point which contradicts what cessationists claim.[144] As Grudem points out, the practice of prophecy in the New Testament was not constrained to the apostles or to those who wrote Scripture.[145] In fact, "ordinary" believers were clearly engaged in prophecy and this necessitates a wider understanding than that proposed by cessationists.

Second, the cessationist interpretation of Ephesians 2:20 is challenged by various continuationists.[146] Ruthven questions interpreting θεμελίῳ as either the canon of Scripture or seeing the apostles and prophets as reposi-

---

142. Hilber, "Diversity of OT Prophetic Phenomena."
143. Carson, *Showing the Spirit*, 180.
144. Turner, *Holy Spirit and Spiritual Gifts*, 212–15.
145. Grudem, *Gift of Prophecy in the New Testament and Today*, 205–6.
146. Grudem, *Gift of Prophecy in 1 Corinthians*, 82–105; Ruthven, "The 'Foundational Gifts' of Ephesians 2:20."

tories of canonical revelation. He rightly points out that Scripture does not claim the sole purpose of apostles and prophets was to write Scripture or to bring the church to a "relative" state of maturity. On the contrary, apostles and prophets are mentioned in Ephesians 4:11–13 together with evangelists and pastor-teachers as having a role in building up the church until it reaches full maturity in attaining the "whole measure of the fullness of God." This seems at odds with the cessationist view that prophets only had a role up to the church attaining a "relative" maturity somewhere in the first century. In any case, the passage nowhere claims the gifts of apostleship and prophecy will cease with the passing away of that generation. Those insisting, as Farnell does, that a foundation once laid cannot be re-laid should recognize that Paul says the Ephesian church was already built (past tense) on the "foundation."[147] This is despite the unfinished canon and the on-going ministry of the apostles and prophets in transmitting further revelation. Thus, the metaphorical use of θεμελίῳ must not be over-stretched.

Third, Ruthven provides a detailed discussion of 1 Corinthians 13:8–13 and counters the arguments put forward by cessationists such as Farnell.[148] Ruthven interprets τὸ τέλειον in its context and sees it as referring to the second coming of Christ. In this sense, the verse may be reasonably associated with 1 Corinthians 1:8 where Paul specifically describes the *parousia*. Ruthven also considers the cessationist claim that the church made a leap from infancy to maturity with the closing of the canon to be historically naïve. Even after the last book of Scripture was completed, the biblical writings were not widely disseminated within the church. Furthermore, debates on recognizing the various writings as canonical continued on for decades and even centuries. This seems contrary to the suggestion that the church had suddenly advanced into a new eschatological epoch and reached "maturity," or even "relative maturity" as Farnell claims.[149]

The discussion above has responded to Farnell's insistence on the cessation of prophecy in church history. In addition, there is ample scriptural evidence to demonstrate an expectation for prophecy and other spiritual gifts to continue till Christ's return.[150] Thus, the view of continuationists like Pentecostals may be considered to be well grounded in Scripture. Furthermore, many non-Pentecostal evangelicals within Asia believe in the

147. Ruthven, "The 'Foundational Gifts' of Ephesians 2:20," 40.

148. Ruthven, *On the Cessation of the Charismata*, 131–51. Also Grudem, *Gift of Prophecy in 1 Corinthians*, 210–19.

149. Not all cessationists interpret 1 Corinthians 13:10 in the same manner. Gaffin acknowledges that it refers to the second coming of Christ. Gaffin, *Perspectives on Pentecost*, 109.

150. Ruthven, *On the Cessation of the Charismata*, 123–87.

continuation of prophecy. Chen Ruoyu from the China Graduate School of Theology in Hong Kong has examined prophecy in the New Testament.[151] He considers the various arguments put forward by cessationists but emphatically declares that they have failed to prove their position. Chen then calls on the church to rediscover and exercise the gift of prophecy so that it might continue to be edified and strengthened.[152] Likewise, Zhou Gonghe from the China Evangelical Seminary in Taiwan has examined the gift of prophecy and believes that prophecy should be active in the contemporary church.[153] He interacts with Gaffin,[154] Grudem,[155] Palmer,[156] and Poythress,[157] and concludes that there is little evidence in support of cessationism. The exegetical conclusions for the continuation of spiritual gifts also agree well with the general worldview of most Asians.[158] Hwa Yung, the Bishop of the Methodist Church in Malaysia, represents most Asians in describing an openness towards prophecy, miracles, faith-healing, and demonic spirits.[159] Anita Chia concurs with this view while examining the various ethnic groups in Singapore.[160] It is perhaps this supernatural worldview that accounts for the appeal of the Pentecostal movement that resulted in its tremendous growth in Asia.

---

151. Chen, "新約教會中的先知恩賜 [The Gift of Prophecy in the New Testament Church]."

152. Ibid., 101.

153. Zhou, "先知恩賜與當代教會 [The Gift of Prophecy and the Contemporary Church]."

154. Gaffin, *Perspectives on Pentecost*.

155. Grudem, *Gift of Prophecy in the New Testament and Today*; Grudem, *Systematic Theology*.

156. Robertson, *Final Word*.

157. Poythress, "Modern Spiritual Gifts."

158. To be clear, it is not suggested that the supernatural worldview of Asians has caused them to ignore the biblical claims for cessationism.

159. Hwa, "Recover the Supernatural"; Hwa, "Endued with Power." Ma makes similar observations in surveying the growth of the Pentecostal movement in Asia. See Ma, "Asian Pentecostalism." Also note the empirical findings of Kay. See Kay, "Empirical and Historical Perspectives," 21–23.

160. Chia, "Biblical Theology on Power Manifestation."

4.3 THE PURPOSE OF PROPHECY

4.3.1 Edification of the Church

The purpose of prophecy should first be considered in the context of the overall purpose of all spiritual gifts. Paul describes this overall purpose in 1 Corinthians 12:7 and 14:26 in that spiritual gifts are meant to build up and strengthen the church. The stress in Paul's epistle is on the corporate benefit of the gifts and there is little to suggest that these gifts are meant for the personal benefit of the one exercising them. In fact, Scripture consistently describes the practice of spiritual gifts in the context of the body of believers rather than in private worship.[161] Ministering to believers through spiritual gifts enables the community to show love to one another.[162] While it is possible for spiritual gifts to be exercised without love, 1 Corinthians 13 shows this is not the intended purpose. Spiritual gifts emphasize the mutual dependence of believers within the church and allows it to experience God's ἀγάπη (*agape*) and the community's κοινωνία (*koinonia*).[163]

Within the context described above, the consensus among scholars is that the purpose of prophecy is to bring οἰκοδομήν (*oikodomen*), παράκλησιν (*paraklesin*), and παραμυθίαν (*paramythian*).[164] This purpose is clearly stated in 1 Corinthians 14:3-4 and 14:31. S. M. Horton expands on each of these individual terms in his description of prophecy:

> When a person prophesies (speaks for God by the Spirit in a language everyone understands), he speaks to men (human beings, including both men and women), not just to God. His words bring edification (that builds up spiritually and develops or confirms faith), exhortation (that encourages and awakens, challenging all to move ahead in faithfulness and love), and comfort (that cheers, revives, and encourages hope and expectation).[165]

Some might suggest that there is a degree of overlap between these purposes, particularly between παράκλησιν and παραμυθίαν. Others might

---

161. Romans 12:4-8; 1 Corinthians 12, 14; 1 Peter 4:10-11.

162. Schatzmann, "Purpose and Function of Gifts in 1 Corinthians," 57-58.

163. Lim, *Spiritual Gifts*, 111-38.

164. Grudem, *Gift of Prophecy in 1 Corinthians*, 181-85; Horton, *Gifts of the Spirit*, 167; Horton, *What the Bible Says about the Holy Spirit*, 225; Lim, *Spiritual Gifts*, 104; Palma, "Prophecy: Regulation and Purpose," 11; Robeck, "Gift of Prophecy in Acts and Paul Part 2," 44; Tyra, *Holy Spirit in Mission*, 89-95. An empirical study of prophecy similarly identified the function as *paraklesis* in edifying, encouraging, and consoling believers. See Muindi, "Nature and Significance of Prophecy," 159, 206.

165. Horton, *What the Bible Says about the Holy Spirit*, 225.

consider παράκλησιν and παραμυθίαν as the means through which οἰκοδομήν is achieved. However, there is no reason why each should not be considered a purpose of prophecy in itself.[166] It was earlier noted that other ministries like preaching and teaching fulfill the purpose of edifying the church. This means that the purpose should not be considered the defining characteristic of what should be considered prophecy. Instead this defining characteristic involves the reception of a spontaneous revelation from God together with the communication of that message.

The message brought through prophecy contains particularistic information addressing the immediate needs and the situation of the assembly. Prophecy is not merely the communication of general principles found through the study of Scripture or acquired through human observation. Muindi describes this as a *"kairological* word for a specific people in specific contextual situations."[167] Soh stresses this aspect when he writes that prophecy "helps us as [God's] people to hear and receive his guidance, counsel, and encouragement or rebuke and correction and know his specific and current plans and actions in particular situations and for particular times."[168] This echoes Grudem's claim mentioned earlier that prophecy brings a "kingdom-perspective" to the situation that the congregation faces.[169] One possibility alluded to in 1 Corinthians 14:24–25 is the revealing of sin within the lives of those present. Paul's example specifically speaks of unbelievers though it is reasonable to believe this occurred for believers as well. Such occurrences bring conviction and conversion and serve as an exhortation to others towards obedience. Chan further notes that the Christian faith believes in a personal God who speaks and works in the life of the congregation.[170] Prophecy underscores this reality and emphasizes that God truly hears the prayers of the church and is intimately interested in their daily lives. It is perhaps this aspect of prophecy that brings a strong sense of encouragement and comfort to the community of believers. This aspect is also closely related with prophecy as a "sign" for believers and will be discussed in the next section.

The particularistic information brought through prophecy could contain information about a future event as shown in the accounts of Agabus (Acts 11:27–28; 21:11). However, prophecy as the prediction of future

166. Grudem attempts to distinguish somewhat between each of these purposes by surveying Paul's use of these terms in his letters. Grudem, *Gift of Prophecy in 1 Corinthians*, 182–83.

167. Muindi, "Nature and Significance of Prophecy," 206.

168. Soh, "Biblical Perspectives on Prophecy," 110.

169. Grudem, *Gift of Prophecy in 1 Corinthians*, 129–31.

170. Chan, "Prophecy and Discernment," 120.

events is not an end in itself. This information is revealed to the church so that they may be edified and strengthened.[171] Information about the impending famine enabled the church in Antioch to practically assist the believers in Judea (Acts 11:29). The prediction of Paul's fate enabled believers to witness his obedience, courage, and sacrifice despite knowing the suffering awaiting him. The account clearly parallels Paul's experience with Jesus's and would encourage the church to imitate Paul even as he sought to follow after Christ.[172] The prophecy also assured Paul of God's presence and strength for the events ahead.

In addition to the points above, some might suggest that prophecy possesses a didactic function that results in the edification of the church.[173] The word μανθάνωσιν (*manthanosin*) in 1 Corinthians 14:31 appears to convey that prophecy was used to instruct the congregation; possibly including instruction in Christian doctrine. However, μανθάνωσιν here is better understood as emphasizing learning on the part of the congregation rather than the teaching aspect of the one prophesying.[174] The communication of a divine revelation will result in some form of learning on the part of the hearers and it is not necessary to insist that doctrinal teaching is implied here.[175]

One last aspect of the edification brought about by prophecy is discussed by Wenk in his proposal to see prophecy initiating a dialogue within the community.[176] Wenk desires to correct the perception of prophecy as simply proclamation and instead calls for prophecy to be understood as a process where God, the prophet, and the community interact. The end goal is to determine the will of God for the community and to bring about a transformation of the congregation so as to live in obedience to God. This understanding sets prophecy within the Pentecostal hermeneutic of the Spirit, Scripture, and the community and helps present the church as a prophetic, eschatological community orientated towards the fulfillment of God's future purpose.[177]

---

171. Grudem, *Gift of Prophecy in 1 Corinthians*, 202; Robeck, "Gift of Prophecy in Acts and Paul Part 1," 15–28.

172. Bruce, *Book of Acts*, 401–2; Polhill, *Acts*, 435; Shade and Nicholls, *Acts*, 313.

173. Palma, "Prophecy: Regulation and Purpose," 12.

174. Fee, *First Epistle to the Corinthians*, 696; Thiselton, *First Epistle to the Corinthians*, 1143.

175. Grudem, *Gift of Prophecy in 1 Corinthians*, 185.

176. Wenk, "Creative Power of the Prophetic Dialogue." Wenk draws inspiration from Overholt's model of prophecy as process and interaction rather than mere proclamation. See Overholt, *Channels of Prophecy*.

177. Archer, *Pentecostal Hermeneutic*; Chan, "Prophecy and Discernment," 114; Wenk, "Creative Power of the Prophetic Dialogue," 129.

4.3.2 Sign of God's Attitude

Paul describes prophecy and tongues as "signs" in the discussion in 1 Corinthians 14:22–25. While Paul's quotation of Isaiah 28:11–12 presents some challenges for understanding tongues as a sign, the case for prophecy is relatively clear.[178] Paul is likely referring to the presence of prophecy as a sign or expression of God's approval towards the community of believers.[179] Prophecy is the manifestation of God's Spirit within the community (1 Cor 12:7). It shows that God is active and concerned with the situation and needs of the believers. The community would then perceive of prophecy as a positive sign of God's blessing upon their community. Even the unbelievers present would be compelled to acknowledge the presence of God in the midst of the congregation (1 Cor 14:25) and it is doubtless that believers would reach the same realization. From a different though related perspective, R. P. Menzies argues from the Acts account that tongues and prophecy indicates God's favor and acceptance of a community.[180] Similarly, Chia presents biblical evidence for considering prophecy and other miraculous phenomena as signs of God's presence, power, and provision.[181]

Prophecy and other spiritual gifts were common in the early church and writings such as the *Didache* and the *Shepherd of Hermas* comment on their activity. Chan points this out and observes that prophecy held an important role within the church even after the apostolic age.[182] Chan examines the writings of the church fathers and concludes that they believed prophecy to be one sign of the "true" church and an indication of its continuity with the apostles. Chan explains:

> In other words, while prophecy alone does not prove that the church is true, it does show at least that if the church is true, it should manifest some form of the prophetic gift. Prophetic gift is a normal part of church life. . . . The true church is the community in which truth is alive and this living truth is evidenced by the presence of prophecies.[183]

---

178. The term σημεῖον is specifically used only of tongues but it is likely that verse 22 contains an *ellipsis* which implies that prophecy also serves as a sign. Fee, *First Epistle to the Corinthians*, 682.

179. Ibid., 680–83; Dunn, *Jesus and the Spirit*, 230–32; Grudem, *Gift of Prophecy in 1 Corinthians*, 192–201; Hiu, *Regulations Concerning Tongues and Prophecy*, 99–102.

180. Menzies, *Empowered for Witness*, 215–18.

181. Chia, "Biblical Theology on Power Manifestation."

182. Chan, "Prophecy and Discernment," 121–22.

183. Ibid., 122.

The Pentecostal movement sees itself as a restoration of the church of the New Testament.[184] In particular, it is the occurrence of prophecy, tongues, and other miraculous phenomena which serve as a sign of the presence of the living God in the movement. Prophecy then serves as an indication to Pentecostals that God is with them and has empowered them for both life and ministry.[185] In this sense, prophecy serves as a sign of blessing to many Pentecostals, much in accordance with Paul's proposition.

4.3.3 Evangelism and Church Growth

The purpose of prophecy described above emphasizes its primary function within the body of believers. At the same time, Paul makes it clear that prophecy has a function in evangelizing unbelievers (1 Cor 14:24–25). Since prophecy communicates revelatory information, this may sometimes be related with the personal secrets of an unbeliever. The prophetic message will then bring conviction and conversion of the unbeliever.[186] The account of Jesus and the Samaritan woman in John 4:4–42 is often cited as an example of this form of prophetic evangelism. Jesus demonstrates knowledge of the Samaritan woman's background and that causes her to acknowledge him as a prophet. It further results in her testifying to others in her hometown and many others end up believing in Jesus.

The Third Wave has emphasized the use of prophecy in evangelism to a greater extent than the Classical Pentecostals.[187] This is largely due to the concept of "power evangelism" introduced by John Wimber and defined as "a spontaneous, Spirit-inspired, empowered presentation of the gospel."[188] Power evangelism includes prophecy though it is more commonly associated with miracles, divine healing, and deliverance from evil spirits. These phenomena are said to authenticate the gospel message and convince unbelievers of the reality of God. At the same time, these miraculous phenomena demonstrate God's power and should be a natural expression of

---

184. Ma, "Pentecostal Worship in Asia"; Stronstad, "Affirming Diversity."

185. Gee, *Concerning Spiritual Gifts*, 29–30. Note also the overall argument by R. P. Menzies. Menzies, *Empowered for Witness*.

186. Gentile, *Your Sons and Daughters Shall Prophesy*, 191–93; Horton, *Gifts of the Spirit*, 170–72; Palma, "Prophecy: Nature and Scope," 12; Stibbe, *Prophetic Evangelism*; Tyra, *Holy Spirit in Mission*, 80–88.

187. The Third Wave refers to a movement which began in the 1980s among evangelical churches stressing the supernatural activity of the Holy Spirit. The movement eschews being labeled as Pentecostal or Charismatic. See Wagner, "Third Wave."

188. Wimber, *Power Evangelism*, 46.

Christian life and ministry.[189] Stibbe's work on prophetic evangelism bears much of the influence of the Third Wave.[190] He rightly emphasizes the value of prophecy in evangelizing unbelievers and carefully appeals to Scripture in support of his arguments. However, Stibbe defines prophetic evangelism as simply God speaking to unbelievers through revelatory phenomena.[191] His broad definition includes even direct revelation to unbelievers through dreams, visions, or impressions. While all revelatory phenomena may be described as "prophetic," they may not be strictly considered as prophecy *per se*. Specifically direct divine revelation without a human intermediary should not be considered prophecy and is not referred to as such in the New Testament.

R. P. Menzies provides a Classical Pentecostal perspective to the "signs and wonders" movement and his insights are relevant to the use of prophecy in evangelism.[192] He acknowledges the efficacy of phenomena such as prophecy in evangelism and church growth but notes that much of Third Wave theology is based on a Pauline view of spiritual gifts. R. P. Menzies provides a Lukan perspective, observing that "signs and wonders" also serve to cultivate the virtues of courage and perseverance in the face of hardship and opposition.[193] He contends that these virtues cause the gospel to flourish and the church to grow in the midst of suffering and persecution. Tan-Chow May Ling concurs with R. P. Menzies and accepts these virtues as a corrective to the dangers of triumphalism in an emphasis on Spirit-empowered ministry.[194] Specifically, she calls for recognition of this in the context of power evangelism in Singapore. This perspective indicates that prophecy results in church growth and evangelism but in an indirect manner. Prophecy stirs courage and perseverance in believers and inspires more evangelistic activity in the midst of challenges. The connection between prophecy and virtue formation will be discussed further in chapter 5.

---

189. For more discussion on the purpose of "signs and wonders," see Greig, "Purpose of Signs and Wonders."

190. Stibbe highlights the strong influence of John Wimber on his ministry. See Stibbe, *Prophetic Evangelism*, 43–58.

191. Ibid., 3.

192. Menzies, "Pentecostal Perspective on 'Signs and Wonders.'" See also Aker, "Gospel in Action."

193. Menzies, "Pentecostal Perspective on 'Signs and Wonders,'" 274–75. Menzies specifically uses the terms "boldness" and "staying power." This study prefers to refer to them as virtues of "courage" and "perseverance."

194. Tan-Chow, *Pentecostal Theology*, 92–93. Tan-Chow was a Pentecostal scholar from Singapore and the Academic Dean of the Theological Centre for Asia.

On a much broader level, Tyra contends for a closer connection between prophetic activity and the missional faithfulness of the church.[195] Tyra surveys both the Old and New Testament to demonstrate that the coming of the Holy Spirit on individuals empowers them in prophetic speech and action. He argues for the necessity of prophetic activity in the church's activities of evangelism, edification, and equipping in order to achieve greater missional faithfulness. The Pentecostal and Charismatic movements are held up as prime examples of church growth that results from the prophetic activity of ordinary believers. Tyra's understanding of prophetic activity is, like Stibbe, broader than the gift of prophecy as defined in the New Testament. However, Tyra's thesis that missional faithfulness and church growth are directly related with the church's prophetic activity is important and significant. It demonstrates that while prophecy is primarily the communication of a revelatory message, its activity results in the transformation of the church's praxis and contributes significantly to the spiritual and numerical growth of the body of believers.

Sociologically, the growth of the Pentecostal movement is attributed to a rejection of modernity and a yearning for a primal spirituality.[196] Tongues within the movement are portrayed as the restoration of primal speech whereas prophecy contributes to the recovery of mystical experiences and a return to primal piety. This presents great appeal to contemporary unbelievers as they seek to find purpose and significance in the midst of postmodern soul-searching.[197] Thus, the practice of prophecy brings church growth by way of the appeal of a mystical spirituality.

4.3.4 Personal Guidance

Classical Pentecostals have shown a strong aversion towards personal prophecy and its use in providing personal direction or decision-making.[198] Gee, for example, notes the modern fascination with personal prophecy as a means of guidance. However, he stresses that the New Testament does not provide a single instance of individuals or churches using the gift of proph-

---

195. Tyra, *Holy Spirit in Mission*. Tyra draws substantially from the work of Menzies and Stronstad in forming his biblical theology of the Holy Spirit. However, he moves beyond a purely Lukan perspective to formulate a broader pneumatology.

196. Cox, *Fire from Heaven*.

197. Alexander, *Signs and Wonders*, 115–30.

198. Gee, *Spiritual Gifts in the Work of the Ministry Today*, 51. Also Gee, *Concerning Spiritual Gifts*, 120–21. For a similar opinion, see Chan, "Prophecy and Discernment," 123; Horton, *Gifts of the Spirit*, 165; Robeck, "Gift of Prophecy in Acts and Paul Part 2," 51.

ecy in such a manner. Prophecy may provide particularistic information but the course of action to take in response is always left to the believer. He claims that the Old Testament provides some instances primarily because the prophet functioned as an intermediary between God and man. In the New Testament, however, all are able to come directly to God to seek His will. Allowances must always be made for God to sovereignly choose to communicate to individuals through prophecy today. However, Gee's main point is that believers should avoid yearning for personal prophecies and churches must refrain from promoting such a practice. Instead, the model of the New Testament church was to use their "sanctified common sense" and to discern God's will through their own prayers. In line with this, the AGUSA specifically cautions against the practice of personal prophecy and warns of potential for abuse.[199]

Elsewhere, Lim examines the various accounts in Acts where prophecy provides some form of guidance to individuals.[200] He rejects the use of prophecy to initiate personal direction but accepts that prophecy may serve to confirm what believers had already felt God was leading them towards. Lim's perspective takes better account of the varied content of prophetic speech in the New Testament, a point also recognized by Turner.[201] Instances such as the missionary call of Barnabas and Saul (Acts 13:2–3) seems to suggest that prophecy has at least some role in decision-making and guidance.[202] Other instances cited by Turner (Acts 15:28; 16:6–13 and 18:10) indicate the revelatory work of the Holy Spirit may be better understood as God speaking directly to individuals rather than as prophecy through a human intermediary.

In contrast to the guarded opinions above, there are several works in popular literature that encourage personal prophecy.[203] These teachings are closely associated with the Apostolic-Prophetic movement and various Apostolic networks worldwide.[204] The teachings exert significant influence within the Pentecostal movement among both clergy and laity as the proponents conduct conferences and workshops in various churches.

199. The Assemblies of God USA, "Prophets and Personal Prophecies."

200. Lim, *Spiritual Gifts*, 249–52.

201. Turner, *Holy Spirit and Spiritual Gifts*, 200–201.

202. A similar case may be made for some form of a ministry call on Timothy (1 Tim 1:18; 4:14) though it is not possible to maintain this conclusively.

203. For example, see Cooke, *Developing Your Prophetic Gifting*; Deere, *Surprised by the Voice of God*; Eckhardt, *God Still Speaks*; Hamon, *Prophets and Personal Prophecy*; Jacobs, *Voice of God*; Joyner, *Prophetic Ministry*.

204. The Apostolic-Prophetic movement is usually associated with Peter Wagner's ministry. See Wagner, *New Apostolic Churches*.

Their teachings are even cited in academic works as representative of the Pentecostal-Charismatic movement.[205] These proponents strongly encourage believers to hear God speak to them through Scripture, prayer, impressions, dreams, and visions. However, they also suggest that God uses believers to prophesy over various areas of an individual's life. For example, Hamon discusses prophecies that cover business endeavors, marriage, and even pregnancies.[206] Hamon does stress extensively on the need for judging prophecy, the possibility of error and abuse, as well as a call to avoid becoming "spooky spiritual" Christians.[207]

It is indeed laudable to call believers to be open to the leading of the Holy Spirit. As Deere points out, contemporary Christianity tends to ignore most of the miraculous phenomena within Scripture and so deny the possibility of any direct, revelatory communication from God.[208] However, discerning God's will for oneself is quite different from prophesying over another person and asserting that it is God's will for them. The issues are more acute if the prophecy demands a particular decision or course of action. Grudem's approach may be seen as a mediating position by describing prophecy as simply expressing something that God brings to mind. Grudem emphasizes that the words of the message and the manner of expression are all the choice of the person prophesying. He calls on believers to avoid using terms such as "thus says the Lord" or to call the message a "word from the Lord."[209] Such an approach avoids making contemporary prophecy the actual words of God and acknowledges the possibility of error on the part of the person prophesying. In any case, the main purpose of prophecy is for corporate exhortation so that the community of believers may be edified. Believers should refrain from viewing prophecy as a form of Christian "fortune-telling" which can be used for their guidance.

4.4 SUMMARY

This chapter has surveyed the literature on New Testament prophecy so as to ascertain its nature and purpose. From this discussion, prophecy can now

---

205. Latham specifically cites Bill Hamon, Rick Joyner, and Graham Cooke as representative of Pentecostal-Charismatic prophecy. Latham, "Is There Any Word from the Lord?" 48–95.

206. Hamon, *Prophets and Personal Prophecy*. For a description of Hamon's ministry, see Grady, "God Spoke through a Man."

207. Hamon, *Prophets and Personal Prophecy*, 163–65. Also see Hamon, *Prophets, Pitfalls and Principles*.

208. Deere, *Surprised by the Voice of God*, 21–29.

209. Grudem, *Gift of Prophecy in the New Testament and Today*, 92–94, 110–12.

be defined as the reception and communication of a spontaneous revelation through an inspired human intermediary. It is not the equivalent of preaching or teaching, though there may be instances where a prophetic element is present in either the preparation or delivery. Prophecy is usually a verbal, intelligible message though tongues with interpretation may be considered a functional equivalent. The main purpose of prophecy is to reveal particularistic information that can then edify, exhort, and encourage the community of believers. It further serves as a sign of God's attitude and to evangelize unbelievers. The next chapter will continue to survey the literature on the practice of prophecy.

5

The Practice of Prophecy

5.1 INTRODUCTION

THIS CHAPTER SEEKS TO review the academic literature on the practice of prophecy amongst Classical Pentecostals from both the biblical and empirical perspectives. The review will cover the ability of believers to prophesy, the process of the actual delivery of prophecy, and the judging of prophetic messages. Psychological aspects of prophecy will also be discussed including empirical studies on personality types and prophecy. Finally, the chapter will consider the place of prophecy within the larger scope of Pentecostal spirituality. The survey will show a gap in the academic literature concerning the practice of contemporary prophecy, particularly within the Asian context.

5.2 THE ABILITY TO PROPHESY

In discussing the practice of prophecy, the first practical consideration concerns who is able to engage in prophecy. Are only certain believers accorded the ability or should all believers expect to be able to prophesy? On this question, Classical Pentecostal writers agree that all believers at least have the potential ability to prophesy.[1] First, it is noted that Paul exhorts all believers to eagerly seek the gift of prophecy in 1 Corinthians 14:1 and 14:39.

---

1. Horton, *Gifts of the Spirit*, 160; Horton, *What the Bible Says about the Holy Spirit*, 276; Lim, *Spiritual Gifts*, 79, 103.

The natural inference is that Paul made such an exhortation because he believed this gift was at least potentially available to all believers.[2] Second, the "all" in 1 Corinthians 14:31 suggests that all believers at the meeting had the potential ability to prophesy and bring edification to the assembly.[3] This is not to suggest that all the believers present at a meeting would actually prophesy given Paul's restriction in 1 Corinthians 14:29 to limit the number of prophecies. Third, Classical Pentecostals point to Acts 2:17-18 where prophecy or inspired utterance is presented as a mark of the outpouring of the Spirit. This is much in line with the "prophethood" of all believers discussed in section 4.2.1.[4]

While all believers may possess the potential ability to prophesy, it is not possible to insist that all believers will actually experience prophesying.[5] Paul clearly explains that the Holy Spirit sovereignly determines the manifestation of the gifts (1 Cor 14:7, 11), so while all believers have the potential to be used, it is not reasonable to insist that all believers will definitely be used in this manner. The same would apply to all the other gifts listed in 1 Corinthians 12:8-10 even though Paul's later discussion does not mention them all explicitly. Furthermore, the rhetorical questions posed in 1 Corinthians 12:29-30 clearly expect a negative answer. This suggests that none of the gifts manifests itself in all believers.[6] In addition, believers may not experience the manifestation of gifts due to a lack of opportunity, unbelief, immaturity, or even sin.[7]

The ability of all believers to engage in prophecy raises an issue on the role and authority of women in the church. Bible passages such as Acts 21:9 and 1 Corinthians 11:5 indicate that women prophesied in the early church. This raises an issue for those who contend that women should not take authority over men in the church. One possible solution proposed by Grudem is to assert that prophecy merely reports a spontaneous revelation and hence

---

2. Fee, *First Epistle to the Corinthians*, 654. See footnote 7. Also note Grudem, *Gift of Prophecy in 1 Corinthians*, 235-36.

3. Barrett, *First Epistle to the Corinthians*, 329; Bruce, *1 and 2 Corinthians*, 134; Fee, *First Epistle to the Corinthians*, 695.

4. Stronstad, *Prophethood of All Believers*. Similar observations are made by Penney, Soh, and Twelftree. See Penney, "Testing of New Testament Prophecy," 55-59; Soh, "Biblical Perspectives on Prophecy," 108; Twelftree, *People of the Spirit*, 157.

5. Grudem, *Gift of Prophecy in 1 Corinthians*, 236-38; Penney, "Testing of New Testament Prophecy," 54.

6. Classical Pentecostals generally view the tongues mentioned in 1 Corinthians 12:30 to refer to the "public" utterance of tongues which are meant to be interpreted for the edification of the assembly. See Hayford, *Beauty of Spiritual Language*, 102-3; Menzies, *Empowered for Witness*, 248-49; Palma, *Holy Spirit*, 159.

7. Deere, *Surprised by the Voice of God*, 235-303.

does not impose any form of authority on the congregation. This position interprets 1 Corinthians 14:34 as restricting women from evaluating prophecy since this would involve assuming an authoritative role.[8] Others who hold to a more egalitarian position between the different genders see little issue with women prophesying in the church or assuming a leadership role.[9] It is beyond the scope of this study to engage in a full discussion on the role of women in the church. Nevertheless, the Pentecostal movement has long recognized the democratization of the Spirit and that both men and women manifest spiritual gifts. Pentecostal churches have acknowledged the significant role played by women in the spread of the gospel and accepted women in leadership positions.[10] Thus, there is little issue with women prophesying or evaluating prophecy within Pentecostal churches.

At this point, some discussion should be made on the designation of individuals as prophets in the New Testament.[11] One view is that the role of a prophet was a formal ecclesiastical role within the church.[12] Proponents of this view usually cite Ephesians 4:11 as the basis for four (or five) offices within the church. In this sense, individuals such as Agabus, Judas, and Silas function as prophets in an appointed office in the New Testament church.[13] Significantly, Ephesians 4:11 refers to people as "gifts" (δόματα) in contrast to 1 Corinthians 12 which highlights the various manifestations as "gifts" (πνευματικά/χαρίσματα). However, opponents to this view highlight an absence of discussion in the New Testament on what qualifies a person to be recognized as a prophet.[14] There are no examples of the church

---

8. Grudem, *Gift of Prophecy in 1 Corinthians*, 239–55.

9. For example, see Gill and Cavaness, *God's Women*; Keener, *Paul, Women & Wives*. Prophecy has also been suggested to serve as divine affirmative action and female empowerment. See Muindi, "Nature and Significance of Prophecy," 170–72.

10. Alexander and Yong, *Philip's Daughters*; Anderson, *Introduction to Pentecostalism*, 273–76; Kay, *Pentecostalism*, 300–302; Warrington, *Pentecostal Theology*, 143–52. Empirical data show that women in Pentecostal churches in Singapore and Hong Kong are not restricted in ministry or leadership opportunities. See Kay, "Where the Wind Blows," 140. In Singapore, the AGS supports the ordination of women and there are several women serving as senior pastors of AGS churches. However, women face greater challenges in other Asian countries. See Ma, "Asian Women and Pentecostal Ministry."

11. Acts 11:27; 13:1; 15:32; 21:10; 1 Corinthians 12:28–29; Ephesians 4:11.

12. Cartledge, *Apostolic Revolution*; Cooke, *Developing Your Prophetic Gifting*, 191–208; Gentile, *Your Sons and Daughters Shall Prophesy*, 187–91; Hamon, *Apostles, Prophets, and the Coming Moves of God*. For a discussion on the five (or four) ecclesiastical offices, see Green, *Understanding the Fivefold Ministry*. For a contrasting perspective, see Fung, "Function or Office"; Resane, "Critical Analysis of the Ecclesiology of the Emerging Apostolic Churches."

13. Hamon, *Apostles, Prophets, and the Coming Moves of God*, 44–45.

14. Lincoln, *Ephesians*, 252–53.

undergoing a process to appoint someone to such a role. Scripture instead contains descriptions and qualifications for individuals to be appointed as deacons, elders, and overseers.[15] In light of this, it may be better to adopt Grudem's position that the term "prophet" was used in a functional sense.[16] A person who prophesies may be called a "prophet" in the same way that a person who teaches may be called a "teacher." Similarly, Gee suggests that prophets should best be seen as those who exercised a frequent and proven gift of prophesying.[17] He argues that insisting on a further distinction would be arbitrary in the absence of clear biblical support. While the contemporary church may choose to recognize individuals with a proven ministry as prophets, care should be exercised in insisting this is a formal ecclesiastical office instituted within the New Testament church.[18]

5.3 THE DELIVERY OF PROPHECY

The process of prophesying is often considered in three stages: reception, analysis, and delivery.[19] Although a high degree of overlap exists between these stages in practice, these stages present a helpful framework by which the practice of prophecy may be investigated. The first stage involves the reception of the prophetic message. This includes the spiritual experiences by which God is believed to be communicating and also the timing of these experiences with respect to the actual delivery. The second stage involves the analysis of the prophecy by the one prophesying. This stage is often described as the interpretation and application of revelation received in the first stage.[20] The third stage of prophesying deals with the relaying of the message to the intended audience. These three stages will be elaborated on in the following sections.

---

15. Fung argues this point and suggests that function and gifts are brought together in an ecclesiastical office-bearer. Fung, "Function or Office."

16. Grudem, *Gift of Prophecy in 1 Corinthians*, 231–34. Also Dunn, *Jesus and the Spirit*, 171.

17. Gee, *Spiritual Gifts in the Work of the Ministry Today*, 43–44. See also Petts, *Body Builders*, 46–56; Lim, *Spiritual Gifts*, 104.

18. The Assemblies of God USA, "Apostles and Prophets." Members of the movement worldwide may differ from this conviction.

19. Pytches, *Prophecy in the Local Church*, 51–94.

20. Bickle, *Growing in the Prophetic*, 23–34; Cooke, *Developing Your Prophetic Gifting*, 91–109; Deere, *Beginner's Guide to the Gift of Prophecy*, 83–84.

5.3.1 The Reception of Prophecy

The first stage of prophesying entails an impetus by which God is believed to be communicating a message through a believer to an audience. This impetus comes in the form of a spiritual experience by which the believer perceives God is speaking. These experiences are well described in popular literature on prophecy.[21] The typical approach of these works is to first survey Scripture to identify the spiritual experiences through which God communicated with the biblical prophets. These experiences are then presented as ways in which God communicates with contemporary believers and through which prophecy is initiated. Several real-life examples are often cited by the literature in support of these claims.[22] A brief survey of these experiences is presented below.[23]

First, prophecy may be initiated by a message coming to the mind of a believer.[24] The message may be in the form of a single word, a phrase, a sentence fragment, or even a complete message. Often as the believer speaks and prophesies, more words and phrases are revealed to the believer. The words may be something that arises spontaneously in their thoughts, a mental image which believers "see," or an audible voice that they "hear."[25] The words may even appear over congregation members or on a person's forehead.[26] The words signal that God wishes to communicate a message and should prompt believers to quieten their minds, seek God, and discern what God wishes to say. Sometimes, the impetus comes in the form of a Scripture verse that is to be shared as part of the prophetic message.[27]

---

21. Cooke, *Developing Your Prophetic Gifting*, 60–68; Deere, *Beginner's Guide to the Gift of Prophecy*, 43–61; Gentile, *Your Sons and Daughters Shall Prophesy*, 364–66; Pytches, *Prophecy in the Local Church*, 51–75; Stibbe, *Prophetic Evangelism*, 94–113.

22. The works by Deere and Pytches are representative of the approach described. See Deere, *Beginner's Guide to the Gift of Prophecy*, 43–61; Pytches, *Prophecy in the Local Church*, 51–75. Gentile provides a summary of how biblical prophets received divine communication. See Gentile, *Your Sons and Daughters Shall Prophesy*, 75.

23. The survey will largely expand on categories outlined by Cartledge. See Cartledge, "Charismatic Prophecy," *JPT*, 83–88.

24. Deere, *Beginner's Guide to the Gift of Prophecy*, 52–53; Kay, *Prophecy!*, 92–93. Biblical examples include 1 Samuel 3:1–14; Isaiah 8; Acts 5:1–11; and Acts 9:4–6.

25. Some authors attempt to distinguish between an "internal" and an "external" voice speaking to the believer. See Deere, *Beginner's Guide to the Gift of Prophecy*, 50–51; Pytches, *Prophecy in the Local Church*, 57–59.

26. Cooke, *Developing Your Prophetic Gifting*, 65–66; Wimber, *Power Evangelism*, 44–45.

27. Cooke, *Developing Your Prophetic Gifting*, 67–68; Kay, *Prophecy!*, 92.

Second, prophecy may be initiated by a mental image which the believer experiences.[28] Occurrences while sleeping are described as dreams and these necessarily occur prior to the delivery of the prophecy. Occurrences while believers are conscious may be described as a vision or a picture. Some experiences are so overwhelming that believers lose consciousness of their surroundings as if in a trance.[29] The mental image may be a static symbol or the dynamic unfolding of a story. These visions, pictures, and dreams communicate the message vividly and forcefully and will be remembered long after the experience.[30] The images may even evoke an emotional response that then becomes part of the prophecy.[31] Mental images contain fairly complex messages with varying degrees of symbolism. Delivery of the prophecy involves describing what was seen and may require further interpretation of the mental image. A special subset of this second category concerns prophecies prompted by a supernatural visitation.[32] Believers experience an encounter with angelic beings who entrust them with a message to relay to others. While some may insist that such experiences are physical encounters, it seems better to consider these experiences as a special type of vision or dream.

Third, the believer may receive the impetus to prophesy through a general impression of what the prophetic message is.[33] In this case, the believer does not receive a word or phrase but rather a distinct idea of what God wants to communicate to the congregation. The impression may be knowledge of a simple fact or an inner conviction to say or do something.[34] This impetus for prophecy has been described as divine promptings from the Holy Spirit within the believer that are then expressed into words and sentences as the believer speaks.[35] This is in line with Grudem's assertion that prophecy is simply reporting or expressing something which God brings to

---

28. Deere, *Beginner's Guide to the Gift of Prophecy*, 55–57; Pytches, *Prophecy in the Local Church*, 54–57. Biblical examples of God communicating in this manner include Judges 7:13–15; Amos 8:1–2; Acts 7:55–56; 10:9–15; and 16:9.

29. Pytches, *Prophecy in the Local Church*, 59–61.

30. Cartledge, "Charismatic Prophecy," *JPT*, 85; Gentile, *Your Sons and Daughters Shall Prophesy*, 365.

31. Deere, *Beginner's Guide to the Gift of Prophecy*, 56–57.

32. Ibid., 48–50; Pytches, *Prophecy in the Local Church*, 61–64. Examples in Scripture can be seen in Daniel 9:21; Luke 1:11–20; and Acts 1:10–11.

33. Cartledge, "Charismatic Prophecy," *JPT*, 84; Deere, *Surprised by the Voice of God*, 151–55. Deere sees God communicating in this manner from Nehemiah 7:5; Mark 2:8; John 14:26 and Acts 14:9.

34. Cooke, *Developing Your Prophetic Gifting*, 65.

35. Hayford, *Beauty of Spiritual Language*, 121–22.

the mind of a believer.[36] The prophecy may not always come in the form of an overwhelming outburst of words but rather be simply a report of a tentative impression that is attributed to God.

Fourth, physical sensations in believers' bodies may serve as a prompt for prophecy. Aches and pains in the body may indicate the presence of people with physical ailments in that particular part of the body.[37] The prophecy may then express God's desire to bring healing or to provide encouragement and comfort in the midst of suffering. There is also the possibility that these physical sensations symbolically represent issues in the congregation's spiritual life. Once the prophecy is delivered, the physical sensation prompting the prophecy disappears. Though practitioners may testify to this experience, biblical support for this form of communication is lacking.

Fifth, prophecies may take the form of a public declaration of a message in tongues followed by an interpretation.[38] This activity was discussed in section 4.2.7 and was noted to be at least functionally equivalent to prophecy. Upon hearing a message in tongues, believers begin to pray quietly and ask God for the interpretation. A believer may then "see," "hear," or receive an impression of the appropriate interpretation.[39] As mentioned, the interpretation is not a translation of the message in tongues and hence it may differ somewhat in length and quality.

The five categories described above cover the main spiritual experiences believed to initiate prophecy. The prophetic message received is often termed as "revelation" in the literature surveyed though efforts are made to distinguish this from biblical revelation.[40] In addition, there is the issue of the timing of these experiences with respect to the relaying of the prophecy.[41] One possibility is where the believer receives the entire revelation pri-

---

36. Grudem, *Gift of Prophecy in the New Testament and Today*, 110–12. In contrast, words may also "'burst forth' under the anointing." See Pytches, *Prophecy in the Local Church*, 88.

37. Cartledge, "Charismatic Prophecy," *JPT*, 86; Deere, *Beginner's Guide to the Gift of Prophecy*, 58–59.

38. 1 Corinthians 14:5, 13.

39. Cartledge, "Charismatic Prophecy," *JPT*, 87; Petts, *Body Builders*, 130. It is observed that much of the popular literature reviewed by this study omit discussing messages given by tongues with interpretation. This possibly reflects the position that tongues with interpretation should not be considered prophecy. More likely, it reflects a reduced emphasis on tongues outside the Classical Pentecostal movement. This is especially true within the Neo-charismatic movement. See Wagner, "Third Wave."

40. Deere, *Surprised by the Voice of God*, 278–86; Horton, *Gifts of the Spirit*, 173; Lim, *Spiritual Gifts*, 105.

41. Cartledge, "Charismatic Prophecy," *JPT*, 82.

or to the actual act of speaking. The second possibility is where the believer receives only part of the message but feels prompted to start speaking. The rest of the message is then received while the believer is speaking. The third possibility is where the believer perceives a strong impulse to speak and prophesy even though the believer does not have any idea what to say. The words and the message then come simultaneously as the believer speaks.

5.3.2 The Analysis of Prophecy

The second stage of prophesying involves an analysis of the revelation received in the first stage.[42] This analysis is often done by the one delivering the prophecy and becomes part of the prophetic message itself. For example, a believer may prophesy by describing a mental image which has come to mind and then continue to interpret the meaning of this image and apply it to the congregation's context. In other instances, the believer simply describes the mental image but refrains from the interpretation and application. The analysis is instead done by other congregation members or by the church leaders who are present. In this case, the analysis becomes part of the process where prophecies are judged.

Interpretation and application are necessary because the prophetic revelation often comes in the form of highly figurative language.[43] Even in cases where the impetus for prophecy comes through words and phrases, the question remains if these sentence fragments should be interpreted literally or figuratively. In the case of visions, pictures, and dreams, the message is often coded in enigmatic symbols which require interpretation. Some popular works even provide extensive guidelines for interpreting prophetic visions and dreams.[44] While some of these guidelines may be useful, many of them are derived from personal experience rather than a clear biblical basis. Human reasoning may logically relate certain symbols with particular meanings but believers ought to realize that prophecy communicates information from a divine or heavenly perspective.[45] Thus, it is essential to seek divine interpretation rather than to rely on human reasoning.

The application of prophecy likewise requires divine guidance as it raises issues of who the prophecy is intended for, the timing of any future

---

42. Cooke, *Developing Your Prophetic Gifting*, 104–8; Pytches, *Prophecy in the Local Church*, 79.

43. Bickle, *Growing in the Prophetic*, 25–28.

44. For example, see Goll and Goll, *Dream Language*; Pierce and Sytsema, *When God Speaks*.

45. Grudem, *Gift of Prophecy in 1 Corinthians*, 129.

fulfillment, and the perceived response which God desires.[46] There is widespread consensus that while the description of the revelation might be accurate, the interpretation and application of the message may introduce some error. Wisdom dictates that believers exercise caution and never be presumptuous or dogmatic regarding their interpretation and application. Prayer and humility in seeking God is essential in arriving at the correct interpretation and application.[47]

The account of Agabus's prophecy (Acts 21:10–14) is often cited as an example of human error in the interpretation and application of a prophetic revelation.[48] It is possible to speculate that Agabus received a revelation of Paul being tied and bound in Jerusalem in the presence of Jews and Gentiles. It is then suggested that Agabus wrongly interpreted this to mean the Jews would bind Paul and hand him over. In reality, the Jews had no desire to deliver Paul to the Gentiles but were instead trying to kill him (Acts 21:27–36). This led to the Romans arresting and binding Paul rather than the Jews. A second error occurred when the believers heard Agabus's prophecy and wrongly interpreted it as a warning for Paul to avoid travelling to Jerusalem (Acts 21:12). Paul instead interpreted this as a confirmation of God's plan for him (Acts 20:22) and he willingly embraced it.

5.3.3 The Relaying of Prophecy

The third stage of prophesying involves the actual delivery of the prophetic message. Scripture seems clear that believers are in control of the gift of prophecy (1 Cor 14:32). Believers are exhorted to regulate the number of prophecies given in a meeting, to cease prophesying if someone else receives a revelation, and even to choose to prophesy rather than speak in tongues when unbelievers are present.[49] These instructions are meaningless if believers surrendered control to the Holy Spirit when prophesying. They also strongly indicate that believers are not in an ecstatic, trance-like state where they lose control and rave violently.[50] Believers may experience a rising ex-

---

46. Bickle, *Growing in the Prophetic*, 31–33; Pytches, *Prophecy in the Local Church*, 80–81.

47. Deere, *Beginner's Guide to the Gift of Prophecy*, 92–94.

48. Gentile, *Your Sons and Daughters Shall Prophesy*, 207–8; Grudem, *Gift of Prophecy in the New Testament and Today*, 77–83; Pytches, *Prophecy in the Local Church*, 81–82; Robeck, "Gift of Prophecy in Acts and Paul Part 2," 25–28.

49. Horton, *Gifts of the Spirit*, 174; Petts, *Body Builders*, 146. See 1 Corinthians 14:23–25, 14:29–30.

50. Grudem, *Gift of Prophecy in the New Testament and Today*, 103–8; Turner, *Holy Spirit and Spiritual Gifts*, 196–200.

citement while prophesying or even some level of mild dissociation, but the experience remains largely within the level of conscious control.

The delivery of prophecy raises a question on the choice of words used to express the prophecy. Does prophecy resemble divine dictation or does the believer choose the words and manner of expressing the prophecy? The practical reality is likely to be somewhere in-between these two extremes. There may be some instances where believers receive specific words and phrases that are incorporated in the prophecy. There may even be instances where the prophecy closely resembles divine dictation.[51] However, in most cases, believers express the prophecy in words of their choice.[52]

Classical Pentecostals have criticized two unhelpful practices with regards the relaying of prophecy. The first issue is where believers express the prophecy in the language of the King James Bible.[53] This unfortunate practice was common in the early days of the Pentecostal tradition, but it ought to be evident to all that God does not speak in Shakespearian English. Believers are instead encouraged to express the prophecy in simple words and phrases so that the congregation might understand and respond. The second issue is where believers choose to express prophecy in first-person language as if God were speaking directly to the congregation.[54] While this is indeed the essence of prophecy, the use of first person expressions may cause believers to overvalue prophecy and to equate it with Scripture. Furthermore, the choice of elevated expressions like, "thus says the Lord" or "I the Lord thy God say to you," suggests a level of infallibility that is inconsistent with a message that requires judging and evaluation by the congregation. This has led some to recommend the use of more tentative expressions such as, "I think the Lord is showing me" or "I sense that God is concerned about."[55] These expressions appear far less presumptuous and naturally invite the evaluation of what was said.

---

51. Cartledge, "Charismatic Prophecy," *JET*, 82.

52. Alexander, *Signs and Wonders*, 119; Grudem, *Systematic Theology*, 1056–57.

53. Petts, *Body Builders*, 147; Hayford, *Beauty of Spiritual Language*, 125. For examples of these expressions, see Horton, *Gifts of the Spirit*, 173–74.

54. Gee, *Spiritual Gifts in the Work of the Ministry Today*, 48; Horton, *Gifts of the Spirit*, 173–74; Petts, *Body Builders*, 146.

55. Gentile, *Your Sons and Daughters Shall Prophesy*, 371; Grudem, *Gift of Prophecy in the New Testament and Today*, 111; Petts, *Body Builders*, 146–47.

5.3.4 Empirical Studies on the Delivery of Prophecy

The literature search revealed two significant empirical studies providing empirical data on the delivery of prophecy. The first study was conducted by Cartledge and was based on a study of thirty-four respondents from nine churches within the Church of England.[56] The second, more recent study was conducted by Muindi and examined the Redeemed Gospel Church in Kenya. Muindi has likewise employed Van der Ven's empirical approach to first study twenty-three respondents followed by a second study of fifty-nine respondents from two congregations.[57] However, Muindi's study utilized focus groups to gather only qualitative data in a departure from Van der Ven's proposal which advocates quantitative analysis for the phase of empirical-theological testing.[58]

Both the studies by Cartledge and Muindi report similar findings. These studies observed that respondents usually received the impetus to prophesy while engaged in prayer.[59] This included private prayer, corporate prayer, or while praying for someone else. Praise and worship, which are a sub-context of prayer, were also observed to be a common setting for prophecy. Respondents reported a variety of ways in which they had received an impulse to prophesy. The most common experiences were the reception of mental pictures and words coming to the mind of believers. Other experiences included inspired prayer, a message in tongues followed by interpretation, dreams and visions, hearing an audible voice, spontaneous reception of knowledge, Scripture verses coming to mind, physical sensations, and subjective impressions.[60] Respondents also recounted varying degrees of internal pressure to speak out and proclaim the prophetic message. This pressure was relieved after delivering the prophecy.[61]

Both the studies found significant correlation between the empirical data and the descriptions in literature. This suggests that the spiritual experiences described in section 5.3 are indeed representative of the actual

---

56. Cartledge, "Charismatic Prophecy," *JET*. Empirical data on the practice of prophecy may also be found in studies by Kay and Poloma. See Kay, *Pentecostals in Britain*; Poloma, *Assemblies of God at the Crossroads*.

57. Muindi, "Nature and Significance of Prophecy."

58. Ibid., 42–43.

59. Cartledge, "Charismatic Prophecy," *JET*, 83; Muindi, "Nature and Significance of Prophecy," 205.

60. Cartledge, "Charismatic Prophecy," *JET*, 79–84; Muindi, "Nature and Significance of Prophecy," 201–2.

61. Cartledge, "Charismatic Prophecy," *JET*, 83–84; Muindi, "Nature and Significance of Prophecy," 175.

experiences of believers. However, more empirical data is needed to form a fuller understanding of practical reality. Much of the rest of current literature on prophecy relies on anecdotal testimonies rather than rigorous empirical investigation. Even the frequency of the spiritual experiences described above is unknown. This is especially true for the Asian setting where there have not been scholarly studies. Such data will assist the church to engage in important practical-theological reflection on the practice of prophecy.[62]

5.4 THE JUDGING OF PROPHECY

Scripture is clear that all prophecies should be judged.[63] This point is strongly advocated throughout Classical Pentecostal literature.[64] The need for testing is due to prophecy being partial and incomplete in revealing God's intentions (1 Cor 13:8–9). As previously mentioned, the interpretation and application of a prophetic message may introduce error. In some instances, a person seeking to manipulate others may even deliver a false prophecy. It is noteworthy that instructions to evaluate prophecy can also be found in extra-biblical works such as the *Didache* and *The Shepherd of Hermas*.[65] Both the biblical and extra-biblical exhortations indicate awareness of possible abuse within the early church and yet it is significant that the response is to evaluate prophecy rather than to abolish the practice.

Robeck provides three common criteria for the testing of prophecy.[66] The first criterion is an assessment of the person prophesying. This involves an evaluation of the person's character and trustworthiness, and necessitates that the person should be part of the local community of faith. It would be difficult to assess or give credibility to prophetic claims made by visitors who are strangers to the community. At the very least, these visitors would need to be recommended by a trusted peer community. The assessment should also include an evaluation of the source inspiring the prophecy (1 John

---

62. For example, see Fuchs, "Charismatic Prophecy and Innovation."

63. Deuteronomy 18:17–22; Matthew 7:15; 1 Corinthians 14:29; 1 Thessalonians 5:19–21 and 1 John 4:1.

64. Chan, "Prophecy and Discernment"; Gee, *Spiritual Gifts in the Work of the Ministry Today*, 47–50; Horton, *What the Bible Says about the Holy Spirit*, 233–34; Lim, *Spiritual Gifts*, 79; Robeck, "Prophecy, Gift of," 1004–5; Warrington, *Pentecostal Theology*, 83.

65. Chan, "Prophecy and Discernment," 121–22; Penney, "Testing of New Testament Prophecy," 75–76; Robeck, "Prophecy, Gift of," 1007–8.

66. Robeck, "Prophecy, Gift of," 1011. Also see Gentile who provides a checklist of 29 questions. Gentile, *Your Sons and Daughters Shall Prophesy*, 318–28.

4:1–3). Gee identifies at least three possible sources—the Holy Spirit, evil spirits, or the human spirit.[67] The χαρίσμα of discernment of spirits (1 Cor 12:10) and general spiritual discernment are possible means by which this may be evaluated.

The second criterion concerns the process by which prophecy is transmitted. Paul's emphasis in 1 Corinthians 14:32–39 is on maintaining peace and order within the assembly. Thus, the one prophesying should be willing to follow the local congregation's guidelines for prophesying and should not attempt to disrupt a meeting. This includes a willingness to allow prophecies to be tested and to submit to the authority of the local church leadership.[68]

The third criterion relates to the actual content of the prophecy. Prophecy should always be in agreement with Scripture and should never contradict it. Pentecostals fully affirm the authority of Scripture over all matters in faith and practice.[69] Higgins, an AG scholar, comments:

> Some elevate a "direct impression" of the Holy Spirit or a manifestation of the Spirit, such as prophecy, above the written Word. The Holy Spirit is the one who inspired the Word and who makes it authoritative. He will not say anything contrary to or beyond what the inspired Word declares.[70]

The canon of Scripture is closed and the revelation brought through contemporary prophecy should never challenge this.[71] Therefore, prophecies which introduce new doctrine or which challenge established biblical truths should be rejected. In any case, the majority of prophecies should concern non-doctrinal matters. These may be evaluated based on whether the message brings edification to the community and whether it glorifies Jesus.[72] This is not to forget the use of common sense in evaluating prophecy.[73] Prophecies which predict a future event can be evaluated based on their fulfillment, though this alone does not authenticate that the message comes from God.[74] All the criteria described should be applied together.

---

67. Gee, *Concerning Spiritual Gifts*, 62–63.
68. Deere, *Beginner's Guide to the Gift of Prophecy*, 127–28.
69. Higgins, "God's Inspired Word."
70. Ibid., 83.
71. For further discussion, see Carson, *Showing the Spirit*, 176–82; Grudem, *Gift of Prophecy in the New Testament and Today*, 27–49.
72. See 1 Corinthians 12:3 and 14:3. Cooke, *Developing Your Prophetic Gifting*, 146; Grudem, *Gift of Prophecy in the New Testament and Today*, 223–24.
73. Warrington, *Pentecostal Theology*, 83.
74. Deuteronomy 13:1–5.

Discussions on prophecy have also differed on who exactly should be judging prophecy. 1 Corinthians 14:29 calls on "the others" to conduct the evaluation. One view suggests that "the others" refers to other prophets who are present.[75] However, it seems more likely that Paul is referring to the entire congregation.[76] The evaluation of prophecy then becomes a corporate activity, permitting the involvement of a variety of spiritual gifts within the congregation.[77] Indeed, some see the gift of discernment of spirits (1 Cor 12:10) as taking the primary role in evaluating prophecy. While this may be true, it seems unnecessary to limit the evaluation to only those with such a gift.[78] Surely all believers have received the Holy Spirit and possess some ability for spiritual discernment. In practice, various churches may provide a protocol for the practice of prophecy within their local assembly.[79] This protocol may determine who is permitted to prophesy at different meetings, how the prophecy is to be delivered, and the people responsible for evaluating the message. Such a protocol may sometimes limit the evaluation of prophecies to the church leadership due to the practical challenge of involving the entire congregation. Jacobs describes the protocol of several churches and these include an AG church and other Pentecostal churches.[80] A common requirement is for believers to approach the pastoral leadership if they feel they have a prophetic word. The pastor or leaders judge the message before allowing it to be shared with the congregation. Sometimes, the pastor shares a summary of the message instead of allowing the believer to address the congregation. This is especially for cases where the congregation does not know the believer. All the churches have guidelines on correcting a prophecy that they feel is inappropriate or to address disorderly conduct.

Section 4.3.4 considered the practice of personal prophecy and concluded that there is little biblical evidence to support this practice. However, it was noted that the Bible does not explicitly rule out this practice and that prophecy may serve to confirm something that God had already spoken to an individual. The issue that then arises is the means by which personal prophecy should be judged. It seems appropriate that personal prophecy should still be delivered in public ministry rather than privately to

75. Aune, *Prophecy in Early Christianity*, 221.

76. Fee, *First Epistle to the Corinthians*, 694; Grudem, *Gift of Prophecy in 1 Corinthians*, 60–62; Hiu, *Regulations Concerning Tongues and Prophecy*, 120–22.

77. Penney, "Testing of New Testament Prophecy," 61.

78. Grudem, *Gift of Prophecy in 1 Corinthians*, 58–60.

79. Cooke, *Developing Your Prophetic Gifting*, 263–80; Gentile, *Your Sons and Daughters Shall Prophesy*, 330–49; Jacobs, *Voice of God*, 141–71; Pytches, *Prophecy in the Local Church*, 102–16.

80. Jacobs, *Voice of God*, 162–66.

an individual.[81] This permits corporate evaluation by the same criteria that were discussed above. This practice also shows respect for, and submission to the authority of the local church pastors. Though the recipient of a personal prophecy would undoubtedly have a key role in evaluating the message, believers must understand that the leadership of a church ultimately bears pastoral responsibility for all prophecies.

Section 4.3.1 further highlighted that prophecy should be seen as a dialogue between God, the one prophesying, and the congregation.[82] This dialogue is necessarily grounded in Scripture and so Scripture becomes the means by which prophecy is judged. It is therefore important to view the judging of prophecy as not simply an act on its own but part of this larger framework of interpersonal interactions. Indeed, the prophetic activities of revelation, proclamation, judging, and response should all be considered within the context of a social dynamic. The legitimization and authority accorded to prophecy can only come when the congregation recognizes its authenticity through corporate evaluation. Within this social dynamic, the aim of judging prophecy is to discern God's specific and immediate will so that the community may live in faithful obedience.

The discussion above highlights the importance of judging prophecy. It is therefore surprising that empirical studies have not described or discussed the actual practice. While one study did describe the self-evaluation of prophecies by the ones prophesying,[83] there remains a lack of studies documenting how prophecies are actually judged in contemporary practice. Furthermore, the contemporary practice of personal prophecies raises questions on how the evaluation of such messages may be conducted, or if this is even done at all.

5.5 THE PSYCHOLOGICAL ASPECTS OF PROPHECY

The psychological aspect of the Pentecostal movement is of great interest to scholars both inside and outside the movement. Studies have sought to examine the experiences and behavior of Pentecostal believers in relation to various psychological theories.[84] Most of these studies have understand-

---

81. Cooke, *Developing Your Prophetic Gifting*, 90; Gentile, *Your Sons and Daughters Shall Prophesy*, 336–38; Jacobs, *Voice of God*, 160–61.

82. Overholt, *Channels of Prophecy*, 17–25; Wenk, "Creative Power of the Prophetic Dialogue."

83. Cartledge, "Charismatic Prophecy," *JET*, 85.

84. Surveys on research in this area may be found in Huber and Huber, "Psychology of Religion"; Kay, "Mind, Behaviour and Glossolalia."

ably focused on *glossolalia* since this is one of the more unique characteristics of the Pentecostal movement. Some others have sought to provide psychological explanations for the practice of prophecy within the movement. These will be discussed next.

5.5.1 The Psychological State of the One Prophesying

From the biblical-historical perspective, discussions have centered on the psychological state of a person while prophesying. This is frequently reduced to whether prophecy should be termed an "ecstatic" phenomenon.[85] This presents an issue since the term "ecstatic" is used somewhat vaguely in these discussions. Turner highlights that the New Testament usage of ἔκστασις (*ekstasis*) may describe the revelatory state whereby the human mind does not contribute to the spoken message.[86] This need not indicate that the one prophesying has lost control and entered into a prophetic frenzy. However, contemporary usage of this term connotes an altered state of consciousness. Even then, there could be varying degrees ranging from mild dissociation to the extreme state where there is loss of self-control and violent raving.[87] Thus, the discussion might be better framed around whether the one prophesying surrenders control and enters into a trance.[88]

In considering the above issue, Grudem notes from 1 Corinthians 14:29–33 that the one prophesying was able to choose when to start and stop prophesying.[89] Paul's clear emphasis in his epistle was that prophecy should be practiced in an orderly manner and not be disruptive. In fact, verse 32 explicitly states that the one prophesying remains in control of the act and the situation. Moreover, prophecy serves to bring edification to the community, thus necessitating that it be intelligible rather than consist of incoherent raving. Grudem goes on to consider and reject in detail the argument that Paul's letter was meant to correct ecstatic, entranced prophecy that was already occurring.[90] These points strongly suggest that the one prophesying maintained a high level of self-control and self-awareness. Turner reaches

85. For a discussion of occurrences in the Old Testament, see Alden, "Ecstasy and the Prophets"; Wilson, "Prophecy and Ecstasy."

86. Turner, *Holy Spirit and Spiritual Gifts*, 197–98. Lindblom would prefer the term "elevated inspiration." Lindblom, *Prophecy in Ancient Israel*, 216–17.

87. Lindblom, *Prophecy in Ancient Israel*, 35–36.

88. Turner, *Holy Spirit and Spiritual Gifts*, 198–99. Grudem centers his discussion around four questions with largely the same focus. Grudem, *Gift of Prophecy in 1 Corinthians*, 150–51.

89. Grudem, *Gift of Prophecy in 1 Corinthians*, 153–55.

90. Ibid., 156–73.

the same conclusions though he suggests some possibility of an ecstatic trance occurring in Acts 10:45–46 and Acts 19:6.[91] Still, there is no reason to insist this was the case or that this should be the normal experience for all forms of prophecy in the New Testament. Likewise, contemporary practitioners provide guidelines for delivering prophecy that indicate the expectation of a high-level of self-restraint and control.[92] Their descriptions of contemporary examples also show little evidence for ecstatic, entranced prophecy.

5.5.2 Psychological Models for Prophecy

Various psychological models have been proposed to explain how prophecy occurs. These attempts should not be seen as a rejection of a divine source for prophecy since the Holy Spirit would be expected to work through natural mechanisms.[93] However, the models described below belong to modern psychology and should not be seen as biblical concepts.

D. Bennett and R. Bennett adopt a tripartite anthropology to distinguish between the human spirit and the soul, the latter consisting of the psychological aspects of the intellect, will, and emotions.[94] In prophecy, the Holy Spirit is seen to by-pass the soul and to communicate directly with the human spirit. A different view is offered by Kelsey that religious introversion exercises the faculty of human imagination and brings up thoughts, images, and fragments from deep within the human unconscious.[95] The voice of the divine is discerned in this activity that is then expressed as prophecy.

Tappeiner builds on Kelsey's psychological model for *glossolalia* by adopting a Platonic-Jungian interpretation of humans as interacting with both objective physical reality and non-objective spiritual reality.[96] He postulates that the Baptism of the Holy Spirit opens up a "channel" between the conscious and deep unconscious of a Pentecostal believer. This deep unconscious is interpreted theologically as the believer's "spirit." The practice of *glossolalia*, deep prayer, and worship quietens the conscious mind and creates a state of even greater sensitivity to the unconscious. Images,

---

91. Turner, *Holy Spirit and Spiritual Gifts*, 199.

92. Gentile, *Your Sons and Daughters Shall Prophesy*, 366–70; Jacobs, *Voice of God*, 182–85.

93. Tappeiner, "Psychological Paradigm," 23–24.

94. Bennett and Bennett, *Holy Spirit and You*, 20–21.

95. Kelsey, *Encounter with God*, 185–95. Similarly Suurmond, *Word and Spirit at Play*, 24.

96. Tappeiner, "Psychological Paradigm." Cf. Kelsey, *Tongue Speaking*.

thoughts, and impressions are found to arise during this "revelatory state" which Tappeiner sees as analogous to the hypnagogic state.[97] These hypnagogic images then form the basis for prophecy. Others within the congregation may likewise experience receiving similar insights simultaneously and this attests to the psychological and spiritual unity created by the worship practices. This corporate witness is then intuitively used in the judging and evaluation of prophecy.

Cartledge has sought to correlate the psychological model proposed by Tappeiner with his qualitative research data.[98] His findings showed a correlation between the reported impulses prompting prophecy and the hypnagogic imagery described by Tappeiner. There was also agreement in that prophecy frequently occurred in the context of corporate prayer, worship, and *glossolalia*. These charismatic practices can be interpreted as the means by which believers enter the revelatory state to access the unconscious. Evidence for a collective corporate insight was found in the corporate confirmation of prophecies through the reception of similar prophetic impressions. However, there were also instances where prophetic experiences occurred in private without other charismatic practices and these are not fully addressed by the model.

5.5.3 Personality and Prophecy

The Pentecostal movement is subject to various criticisms from within the Christian church, most of them directed at an over-emphasis on the subjective experience of the Holy Spirit.[99] These critics assert that the movement stresses unhealthy emotionalism resulting in the pursuit of emotional excesses. They claim that Pentecostal spirituality is superficial and that believers tend to be overly preoccupied with the pursuit of spiritual gifts, particularly the more spectacular ones like prophecy. Some have even dubbed the movement "charismania."[100] It is claimed that the emotional experience of spiritual gifts becomes an end in itself and that Pentecostals measure their spirituality in terms of the subjective liveliness of their religious life. MacArthur sums up this negative assessment when he writes:

97. Kelsey has also noted the similarity between *glossolalia* and dreams which is a parallel to Tappeiner's hypnagogic imagery. See Kelsey, *Tongue Speaking*, 211–15.

98. Cartledge, "Charismatic Prophecy," *JET*, 86–87.

99. Hanegraaff, *Christianity in Crisis*; Khoo, *Charismatism Q&A*; Logan, "Controversial Aspects of the Movement"; MacArthur, *Charismatic Chaos*; MacArthur, *Strange Fire*; Vines, *Spirit Works*.

100. Logan, "Controversial Aspects of the Movement," 38–39; Smith, *Charisma vs Charismania*.

> There is nothing wrong with being happy; there is nothing wrong with praising God and feeling fulfilled. Unfortunately, however, many in the charismatic movement seem so determined to pursue the emotional high, the quick thrill, the exciting event, the electrifying moment, the exhilarating conference—that they have given up the rich rewards of a consistent walk with God in favor of the superficial gaiety of a public spectacle.[101]

Indeed, this negative view of the movement is not new. S. Huber and O. Huber have noted that earlier psychological studies hypothesized that Pentecostal behavior and practices were the result of underlying psychological disorders.[102] These claims are highly significant and relevant to this present study since it suggests a correlation between the practice of prophecy and specific personality types. Several studies have already researched more generally on the personality types of Pentecostal believers and these will be reviewed below.

The personality theory of Hans Eysenck possesses strong psychometric and biological components and this theory is widely used in the study of religion.[103] The theory proposes three independent personality dimensions of extraversion (E), neuroticism (N), and psychoticism (P). Each factor is bipolar with unimodal distribution, and satisfies Eysenck's criteria of psychometric evidence, heritability, theoretical meaning, and social relevance. The factor of extraversion/introversion reflects the individual's sociability; neuroticism/stability reflects emotional stability; and psychoticism/superego reflects impulse control and whether an individual is tough-minded or tender-minded. All personality types are then accounted for by the interplay of these factors. Various personality inventories have been developed based on this theory with some including a Lie Scale (L).[104] This Lie Scale

---

101. MacArthur, *Charismatic Chaos*, 254. See also MacArthur, *Strange Fire*, 72. Elsewhere, Packer once described Pentecostalism in this manner: "It's warmth and liveliness attract highly emotional and disturbed people to its ranks, and many others find in its ritual emotionalism some relief from strains and pressures in other areas of their lives (marriage, work, finance, and so forth). But such sharing in group emotion is a self-indulgent escapist 'trip' that must debilitate in the long run. Generally the movement seems to teeter on the age of emotional self-indulgence in a decidedly dangerous way." Packer, *Keep in Step with the Spirit*, 192. Packer has since changed his stance on the movement. See Kennedy, "J. I. Packer: Knowing God Is a Lifelong Process."

102. Huber and Huber, "Psychology of Religion," 135.

103. Eysenck, "Personality and the Psychology of Religion."; Eysenck, *Dimensions of Personality*; Eysenck, *Biological Basis of Personality*; Feist and Feist, *Theories of Personality*, 408–18.

104. For example, see Barrett et al., "Eysenck Personality Questionnaire"; Eysenck, Eysenck, and Barrett, "Revised Version of the Psychoticism Scale."

was originally conceived to reflect the respondent's honesty in answering the questionnaire but has been variously interpreted as reflecting other-deception, self-deception, immaturity, or social conformity.[105]

A variety of theories have been postulated regarding the relationship between charismatic activity and personality dimensions.[106] Due to the liveliness and expressiveness of the movement, one position hypothesizes a positive correlation between extraverts and charismatic activity.[107] However, a second position postulates that charismatic activity correlates with introversion since it serves as a cathartic outlet for suppressed behavior.[108] Conflicting views also arise with regards to neuroticism. Those who see charismatic activity as an expression of emotional instability would postulate a positive correlation with neuroticism.[109] Alternatively, charismatic activity may be theorized as tension-reducing and therapeutic, leading to greater emotional stability and lower neuroticism scores.[110] Lower scores for psychoticism have been found to correlate with positive attitudes to religion and this suggests a negative relationship between charismatic activity and psychoticism. This is further supported by studies showing Pentecostals demonstrating submissiveness and suggestibility which correspond to lower psychoticism scores.[111] Hypotheses on correlations with the Lie Scale depend on what trait the scale is understood to measure. Religious individuals usually report higher Lie Scale scores so this may indicate greater social conformity, or greater self-deception and immaturity, or that religious individuals are simply more honest.

The hypotheses above were investigated in a series of studies. Francis and Kay conducted a study on 259 male and 105 female Pentecostal ministry candidates studying at Bible Schools in England.[112] The Eysenck Personality

---

105. Jackson and Francis, "Interpreting the Correlation between Neuroticism and Lie Scale Scores."

106. For further discussion, see Gritzmacher, Bolton, and Dana, "Psychological Characteristics of Pentecostals"; Huber and Huber, "Psychology of Religion"; Kay, "Mind, Behaviour and Glossolalia."

107. Kelsey, *Tongue Speaking*, 220–21.

108. Gritzmacher, Bolton, and Dana, "Psychological Characteristics of Pentecostals," 240.

109. Hutch, "Personal Ritual of Glossolalia"; Kildahl, *Psychology of Speaking in Tongues*; Kildahl, "Psychological Observations."

110. Smith and Fleck, "Personality Correlates of Conventional and Unconventional Glossolalia."

111. Gritzmacher, Bolton, and Dana, "Psychological Characteristics of Pentecostals," 242–43.

112. Francis and Kay, "Personality Characteristics of Pentecostal Ministry Candidates."

Questionnaire (EPQ) was used to assess personality and to compare the scores with the general population. This study showed that the candidates differed in personality characteristics with religious professionals in other denominations. This difference may be accounted for by the unique charismatic experience within the Pentecostal tradition. The candidates did not demonstrate significant difference in extraversion with population norms but showed significantly lower neuroticism scores. The female candidates did not differ in psychoticism or Lie Scale scores but the male candidates scored lower in psychoticism and higher on the Lie Scale.

In a second study, Francis and Thomas surveyed 222 male Anglican clergy from the Church of Wales.[113] The short form of the Revised Eysenck Personality Questionnaire (EPQR-S) was used to assess personality and a fourteen-item scale was used to assess charismatic experience (Cronbach α = 0.90). Prophecy was not explicitly listed in the charismatic scale though it may be reasonably related with the items in the scale.[114] Their study revealed that charismatic experience is positively correlated with extraversion ($r = 0.2474, p \leq 0.001$) but negatively correlated with neuroticism ($r = -0.1703, p \leq 0.01$). There was no correlation observed between charismatic experience and psychoticism or the Lie Scale.

A third study was conducted by Francis and Jones on 243 male and 125 female adults who were described as committed Christians.[115] These participants were mainly from Anglican and Pentecostal backgrounds, with the rest from other denominations. The participants completed the EPQR-S and a five-item Index of Charismatic Experience (Cronbach α = 0.8720). This study yielded similar results in finding that charismatic experience was positively correlated with extraversion ($r = 0.1208, p \leq 0.05$), negatively correlated with neuroticism ($r = -0.1874, p \leq 0.001$) and unrelated to psychoticism.

In a fourth study, Robbins, Hair, and Francis surveyed 172 male clergy within the Church of England.[116] The longer Eysenck Personality Questionnaire (EPQ) was used to assess personality and a fifteen-item scale was used to assess charismatic experience (Cronbach α = 0.92). The study showed that charismatic experience was correlated with extraversion ($r = 0.2516, p \leq 0.01$). No relationship was found with neuroticism and psychoticism.

113. Francis and Thomas, "Are Charismatic Ministers Less Stable?"

114. One item listed "receiving a 'word of knowledge'" while another was "hearing God speak to me."

115. Francis and Jones, "Personality and Charismatic Experience among Adult Christians."

116. Robbins, Hair, and Francis, "Personality and Attraction to the Charismatic Movement."

Francis and Robbins contributed a fifth study which focused on glossolalia in relation with personality.[117] Their sample consisted of 991 male clergy from the Evangelical Alliance which is an inter-denominational society in Britain. The clergy came from Baptist, Methodist, Anglican, and Pentecostal churches with some from independent churches. Participants reported how frequently they practiced *glossolalia* and this was correlated with their scores from the EPQR-S. This study showed that *glossolalia* was correlated positively with extraversion ($r = 0.1513$, $p \leq 0.001$), negatively with neuroticism ($r = -0.1015$, $p \leq 0.001$), and unrelated to psychoticism.

Related information may also be drawn from an extensive study conducted by Kay on Pentecostal ministers in Britain to document their characteristics, beliefs and practices.[118] This study covered 907 male ministers and twenty-three female ministers across four Pentecostal denominations. The research is relevant to this present study since his measure of charismatic activity explicitly included the practice of prophecy. The data showed a significant, strong, positive correlation between ministerial charismatic activity and extraversion but no correlation with neuroticism and psychoticism. Kay observed that if the tests were made less rigorous, a likely trend would be higher charismatic activity correlated with lower neuroticism and higher psychoticism. This suggests that ministers who are more emotionally stable and tough-minded would be willing to "risk" being involved in charismatic activity. The Lie Scale scores also showed less conformist ministers were more likely to become charismatically active.

A summary can now be made of the studies surveyed above. First, there seems to be a clear indication of a positive correlation between charismatic activity and extraversion. Second, there is some indication of a negative correlation between charismatic activity and neuroticism. Some studies showed they were unrelated but none of the studies showed a positive correlation. This indicates that charismatic activity is associated with emotionally stable personalities. Third, the studies all showed that charismatic activity is unrelated with psychoticism. These findings demonstrate that charismatic activity should not be associated with psychopathology but rather with psychological stability. The allusions of "charismania" reported at the start of this section seem to be a popular caricature focused on extremes of the movement rather than the norm.[119]

---

117. Francis and Robbins, "Personality and Glossolalia."

118. Kay, *Pentecostals in Britain*, 268–97.

119. To be clear, Pentecostals have acknowledged the emotional appeal of the movement as well as its excesses. See, for example, Gee, *Pentecostal Experience*, 89–92; Menzies, *Pentecost*, 137.

The studies surveyed were focused on the movement within the United Kingdom and presents an opportunity for replication in other countries.[120] Significantly, empirical studies on the fast-growing Pentecostal movement in Asia are lacking. In addition, the studies surveyed did not significantly examine the practice of prophecy in relation to personality dimensions. This study hopes to meet this gap in the literature.

5.6 PROPHECY AND PENTECOSTAL SPIRITUALITY

Pentecostal spirituality refers to the beliefs, values, habits, and spiritual practices that characterize the Pentecostal faith community.[121] Perhaps the central characteristic of Pentecostalism is the expectation of a radical encounter with God.[122] Pentecostals have a fundamental desire to know God experientially so as to deepen their understanding of the faith. This not merely refers to cognitive beliefs but also an affective understanding of God, the believer's identity, and the Christian life. Within the church, the congregational service is meant to move worshippers into an encounter with the divine.[123] This process can be viewed within a search-encounter-transformation framework where the church seeks after God, encounters the divine, and experiences edification, healing, and empowerment for life and ministry.[124] From this perspective, prophecy itself is very much a part of Pentecostal spirituality and the search for an experiential encounter with the divine. There are indications that the practice of prophecy is correlated with other spiritual practices and values within the shared community of faith. Three aspects will be examined in this section—prayer, evangelism, and the Pentecostal affections.

5.6.1 Prophecy and Prayer

Prophecy is commonly observed to occur in the context of prayer. Prayer here should be understood as a dialogue rather than mere human petition. To Pentecostals, the purpose of prayer is to encounter with a transcendent

---

120. Francis and Robbins specifically call for replication of their study in other countries. Francis and Robbins, "Personality and Glossolalia," 395.

121. Sheldrake, *Brief History of Spirituality*; Smith, *Thinking in Tongues*, 17–47; Spittler, "Spirituality, Pentecostal and Charismatic."

122. Warrington, *Pentecostal Theology*, 26–27. Also see Neumann, *Pentecostal Experience*.

123. Albrecht, *Rites in the Spirit*, 141–49.

124. Cartledge, *Encountering the Spirit*, 25–27.

God and this is engaged both individually and corporately.[125] Since prophecy is concerned with communication from God and discerning what God wants to say to others, it therefore seems logical for prophecy to be related with prayer.[126] The spiritual experiences which initiate prophecy are the same revelatory experiences expected in prayer. Prophecy also often occurs in the midst of corporate praise and worship, and this too should be understood as an expression of prayer. This relationship between prophecy and prayer is examined in various empirical studies which are reviewed below.

Poloma and Gallup conducted an extensive research on the American public in the United States.[127] Using factor analysis, they identified four main types of prayer from their survey data. These prayer types are ritual prayer, petitionary prayer, conversational prayer, and meditative prayer. The last prayer type is of particular interest to this present study. The four items reflecting meditative prayer were: "spending time quietly thinking about God"; "'feeling' the presence of God"; "worshipping and adoring God"; and "trying to listen to God speaking."[128] Meditative prayer appears more passive than the other types of prayer but the researchers reported that it had the most potential for dialogue with God. The researchers used multiple regression to analyze the four types of prayer and found that only meditative prayer had a positive correlation with a respondent's sense of feeling close to God.[129] The study also found that people who were engaged in meditative prayer tend to score higher on a prayer experience scale which the researchers constructed.[130] These results indicate that people who engage in meditative prayer are more likely to feel close to God and undergo more prayer experiences where they perceive communication from God. This suggests that believers who engage in meditative prayer are more likely to practice prophecy. Interestingly, the study's description of "meditative prayer" bears a similarity to Pentecostal spirituality though one would not normally describe Pentecostal prayer as "meditative."

An extensive empirical study was conducted by Poloma across the AG denomination in the United States.[131] In this study, she used a seven-item

---

125. Warrington, *Pentecostal Theology*, 214–15.

126. Cartledge, "Charismatic Prophecy," *JPT*; Cartledge, "Charismatic Prophecy" *JET*; Cooke, *Developing Your Prophetic Gifting*, 50–57; Deere, *Surprised by the Voice of God*, 97; Pytches, *Prophecy in the Local Church*, 31; Robeck, "Prophecy, Gift of," 1004.

127. Poloma and Gallup, *Varieties of Prayer*.

128. Ibid., 35.

129. Ibid., 40.

130. Ibid., 61–63. The index of prayer experience was based on work by Stark. See Stark, "Taxonomy of Religious Experience."

131. Poloma, *Assemblies of God at the Crossroads*.

scale to measure the charismatic experiences of AG ministers (Cronbach α = 0.74). Two of the items in this scale were: "given a prophecy in a church service" and "given a prophecy privately to another."[132] The study found that believers who regularly read the Bible and pray, confess to traditional Pentecostal beliefs, and had a higher level of education, tend to score higher on the charismatic experience scale.[133] In a further analysis, multiple regression was used with demographic, attitudinal, and behavioral measures regressed against charismatic experience. The results showed that the devotion measure demonstrated the strongest partial-correlation with charismatic experience, implying that private prayer and Bible-reading is very important in accounting for charismatic experiences. The study did not find any significant correlation between charismatic experience and age, gender, income, attitudes towards holiness taboos, or participation in ritual.

In a more recent study, Poloma surveyed 1,827 adherents from twenty-one AG congregations in the United States.[134] The study included separate measures for *glossolalia*, healing prayer, and prophetic prayer. This last prayer measure consisted of "receiving divine revelation from another person," "giving prophecy to another person," and "receiving direct revelation from God" (Cronbach α = 0.81). The study showed a strong correlation between prophetic prayer and *glossolalia* ($r = 0.48$, $p \leq 0.001$) and between prophetic prayer and healing prayer ($r = 0.43$, $p \leq 0.001$). This led Poloma to suggest that the practice of *glossolalia* leads believers to pray expectantly for healing and to experience prophetic or revelatory prayer.

The studies reviewed above show evidence of a relationship between prayer and charismatic activity. The research also indicates that certain types of prayer may display a stronger correlation than others. For example, Poloma and Gallup suggested that what they termed as "meditative prayer" would result in prophetic experiences. Thus, possibilities exist to study prophecy and charismatic experiences in relation to a broader framework of prayer. Several studies have sought to empirically identify the various types of prayer.[135] One proposal by Ladd and Spilka presents such an opportunity and will be briefly discussed.[136]

---

132. Ibid., 255.

133. Ibid., 33.

134. Poloma, "Pentecostal Prayer."

135. For example, see Janssen et al., "Structure and Variety of Prayer"; Laird et al., "Measuring Private Prayer"; Poloma and Pendleton, "Exploring Types of Prayer." For further discussion on the dimensionality of prayer, see Spilka, "Religious Practice, Ritual, and Prayer," 372–74.

136. Ladd and Spilka, "Inward, Outward, and Upward"; Ladd and Spilka, "Inward, Outward, Upward Prayer."

Ladd and Spilka's proposal builds on work by Foster who suggests that prayer is a means of forming cognitive connections.[137] Specifically, these cognitive connections may be directed inward, outward, or upward. Inward prayers emphasize self-examination, outward prayers stress human-human connections, and upward prayers focus on the divine-human relationship. Ladd and Spilka constructed various sub-scales based on prayer types to measure prayer in these three directions. Inward prayer consisted of the prayer types Examination and Tears; outward prayers consisted of the prayer types Radical, Suffering, Intercession, and Petition; whereas upward prayers consisted of the prayer types Sacramental and Rest.[138] This model thus suggests that there are eight primary prayer factors, each measured by asking respondents to rate how often they think of the respective survey item while engaged in prayer. The instrument was validated and found to have good psychometric properties. This instrument presents an opportunity to test relationships between the practice of prophecy and other charismatic activities with the various types of prayer. Face-value examination of the items in the instrument suggests a possible correlation between these prayer content and the Pentecostal affections that are discussed in section 5.6.3.

5.6.2 Prophecy and Evangelism

Section 4.3.3 discussed and suggested that one of the purposes of prophecy is evangelism and church growth. Popular Christian literature was found to encourage the use of prophecy in the context of evangelism.[139] The activity of spiritual gifts, including prophecy, is also identified as an important component in evangelism amongst Pentecostals in Singapore.[140] A search of the literature provided some empirical evidence in support of this relationship.

A study by Poloma on the AGUSA demonstrated a relationship between charismatic activity and evangelism.[141] Aside from the index measuring charismatic experience, an evangelism index was constructed to measure the respondent's evangelistic activities. This evangelism index consisted of eight items with a Cronbach alpha of 0.82. Poloma noted a strong correlation between charismatic experience and evangelism ($r = 0.45$, $p \leq$

---

137. Foster, *Prayer*.

138. Ladd and Spilka, "Inward, Outward, and Upward," 480.

139. Blasi, *Prophetic Fishing*; Stibbe, *Prophetic Evangelism*; Wimber, *Power Evangelism*.

140. Chan, "Urban Evangelistic Strategies," 45–47; Ong, "Historical Analysis of the Factors of Growth," 50–54.

141. Poloma, *Assemblies of God at the Crossroads*.

0.05) which led her to hypothesize that believers who have more frequent charismatic experiences are also more likely to engage in evangelistic activities.[142] This is not to conclude that one activity is the cause of the other since a bivariate correlation does not indicate causation. However, since evangelism occurs outside the Pentecostal tradition, it seems more reasonable to propose that charismatic experience strengthens evangelistic activity and is contributing to church growth within the AG.

In a separate study, Kay sought to replicate Poloma's research in a survey of Pentecostal ministers in Britain, though with some modification.[143] Scales with similar items measuring charismatic experience and evangelism were used but Kay's sample consisted exclusively of ministers whereas Poloma's sample contained both ministers and congregation members. Kay's sample also included data from four Pentecostal denominations whereas Poloma studied only the AG. Kay reported similar findings to Poloma in that ministers who scored higher in charismatic experience also scored higher in evangelistic activity. Kay sought to indirectly measure the various congregations by asking the ministers to assess their congregation in terms of charismatic activity and in church growth. He found a clear positive correlation between the reported percentage of a congregation exercising spiritual gifts and the reported growth of that congregation. He also showed a relationship between the charismatic experience of the minister and that of the congregation with ministers scoring higher on the charismatic experience scale reporting a higher percentage of their congregation exercising spiritual gifts.

Kay conducted a further study on church growth in Singapore and Hong Kong.[144] Similar to his study in Britain, Kay asked ministers to assess their congregation's charismatic activity and church growth. He reported a large and significant positive correlation between reported church growth and the reported percentage of the congregation exercising spiritual gifts. Kay's study also reported a positive correlation between church growth and belief in divine healing.

The studies by Poloma and Kay show a correlation between charismatic activity and evangelistic activity within a congregation. This further suggests that the practice of prophecy, which was included in their studies' measure of charismatic experience, should also have a positive correlation with evangelistic activity. The empirical data corresponds well with the historical growth and worldwide spread of the Pentecostal movement. The

---

142. Ibid., 31–33.
143. Kay, *Pentecostals in Britain*, 245–64.
144. Kay, "Where the Wind Blows."

activity of spiritual gifts, the prevalence of a supernatural worldview, and ministry to physical needs have long been recognized as major factors in the growth of the movement.[145]

5.6.3 Prophecy and the Pentecostal affections

The uniqueness of Pentecostal spirituality has long been recognized in studies on the movement.[146] Spittler suggests that five implicit values govern this spirituality.[147] These are: the value of personal experience, orality, spontaneity, otherworldliness, and a commitment to biblical authority. Smith offers a similar proposal in describing the elements of the Pentecostal worldview.[148] In Asia, Ma's description of Pentecostal worship highlights its intensity and liveliness, group participation, spontaneity, and experience of the transcendental.[149] More importantly, Ma notes that Pentecostal experiences and practices serve both as theological expression and also as theological formation of the community. With this understanding, the practice of prophecy would affirm, reinforce, and strengthen Pentecostal spirituality. Research done by McGuire and Cartledge supports this role of prophecy in both reflecting and perpetuating this unique spirituality.[150]

Steven Land has made a landmark proposal that sees Pentecostal spirituality as the starting point for Pentecostal theology.[151] This proposal highlights the need to integrate the beliefs and practices of the movement and suggests that this should be done through explicating the Christian affections. For Land, salvation is participation in the divine life brought through union with God and the resulting transformation into the likeness of Christ. This transformation is primarily accomplished through the affections as the integrating center of Pentecostal spirituality. Land explains that these affections are objective since they are focused on God who is both the source and *telos* of these affections.[152] They are also relational since the affec-

---

145. Alexander, *Signs and Wonders*; Chan, "Urban Evangelistic Strategies," 45; Kay, "Empirical and Historical Perspectives," 18; Ma, "Asian Pentecostalism," 200–201; Wagner, "Church Growth Perspective."

146. For example, see Albrecht, *Rites in the Spirit*; Cettolin, "AOG Pentecostal Spirituality in Australia"; Cox, *Fire from Heaven*.

147. Spittler, "Spirituality, Pentecostal and Charismatic."

148. Smith, *Thinking in Tongues*, 17–47.

149. Ma, "Pentecostal Worship in Asia."

150. Cartledge, "Charismatic Prophecy," *JET*; McGuire, "Social Context of Prophecy."

151. Land, *Pentecostal Spirituality*.

152. Ibid., 130–33.

tions require an on-going relationship with God, the Christian community, and the world. The affections are not mere feelings or subjective emotions but rather dispositions which characterize the believer. Land proposes that the three core Pentecostal affections are gratitude, compassion, and courage.[153] Gratitude stems from the salvific work of God in the life of a believer and is grounded in the righteousness of God. Compassion draws its source from the love of God and encompasses the believer's devotion to God and love for others both inside and outside the church. Courage comes from the assurance of God's final victory and is grounded in God's power. These affections manifest in believers as a passion for God's kingdom; a longing for the kingdom that is yet to come but is already encountered within the faith community.[154]

Of specific interest to this study is Land's assertion that the formation and expression of these affections is primarily through prayer.[155] Land views prayer as the primary theological activity of Pentecostals where the heart is formed for both worship and witness. The earlier discussion highlighted that prophecy occurs within the context of prayer and fits in well with the Pentecostal expectation of divine encounter. The impact of prophecy obviously extends beyond the cognitive to include the affective and behavioral as believers respond to what they interpret as God's expressed desires. Therefore, it is quite logical to see prophecy stirring and cultivating the affections of gratitude, compassion, and courage. Believers often respond to prophecy in gratitude and joy as they perceive the transcendent God has heard and responded to their prayers. Compassion is evoked through prophecies that encourage the church to fulfill its mission in the world. Courage is stirred as the community understands that the almighty God is for them and with them. In addition, the very act of prophecy itself demands the one prophesying to display gratitude, compassion, and courage as one speaking on behalf of God who is the perfect embodiment of these affections.

The Pentecostal affection of compassion, in particular, has been discussed by various authors in relation with spiritual gifts; not least because Paul's discussion of spiritual gifts includes an exposition of love in 1 Corinthians 13. Gee notes that the supernatural manifestation of the gifts is reduced to utter worthlessness without love.[156] In fact, he claims that gifts exercised without love is abnormal spirituality and inexcusable for any believer. In teaching on prophecy, Gee specifically states that prophetic revela-

---

153. Ibid., 135–39.
154. Ibid., 173–80.
155. Ibid., 163–72.
156. Gee, *Fruit of the Spirit*, 15.

tion is given to those who are in close communion and loving devotion to God.[157] Lim likewise views love as the true authenticator of spiritual maturity in the exercise of spiritual gifts.[158] Paul is interpreted as correcting the Corinthians' mistaken notion that spiritual gifts were a sign of spiritual attainment. Even then, this love must not be mistaken for human effort but rather it is love poured out by God through the power of the Holy Spirit (Rom 5:5).[159]

Elsewhere, Macchia calls for a renewed understanding of Pentecostal Spirit-baptism as a baptism in divine love.[160] Macchia asserts that Spirit-baptism enables believers to participate in the *koinonia* of God and to be empowered through love to serve in God's mission in the world. It is this experience of *koinonia* that brings intimacy and joy and enables believers to catch God's divine compassion for the world. Macchia thus makes claims similar to Land in seeing the experience of the vertical dimension of God's love for humanity expanding the horizontal dimension of neighborly love for others. The out-pouring of God's love shapes the believer into the likeness of God as a source of self-giving love. Spiritual gifts, like prophecy, should then be understood as the expression of self-transcending, self-giving compassion rather than merely raw power to fulfill a function. To experience spiritual gifts is to experience the love and grace of God expressed through another believer.

The association between spiritual gifts and the Pentecostal affections finds support in various empirical studies. Kay's research on Pentecostal ministers in Britain reported an extremely high concern for the poor and disadvantaged groups in society.[161] This indicates a desire for Pentecostal churches to be engaged in compassionate social action; a desire likely motivated by the Pentecostal affection of compassion. Miller and Yamamori found this same emphasis on compassionate social action in their study of global Pentecostalism.[162] In fact, they suggest that this is one of the reasons for the explosive growth of the movement worldwide. Koning and Dahles's study of ethnic Chinese managers in Indonesia and Malaysia who converted to Pentecostal/Charismatic Christianity found that almost all of them were heavily engaged in charity, once again demonstrating the affection of

---

157. Gee, *Spiritual Gifts in the Work of the Ministry Today*, 50.
158. Lim, *Spiritual Gifts*, 108–9.
159. Hemphill, *You Are Gifted*, 66.
160. Macchia, *Baptized in the Spirit*, 257–82.
161. Kay, *Pentecostals in Britain*, 238–39.
162. Miller and Yamamori, *Global Pentecostalism*.

compassion.[163] From a broader perspective within the psychology of religion, helping and prosocial behavior is acknowledged to be correlated with religious belief.[164]

Poloma and Hood's study on a Pentecostal emerging church named Blood-n-Fire has led to the most distinctive evidence of a correlation between compassion and charismatic experience. The study combined both qualitative and quantitative data in an investigation of what was termed as "godly love." They defined godly love as "the dynamic interaction between human responses to the operation of perceived divine love and the impact this experience has on personal lives, relationships with others, and emergent communities."[165] This concept is partly drawn from Sorokin's theory of "love energy" which flows from a higher, possibly divine, source into an individual and results in altruistic and compassionate behavior.[166] The quantitative study included scales to measure altruism, empathy, charismatic experience, and mysticism. They reported a positive correlation between altruism and charismatic experience ($r = 0.41$) and between altruism and mysticism ($r = 0.40$). A positive correlation was also found between empathy and charismatic experience ($r = 0.36$) and between empathy and mysticism ($r = 0.28$). These findings corroborate Sorokin's theory and led the researchers to suggest that charismatic experiences, including prophecy, allows believers to experience a loving God resulting in a vertical transfer of "love energy." This is then distributed horizontally through the believers out to society in the form of compassionate and loving behavior.[167]

A subsequent work by Lee and Poloma sought to further explore the concept of godly love through a qualitative investigation.[168] The researchers selected and interviewed seventy-two exemplars of godly love and twenty-nine of their collaborators to develop a grounded theory of benevolent service. At the same time, the researchers sought to compare their findings with a theological model derived from Macchia's work.[169] This theological model suggests that "a vision of the Kingdom of God interacts with a series of spiritual transformations in a way that fosters or impacts benevolent service."[170] Spiritual transformation is seen to occur at conversion, at charis-

---

163. Koning and Dahles, "Spiritual Power."
164. Hood, Hill, and Spilka, *Psychology of Religion*, 404–11.
165. Poloma and Hood, *Blood and Fire*, 4.
166. Sorokin, *The Ways and Power of Love*.
167. Poloma and Hood, *Blood and Fire*, 115–16.
168. Lee and Poloma, *Sociological Study of the Great Commandment*.
169. Macchia, *Baptized in the Spirit*.
170. Lee and Poloma, *Sociological Study of the Great Commandment*, 66.

matic experiences like Spirit-baptism, and at other unexpected experiences that the study called "anomalies." The qualitative analysis of the interviews provided support for the theological model, illustrating how benevolent service is produced. The study also allowed the researchers to corroborate their proposed "diamond model" which treats God as an actual partner humans interact with.[171] This sociological model then enables a framework for understanding how dynamic interactions between divine love and human love generates benevolence and compassionate action. An important caveat to this work is that several of the interviewees do not practice *glossolalia* or even report experiencing a baptism in the Holy Spirit.[172] Thus, the study's claim to focus on "Pentecostals" would not be accurate with regard to Classical Pentecostal beliefs.

One key question centers on using an appropriate tool to measure love and compassion. Poloma and Hood sought to measure altruism and empathy whereas Kay sought to measure concern for social issues. Other instruments have been developed to measure empathy, altruism and compassion though these scales usually do not consider the role of faith.[173] The Faith Maturity Scale (FMS) may be useful in this regard though it was not explicitly developed to measure compassion.[174] This scale consists of thirty-eight items that seek to measure "the degree to which a person embodies the priorities, commitments, and perspectives of vibrant and life-transforming faith, as these have been understood in 'mainline' Protestant denominations."[175] The items in the scale focus on values and behavioral indicators and so the scale remains relevant to Pentecostals even though Pentecostal denominations were not involved in its development. Furthermore, a Chinese version of the scale was found to have validity among Asian Christians who did not come from a mainline denomination.[176] The FMS demonstrated good psychometric characteristics with Cronbach alpha scores ranging from 0.84 to 0.9. The FMS may be broken down into two sub-scales measuring vertical religion and horizontal religion. The vertical sub-scale (FMS-V) mea-

---

171. Ibid., 26–31.

172. Ibid., 125–26.

173. For example, see Brems, "Dimensionality of Empathy"; Lee, Lee, and Kang, "Development and Validation of an Altruism Scale for Adults"; Rushton, Chrisjohn, and Fekken, "Altruistic Personality"; Sprecher and Fehr, "Compassionate Love."

174. Benson, Donahue, and Erickson, "Faith Maturity Scale."

175. Ibid., 3. Six denominations in the United States were involved in its development. These denominations are: Christian Church, Disciples of Christ; Evangelical Lutheran Church in America; Presbyterian Church, U.S.A.; Southern Baptist Convention; United Church of Christ; and United Methodist Church.

176. Hui et al., "'Faith Maturity Scale' for Chinese."

sures "the degree to which a person emphasizes maintaining, honoring, or heeding the relationship between self and transcendent reality" while the horizontal sub-scale (FMS-H) measures "the degree of emphasis a person places on serving humanity, as evidenced by prosocial values and acts of mercy and justice."[177] A face-value examination of the scale items suggests that the FMS-V may be used to measure a respondent's devotion and love for God while the FMS-H may be used to measure a respondent's compassion for others. In particular, the items in the FMS-H describe altruistic and compassionate social actions. Therefore, the FMS may be interpreted to measure both the vertical and horizontal dimensions of love described by both Land and Macchia mentioned earlier.

The literature surveyed above suggests that a relationship exists between charismatic experience and the Pentecostal affections, especially the affection of compassion. There are theological grounds for making such an assertion and empirical studies seem to corroborate the relationship. There are possibilities for expanding the investigation of this relationship to specific Pentecostal practices such as prophecy. There is also a need for research in Asia as all the current research is located within the West.

5.7 SUMMARY

This chapter has reviewed the literature on the practice of prophecy. This literature review shows that Pentecostals generally see all believers having the potential ability to engage in prophecy. The literature review described various spiritual experiences initiating prophecy and considered the interpretation and application of these revelatory messages. It further discussed the delivery of prophecy and found that believers choose the words and manner in relaying a prophetic message. The criteria for judging prophecy include an assessment of the person prophesying, the process by which the prophecy is delivered, and the actual content of the prophecy. The discussion continued to consider psychological aspects of prophecy, concluding that the one prophesying largely maintains self-control and is not in an entranced state. Personality studies suggest that prophecy is positively correlated with extraversion and unrelated with psychoticism. Prophecy may either be unrelated with neuroticism or negatively correlated. Empirical studies suggest a possible correlation between prophecy and certain types of prayer and also a positive correlation between prophecy and evangelism. Lastly, prophecy is believed to be correlated with the Pentecostal affections of gratitude, compassion, and courage. The affection of compassion, in

---

177. Benson, Donahue, and Erickson, "Faith Maturity Scale," 18.

particular, holds potential for further investigation. A gap in the literature exists for empirical studies on the practice of prophecy. In particular, studies within the Asian context are severely lacking. This present study attempts to fill this gap.

6

A Quantitative Study on Prophecy

6.1 INTRODUCTION

THIS STUDY HAS COMPLETED the phases of theological problem and goal development in the previous chapters. The study continued with theological induction as the second phase of the empirical-theological cycle. Interviews were conducted with ten senior pastors of AGS churches and the data was analyzed to identify themes characterizing the practice of prophecy. An extensive literature survey was also carried out to determine the nature, purpose, and practice of prophecy described within Pentecostal literature. The interviews and literature survey fulfill the necessary conditions for theological perception, enabling the study to continue with theological reflection.

6.2 THEOLOGICAL REFLECTION

There was much agreement between data from the qualitative interviews and the literature survey. The study found congruity in the areas of the understanding and purpose of prophecy, the spiritual experiences that initiate prophecy, the delivery of prophecy, and the judging of prophecy. These areas are discussed in turn below.

The interviews and the literature survey both showed that Pentecostals understand prophecy to be the reception and communication of a spontaneous revelation from God. The interviews provided clear descriptions of actual examples of the phenomenon. Prophecy was mostly found to occur in congregational meetings though it also takes place in more personal settings. To Pentecostals, prophecy need not contain any prediction of future events but rather entails the communication of a message on God's behalf. Both sets of data showed that Pentecostals distinguished prophecy from preaching or charismatic exegesis. There was some uncertainty amongst the interviewees if a message in tongues with interpretation should be considered the equivalent of prophecy. Likewise, the literature showed a difference in opinion on this matter. Intriguingly, the practice of tongues with interpretation seems more widespread and common in the research context than what one author suggests should be the case.[1]

The analysis of the interviews identified the various themes associated with the purpose of prophecy: spiritual edification, confirmation and direction, warning and correction, healing, and evangelism. Interestingly, doctrinal teaching was not found to be characteristic of contemporary prophecy. While the literature provided biblical support for these themes, little is said of the prevalence of these themes in the actual practice of prophecy. This presents opportunity to examine how frequently the identified themes appear in the content of prophecy. There is also opportunity to compare the prevalence of these themes within congregational prophecy and personal prophecy.

The previous analysis revealed several interesting elements in the reception, analysis, and delivery of prophecy. These elements include the spiritual experiences initiating prophecy, the interpretation and application of prophetic revelation, the choice of the actual words to express the prophecy, and the psychological state of the one prophesying. The interviews and literature survey were much in agreement on these areas. A survey with a larger sample of AGS ministers will be able to further test these findings and identify prevalent patterns of praxis.

A conviction that all prophecy should be evaluated was evident in both the interviews and the literature. While various criteria were cited for the evaluation process, there is prospect to examine the relative importance of each criterion in actual practice. A wider investigation will also reveal the actual people involved in evaluating congregational prophecy and personal prophecy. A related aspect to the judging of prophecy concerns the authority accorded to prophetic messages by recipients. A further study will clarify the authority given to prophecy as compared with Scripture and church leadership.

The analysis of the interviews revealed three themes that seemed to enhance the practice of prophecy. These themes of compassion, courage,

---

1. Gee, *Spiritual Gifts in the Work of the Ministry Today*, 52–53.

and intimacy with God appeared to characterize believers who engaged regularly in prophecy. These themes can also be found mentioned in various ways within the literature. Of particular note is that these themes are similar to the Pentecostal affections of gratitude, compassion, and courage described within Pentecostal spirituality.[2] The literature survey further showed various empirical studies that suggest a correlation between these themes and charismatic phenomena such as prophecy. In particular, the themes of compassion for others and intimacy with God present a horizontal and vertical dimension of love relationships. This bears similarity to correlations found from empirical studies in the literature.[3] This suggests that these themes are variables associated with the practice of prophecy.

The literature review further suggests other variables associated with the practice of prophecy. The personality types of believers were found to correlate with charismatic practices. In particular, empirical studies show that extraversion is positively correlated with charismatic phenomena. It is then likely that prophecy would display a similar relationship. Furthermore, since prophecy itself is a charismatic phenomenon, it is likely that prophecy would be positively correlated with other charismatic experiences. The literature review also suggests that prophecy is correlated with certain types of prayer and evangelistic activity. However, the earlier interviews show limited evidence of these correlations and further testing is needed to elucidate the relationships.

Based on the data collected thus far, the theological-conceptual model in figure 6.1 was constructed. The conceptual model proposes various causal relationships between the variables as indicated from the literature survey and interviews. The model also includes background variables such as age and sex even though there was no indication that they are correlated with the practice of prophecy. These background variables should still be included in the phase of empirical-theological testing to corroborate this finding.

---

2. Land, *Pentecostal Spirituality*, 135–39.
3. Lee and Poloma, *Sociological Study of the Great Commandment*.

Figure 6.1 The theological-conceptual model for the practice of prophecy

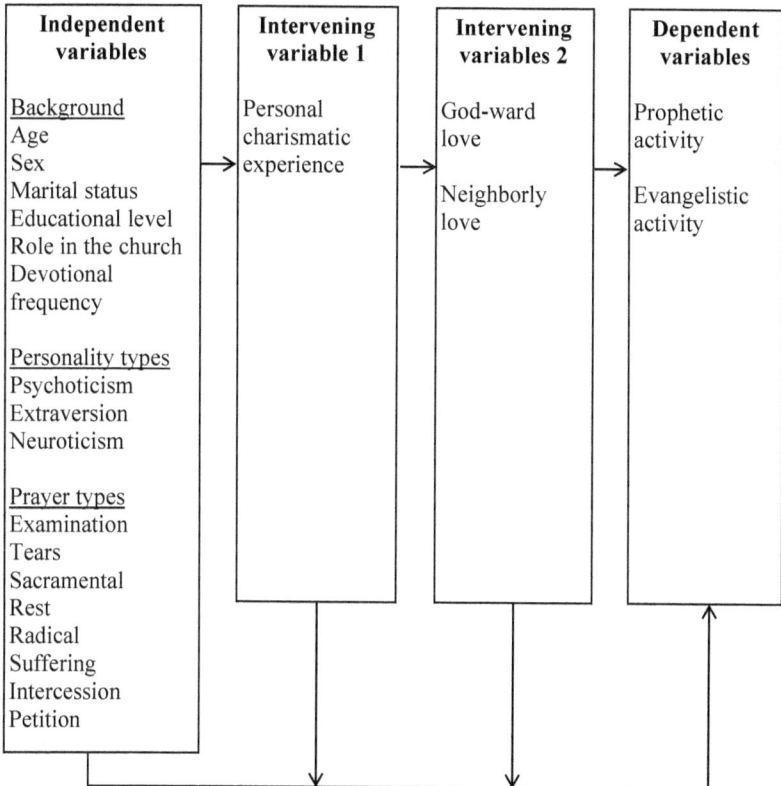

6.3 SURVEY AIMS

Theological perception and reflection have raised several opportunities for further investigation in the next phase of empirical-theological testing. Using the continuum of research forms proposed by Van der Ven, the aims of the survey are divided into the categories of description and hypothesis-testing.[4]

6.3.1 Survey Aims: Descriptive

The interviews and literature survey provided rich descriptions of the phenomenon of prophecy. These descriptions can now be tested on a larger sample of AGS ministers so that generalizations may be made about the survey population. In addition, it would permit triangulation between the

---

4. Van der Ven, *Practical Theology: An Empirical Approach*, 125–26.

data obtained from the literature review, the qualitative interviews, and the quantitative survey.[5] The earlier section on theological reflection highlighted several areas that may be tested and also suggested further possibilities for obtaining descriptive data. The survey will attempt to answer the questions listed below.

The understanding of prophecy

D_1: Is a message in tongues with interpretation considered the equivalent of prophecy?

D_2: Is inspired preaching considered the equivalent of prophecy?

D_3: What authority do recipients accord to prophecy?

The reception of prophecy

D_4: What spiritual experiences initiate prophecy and how common are these spiritual experiences in relation to prophecy?

D_5: How is the prophetic message revealed to the person prophesying?

The delivery of prophecy

D_6: What is the psychological state of the person prophesying?

D_7: How are the actual words to express the prophecy determined?

The judging of prophecy

D_8: What criteria are used to judge prophecy and who is involved in the evaluation of prophecy?

The purpose of prophecy

D_9: What is the content of prophecy?

D_{10}: What is the effect of prophecy on the church?

6.3.2 Survey Aims: Hypothesis-testing

Theological perception and induction revealed possible correlations between the practice of prophecy and other variables. These relationships are tentatively reflected within the theological-conceptual model. This study will first focus on analyzing the simple direct correlation of the variables with the practice of prophecy. The model also proposes some complex causal paths with intervening variables and these causal paths will be tested as well. The hypotheses for testing are described below.

---

5. Creswell and Plano Clark, *Mixed Methods Research*, 213–14.

H1: Background variables are correlated with prophetic activity.

The background variables included in the theological-conceptual model are age, sex, marital status, educational level, role in the church, and devotional frequency. The literature review did not suggest any direct correlation between demographic variables and the practice of prophecy. Still, these variables are included within the model for further investigation. The practice of prophecy was often mentioned in association with church leaders in the earlier exploration and so the respondent's role in the church is included in the model. The earlier interviews identified compassion, courage, and intimacy with God as themes that serve to enhance the practice of prophecy. These themes may be related with the respondents' age and devotional frequency. Hence the model includes these variables for testing.

H_2: Personality types are correlated with prophetic activity.

The personality types included in the model are psychoticism, extraversion, and neuroticism. Studies in literature show a positive correlation between extraversion and charismatic experience. There is also some suggestion of a negative correlation between neuroticism and charismatic experience. This study will analyze the sample data for evidence of these relationships. Furthermore, prophecy itself is a charismatic phenomenon and so this study will explore relationships between prophecy and the personality types.

H_3: Prayer types are correlated with prophetic activity.

The eight prayer types included in the model are examination, tears, sacramental, rest, radical, suffering, intercession, and petition. Earlier studies in literature suggest possible correlations between certain types of prayer and the practice of prophecy. In addition, the identified theme of courage would broadly correspond to certain prayer types. These possible relationships between prayer types and prophecy will be assessed through this hypothesis. This study also previously noted that certain prayer types are emphasized within Pentecostal spirituality. This association can be explored through the relationship between prayer types and personal charismatic experience.

H_4: Personal charismatic experience is correlated with prophetic activity.

The earlier investigation showed a relationship between the practice of prophecy and charismatic experience. This seems likely since prophecy itself is a charismatic phenomenon. Thus, this hypothesis seeks to test the relationship between prophecy and other charismatic phenomena. However, the charismatic phenomena will be limited to what is experienced on a personal basis and will exclude charismatic ministry to others. This is to prevent a possible overlap between prophecy and the items measured under personal charismatic experience.

H_5: God-ward love and neighborly love are correlated with prophetic activity.

This study has noted that prophetic activity is viewed as a ministry to believers within the faith community. This suggests that prophetic activity is correlated and actually motivated by God-ward love and neighborly love within the person prophesying. Furthermore, the theme of compassion that was identified earlier would broadly correspond with neighborly love. The relationship will be tested through this hypothesis.

H_6: Evangelistic activity is correlated with prophetic activity.

The previous investigation suggested a positive correlation between evangelism and prophecy. The theological-conceptual model hypothesizes both evangelism and prophecy as dependent variables that are influenced by the same explanatory variables. Thus, this would explain the empirical correlation between evangelism and prophecy.

H_7: Independent variables influence prophetic activity and are mediated through the intervening variables personal charismatic experience, God-ward love, and neighborly love.

Previous studies have shown that charismatic experience is correlated with some of the independent variables included in the model. Likewise, the independent variables are postulated to have an influence on God-ward love and neighborly love. It is thus hypothesized that personal charismatic experience, God-ward love, and neighborly love serve as intervening variables in the proposed model. This is in line with the literature that suggests that personal charismatic experience leads to the transfer of divine love energy that was termed "godly love" in literature. This love energy may then be expressed in forms of ministry such as in prophecy. Such a causal pathway would further affirm the themes of intimacy and compassion in the practice of prophecy.

H_8: Independent variables influence evangelistic activity and are mediated through the intervening variables personal charismatic experience, God-ward love, and neighborly love.

Studies in literature point to a correlation between evangelistic activity and charismatic experience. Evangelistic activity can also be considered an expression of divine love energy that is termed "godly love" in literature.

Therefore, it is hypothesized that the independent variables in this study have a causal relationship with evangelistic activity that is mediated through the intervening variables of personal charismatic experience, God-ward love, and neighborly love. This hypothesis would also explain any possible correlation between evangelistic activity and prophetic activity.

6.4 THEOLOGICAL OPERATIONALIZATION

The theological-conceptual model was operationalized in the survey through the use of various survey questions. The background variables of spiritual age, sex, marital status, educational level, and the role in church were operationalized through questions asking for the respondents' personal data. Some variables were operationalized through the use of established instrument scales drawn from literature. The short-form of the Revised Eysenck Personality Questionnaire (EPQR-S) was used to measure the personality types extraversion, neuroticism, and psychoticism. Prayer types were operationalized through the use of prayer scales developed by Ladd and Spilka.[6] The variables God-ward love and neighborly love were operationalized through the use of the Faith Maturity Scale (FMS).[7] This instrument contains a vertical and horizontal scale which can be understood to reflect God-ward love and neighborly love respectively.

Other instrument scales had to be constructed to measure the remaining variables as suitable scales could not be found in literature. This approach was common in other empirical studies reviewed in the literature. The constructed scales are briefly mentioned here and will be discussed in detail in section 6.7. The practice of prophecy is represented by the variable prophetic activity in the theological-conceptual model. This was operationalized through questions on the frequency of respondents engaging in practices that this study has defined as prophecy. A scale for prophetic activity was subsequently constructed from these questions.

Personal charismatic experience was operationalized through a scale measuring the frequency of specified charismatic phenomena. Devotional frequency was operationalized through questions on the frequency of the respondents engaging in prayer, reading the Bible, and reading Christian materials. Evangelistic activity was operationalized through a scale measuring the frequency of respondents engaging in evangelistic practices.

---

6. Ladd and Spilka, "Inward, Outward, and Upward"; Ladd and Spilka, "Inward, Outward, Upward Prayer."

7. Benson, Donahue, and Erickson, "Faith Maturity Scale."

6.5 CONDUCTING THE SURVEY

Ethical considerations are an important factor for all investigations with human subjects. The survey followed the same ethical principles and code of practice discussed earlier in section 3.2.3. In particular, the surveys were all done anonymously so that the researcher would not be able to identify any of the respondents.

A pilot study was first conducted among twenty volunteers at a Bible School. There were no AGS ministers involved in this exercise though the volunteers came from charismatic backgrounds. The pilot study sought to ensure that the survey questions were clearly expressed and easily understood by the volunteers. Changes were then made to the questionnaire based on feedback from these respondents. Some minor changes were made to the wording of questions. Three changes were also made to the FMS so that it was contextualized to the respondents' sociological and cultural context. These changes are described in the next section.

Once the questionnaire was finalized, the study proceeded to carry out the actual data collection. This study sought to invite all credentialed ministers in the AGS to participate in the survey. Permission was obtained from the AGS General Council to conduct the survey. The list of AGS credentialed ministers was obtained from the 2009 AGS directory. The survey questionnaires were distributed to the credentialed ministers in two ways. First, questionnaires were distributed at one of the monthly prayer meetings attended by AGS ministers. Second, questionnaires were mailed to ministers who were absent from the prayer meeting. The collected questionnaires were then prepared for collation and analysis. All data analysis for this study was performed using the Statistical Package for Social Sciences (SPSS) version 21.

6.6 DESCRIPTION OF THE SURVEY POPULATION

The survey population consisted of all credentialed members of the AGS who were residing and ministering in Singapore at the time of the survey. The 2009 AGS directory lists a total of 359 credentialed members and forty-nine AGS churches. Ministers who were found to be residing or ministering outside of Singapore on a long-term basis were excluded from the study as their responses would not be representative of ministry in the Singapore context. The ten senior pastors who participated in the first phase of interviews were also excluded from this second phase. This resulted in a population of 321 credentialed ministers for the quantitative survey. This consisted of 133 ordained ministers, eighty-two licensed ministers, thirty-one associate ministers, forty-two exhorters, thirty-two Christian workers, and one special licensed minister.

The data collection produced a total of 168 responses. In reviewing the data, twenty questionnaires were rejected. This left a sample size of 148 respondents that represents 46.11 percent of the survey population. The sample consisted of 56.76 percent men and 42.57 percent women. The rest (0.68 percent) did not indicate their sex. This compares favorably with the overall population ratio of 60 percent men and 40 percent women reported by the AGS office.[8] There were 70.27 percent respondents who were married, 27.03 percent who were single, and 2.70 percent who failed to indicate their status. More than 60 percent of the respondents are between forty to fifty-nine years old. The age distribution of the sample can be seen in table 6.1. The mean age of the sample is 46.61 years. This compares favorably with the average age of fifty years for the population as reported by the AGS office.[9]

Table 6.1 Age distribution of respondents

Age	Frequency	Proportion of respondents (%)
≤ 29	2	1.35
30–39	35	23.65
40–49	46	31.08
50–59	45	30.41
60–69	8	5.41
≥ 70	4	2.70
Not reported	8	5.40
Total	148	100.00

The highest educational level of the survey respondents is seen in table 6.2. The analysis showed that 70.27 percent of the sample held a bachelor degree or a higher degree. This is in contrast with the overall Christian population in Singapore where 32.2 percent were university graduates.[10] It also contrasts with the overall resident population in Singapore where 22.8 percent were university graduates.[11] The higher educational level of the

---

8. Obtained from personal communication with the AGS office.
9. Obtained from personal communication with the AGS office.
10. Department of Statistics, *Census of Singapore 2010*.
11. Ibid.

respondents is expected since this is usually the requirement for leadership roles in the church.

Table 6.2 Highest educational level of respondents

Highest qualification	Frequency	Proportion of respondents (%)
O-level	16	10.81
A-level	9	6.08
Polytechnic diploma	10	6.76
Bachelor degree	55	37.16
Master degree and above	49	33.11
Others	8	5.41
Not reported	1	0.68
Total	148	100.00

The respondents served in various roles in their local churches as seen in table 6.3. The majority of the respondents served as pastors in their churches. In the Singapore context, this would likely mean the respondents formed part of a team of pastors overseeing the ministries of a local church.

Table 6.3 Respondents' role in their churches

Role in the church	Frequency	Proportion of respondents (%)
Congregation member	1	0.68
Ministry/Cell group leader	19	12.84
Ministry staff	14	9.46
Pastor	97	65.54
Itinerant minister	12	8.11
Missionary	4	2.70
Not reported	1	0.68
Total	148	100.00

6.7 DESCRIPTION AND RELIABILITY OF SURVEY INSTRUMENTS

The study employed a variety of survey instruments to measure the variables in the theological-conceptual model. Some of these instruments were drawn from literature while the others were constructed from the questionnaire.

The following sections will provide a description of these instruments together with an analysis of scale reliability. In addition, factor analysis was performed on scales that were constructed by this study to ensure that they are unidimensional.

6.7.1 Faith Maturity Scale

The Faith Maturity Scale (FMS) was described in the literature review earlier.[12] The scale defines faith maturity as "the degree to which a person embodies the priorities, commitments, and perspectives characteristic of vibrant and life-transforming faith, as these have been understood in 'mainline' Protestant traditions."[13] The FMS consists of a thirty-eight-item scale and has two twelve-item subscales. The vertical sub-scale (FMS-V) and the horizontal sub-scale (FMS-H) may be used to reflect the variables Godward love and neighborly love respectively.

The FMS used for this study can be found in appendix B. It contains three amendments due to feedback obtained from the pilot study. The first amendment concerned changing the instructions to "How true are each of these statements for you?" instead of "Be as honest as possible, describing how true it really is and not how true you would like it to be." Some of the pilot study participants were offended by the original instructions, feeling it implied that they were dishonest. The second amendment involved changing the term "political" to "national" for items twenty-nine and thirty-five. There is a clear separation between religion and political issues in Singapore due to a population which is multi-ethnic and multi-religious. The use of the term "national" would therefore be more appropriate. The third amendment involved changing item twenty-two to "I speak out for equality for the underprivileged." The use of the term "underprivileged" instead of "women and minorities" would better measure prosocial behavior in Singapore.

The Cronbach alpha, mean, and standard deviation for the FMS and its sub-scales were obtained from the data sample and found to be comparable to two other studies.[14] The scales are found to be reliable with Cronbach alpha values of 0.84, 0.80, and 0.85 for the FMS, FMS-V, and FMS-H respectively.

---

12. Benson, Donahue, and Erickson, "Faith Maturity Scale."

13. Ibid., 3.

14. Benson, Donahue, and Erickson, "Faith Maturity Scale"; Salsman and Carlson, "Religious Orientation, Mature Faith, and Psychological Distress."

6.7.2 Personality Scales

This study used the short-form of the Revised Eysenck Personality Questionnaire (EPQR-S) to measure the personality dimensions of psychoticism, extraversion, and neuroticism. Each of these dimensions was measured with a twelve-item scale where respondents had to answer "yes" or "no" to each question. The EPQR-S further includes a twelve-item Lie Scale.

The Extraversion, Neuroticism, and Lie Scales are found to be reliable with Cronbach alpha values of 0.80, 0.81, and 0.73 respectively. The mean and standard deviation for the scales were also obtained and found to be comparable with data from literature.[15] This affirms the psychometric properties of the test. However, the Psychoticism Scale produced a low Cronbach alpha of 0.30 indicating poor reliability. This is in line with other studies in literature and suggests that further improvement to the Psychoticism Scale is necessary.[16]

6.7.3 Prayer Scales

The prayer scales developed by Ladd and Spilka were discussed in the literature review earlier.[17] The instrument provides survey participants with a list of twenty-nine words or phrases. Participants had to score on a scale of 1 to 6 how often they thought of each of the words or phrases during their prayers.

Ladd and Spilka have proposed eight primary prayer factors: examination, tears, sacramental, rest, radical, suffering, intercession, and petition. The Examination Prayer Scale (ExamPray) consists of five items emphasizing personal examination, evaluation, and commitment. The Tears Prayer Scale (TearsPray) comprises of three items focused on expressions of sadness and grief. The Sacramental Prayer Scale (SacraPray) has three items and centers on rituals, traditions, and sacraments. The Rest Prayer Scale (RestPray) consists of four items emphasizing stillness and quietude in the presence of the divine. The Radical Prayer Scale (RadPray) has four items centering on a bold, assertive nature during the prayer activity. The Suffering Prayer Scale (SuffPray) comprises of three items which show connection with others experiencing distress. The Intercession Prayer Scale (InterPray)

---

15. Francis and Robbins, "Personality and Glossolalia"; Francis, Brown, and Philipchalk, "Development."

16. Miles and Hempel, "Eysenck Personality Scales," 102.

17. Ladd and Spilka, "Inward, Outward, and Upward"; Ladd and Spilka, "Inward, Outward, Upward Prayer."

has three items describing prayer activity which seeks to help or assist others. The Petition Prayer Scale (PetPray) comprises of four items focused on requesting for personal physical and material needs.

The Cronbach alpha values for all the prayer scales were obtained for the data sample. They are reflected in table 6.4 and are comparable with the values reported by Ladd and Spilka.[18] The alpha values are acceptable for short scales and affirm the psychometric properties for each of the scales.

Table 6.4 Reliability analysis of prayer scales

	No. items in the scale	Cronbach α
ExamPray	5	0.74
TearsPray	3	0.71
SacraPray	3	0.71
RestPray	4	0.76
RadPray	4	0.70
SuffPray	3	0.72
InterPray	3	0.71
PetPray	4	0.81

6.7.4 Devotion Frequency Scale

The devotional frequency of respondents was measured by constructing the Devotion Frequency Scale (DevoFreq). This scale consists of three items describing the devotional activities of prayer, reading the Bible, and reading Christian materials other than the Bible. Respondents indicated on a scale of 1 to 5 how frequently they engaged in the described activity. The scale can be found in appendix B.

Table 6.5 shows the reliability analysis for the scale. The scale was found to have a Cronbach alpha of 0.60 which is acceptable for a three-item scale.[19] The corrected item-total correlations for the scale items were above 0.3, indicating good internal correlation between the scale items.[20] While the third item of the scale shows a smaller correlation with the other items, all three items were included so that the scale could have a broader measure of devotional activity.

18. Ladd and Spilka, "Inward, Outward, and Upward"; Ladd and Spilka, "Inward, Outward, Upward Prayer."
19. Van der Ven, *Practical Theology: An Empirical Approach*, 146.
20. Pallant, *SPSS Survival Manual*, 92.

Table 6.5 Reliability analysis for DevoFreq

How often do you ...	Item mean	Item std. deviation	Corrected item-total correlation
Pray	4.62	0.67	0.44
Read the Bible	4.43	0.76	0.58
Read Christian materials other than the Bible	3.64	1.14	0.30

Cronbach $\alpha = 0.60$

6.7.5 Prophetic Activity Scale

This study sought to measure the frequency of prophetic activity by constructing the Prophetic Activity Scale (ProphAct). This scale consists of six items describing activities which are defined as prophecy in this study. Respondents were asked to indicate on a scale of one to seven how frequently they engaged in the described activity. The scale can be found in appendix B.

Table 6.6 shows the reliability analysis for the prophetic activity scale. The scale was found to be reliable with a Cronbach alpha of 0.77. The corrected item-total correlations for the scale items are above 0.3, indicating good internal correlation between the scale items.[21]

Table 6.6 Reliability analysis for ProphAct

How often do you ...	Item mean	Item std. deviation	Corrected item-total correlation
prophesy in a church service or group setting?	4.04	2.00	0.67
prophesy to an individual in private?	3.94	1.93	0.48
sing out a prophetic message?	2.57	2.02	0.51
utter a message in tongues (glossolalia) which is then interpreted?	2.33	1.62	0.42
interpret an utterance of tongues (glossolalia)?	2.20	1.53	0.49
receive a message or impression from God for someone else?	4.39	1.69	0.50

Cronbach $\alpha = 0.77$

---

21. Ibid.

The study proceeded to assess the factorial validity of the scale based on the sample data. This is necessary to ensure the scale items are measuring the same underlying construct.[22] The Kaiser-Meyer-Olkin (KMO) value was found to be 0.67, exceeding the recommended value of 0.6. The Bartlett's Test of sphericity was also significant (p = 0.00). This indicated the data met the criteria for exploratory factor analysis.[23] Principal component analysis was then applied to the data. Using Kaiser's criterion, components with eigenvalues above one should be extracted. Two components were identified, together accounting for 71.66 percent of the variance. Examination of the screeplot showed an inflexion point after the second component, again suggesting that there were two components present. The component matrix further showed the scale items loading on one of two factors (table 6.7). Varimax rotation of the data was performed to further aid in interpretation of the components. The rotated solution again showed the scale items loading on one of two components (table 6.8). The first component describes activity where a prophetic message is directly communicated to the recipients. The second component describes activity where a prophetic message in tongues is first delivered followed by an inspired interpretation. Both these components are within this study's definition of prophecy. Furthermore, the survey results will later show that the large majority of respondents consider tongues with interpretation to be equivalent to prophecy. Hence the Prophetic Activity Scale may be said to be unidimensional for the purpose of this study.

Table 6.7 Component matrix for ProphAct

Scale item	Component 1	Component 2
prophesy in a church service or group setting	.812	
sing out a prophetic message	.678	
interpret an utterance of tongues (glossolalia)	.668	.640
receive a message or impression from God for someone else	.668	-.455
prophesy to an individual in private	.646	-.581
utter a message in tongues (glossolalia) which is then interpreted	.620	.701

---

22. Hair et al., *Multivariate Data Analysis*, 117.
23. Pallant, *SPSS Survival Manual*, 174.

Table 6.8 Rotated component matrix for ProphAct

Scale item	Component 1	Component 2
prophesy to an individual in private	.866	
receive a message or impression from God for someone else	.806	
prophesy in a church service or group setting	.765	.338
sing out a prophetic message	.558	.387
utter a message in tongues (glossolalia) which is then interpreted		.934
interpret an utterance of tongues (glossolalia)		.915

Rotation Method: Varimax with Kaiser Normalization

6.7.6 Personal Charismatic Experience Scale

This study sought to measure the frequency of charismatic experiences by constructing the Personal Charismatic Experience Scale (CharExp). The scale was limited to individual personal experiences rather than experiences which involved charismatic ministry to others. Hence, the scale did not include activities such as praying for someone else to be supernaturally healed. This scale consists of six items describing charismatic phenomena. Respondents were asked to indicate on a scale of 1 to 7 how frequently they experienced the described phenomena. The Personal Charismatic Experience Scale can be found in appendix B.

The reliability analysis of the scale can be found in table 6.9. The Cronbach alpha for the scale is 0.73, indicating that it is statistically reliable. The alpha value could be marginally improved if the scale item for singing in tongues was removed. However, this phenomenon is an important aspect of charismatic experience and was kept in the scale. The corrected item-total correlations for the scale items are above 0.3, indicating good internal correlation between the scale items.[24] The scale did not include speaking in tongues as one of the scale items even though this is an important and common charismatic experience. This decision was made because almost all respondents in the sample reported speaking in tongues every week. Thus, speaking in tongues did not correlate with any of the other scale items and would have affected the scale reliability if it was included. However, speaking in tongues should be included in the scale if the study was performed

24. Ibid., 92.

on a different population where members speak in tongues with varying frequency.

Table 6.9 Reliability analysis for CharExp

How often do you ...	Item mean	Item std. deviation	Corrected item-total correlation
experience being "slain in the Spirit"?	3.00	1.37	0.30
experience a fresh "infilling" of the Spirit?	5.34	1.64	0.60
experience a miracle from God?	4.05	1.60	0.46
sing in tongues (glossolalia)?	5.28	2.30	0.36
receive divine knowledge for yourself about something you did not know previously?	3.79	1.70	0.50
receive divine guidance for yourself to make a specific decision?	4.45	1.64	0.63

Cronbach α = 0.73

The study proceeded to assess the factorial validity of the Personal Charismatic Experience Scale. A value of 0.735 was obtained for the KMO measure and this exceeded the recommended value of 0.6. The Bartlett's Test of sphericity was also found to be significant (p = 0.00). The data thus met the criteria for exploratory factor analysis.[25] Principal component analysis was performed on the data. Only one component was found with an eigenvalue above 1. This component accounted for 44.08 percent of the variance. The screeplot showed a clear break after the first component, indicating there was only one component present. The component matrix showed all the scale items loading on this one component (table 6.10). Therefore, the factor analysis indicates that the scale is clearly unidimensional.

25. Ibid., 174.

Table 6.10 Component matrix for CharExp

Scale item	Component 1
receive divine guidance for yourself to make a specific decision?	.800
experience a fresh "infilling" of the Spirit?	.779
receive divine knowledge for yourself about something you did not know previously?	.702
experience a miracle from God?	.657
sing in tongues (glossolalia)?	.516
experience being "slain in the Spirit"?	.457

6.7.7 Evangelistic Activity Scale

The Evangelistic Activity Scale (EvangAct) was constructed from the questionnaire to measure the frequency in which respondents engaged in evangelistic practices. The scale consists of five items. Respondents were asked to indicate on a scale of 1 to 7 how frequently they engaged in the described activity. The scale can be found in appendix B.

The reliability analysis for the scale can be found in table 6.11. The Cronbach alpha for the scale is 0.91, indicating that the scale is statistically reliable. The corrected item-total correlations for the scale items are well above 0.3, indicating good internal correlation between the scale items.[26]

Table 6.11 Reliability analysis for EvangAct

How often do you engage in the following activities with non-Christians or "back-slid" Christians?	Item mean	Item std. deviation	Corrected item-total correlation
Invite them to Christian events or activities	4.72	1.36	0.77
Share about Christianity with them	5.10	1.35	0.84
Share a testimony with them	5.11	1.38	0.84
Pray with them	5.14	1.45	0.78
Give them Christian resources (books, music, sermons)	4.28	1.57	0.62

Cronbach α = 0.91

The study proceeded to test the factorial validity of the scale. A value of 0.84 was obtained for the KMO measure and this exceeded the

26. Ibid., 92.

recommended value of 0.6. The Bartlett's Test of sphericity was found to be significant (p = 0.00). Exploratory factor analysis could thus be carried out since these criteria are met.[27] Principal component analysis was performed on the data. Only one component was found with an eigenvalue above 1. This component accounted for 73.63 percent of the variance. The screeplot showed an inflexion point after the first component, indicating there was only one component present. The component matrix showed all the scale items loading substantially on this one component (table 6.12). Therefore, the factor analysis indicates that the scale is unidimensional.

Table 6.12 Component matrix for EvangAct

Scale item	Component 1
Share a testimony with them	.914
Share about Christianity with them	.913
Pray with them	.866
Invite them to Christian events or activities	.856
Give them Christian resources (books, music, sermons)	.729

6.8 SURVEY RESULTS: DESCRIPTIVE

An analysis of the data showed the respondents had a large degree of experience with prophecy. As seen in table 6.13, 87.16 percent of the sample reported having delivered a prophecy. The results show that 99.32 percent of the sample had witnessed the delivery of a congregational prophecy while 97.30 percent of the sample had witnessed the delivery of a personal prophecy. The results also show 73.65 percent of the sample were from churches which encourage prophecies in meetings. Likewise, personal prophecy seems to be widely encouraged (62.16 percent) though this figure is lower than for congregational prophecy. The data indicates that prophecy is a common practice within the AGS churches. In fact, 82.43 percent of the sample agree or strongly agree that all believers can prophesy (table 6.14). This displays a widespread belief within the population that prophecy is not limited to only certain believers.

27. Ibid., 174.

Table 6.13 Experience with prophecy

Item	Yes (%)	No (%)	Missing (%)
Have you ever delivered a prophecy?	87.16	9.46	3.38
Have you ever witnessed a prophecy?	99.32	0.68	0.00
Have you ever witnessed a personal prophecy given to someone?	97.30	2.03	0.68
Do you know someone who prophesies regularly?	82.43	16.22	1.35
Does your church encourage prophecies in meetings?	73.65	25.00	1.35
Does your church encourage personal prophecies to individuals?	62.16	35.14	2.70

6.8.1 The Understanding of Prophecy

6.8.1.1 D_1: Is a message in tongues with interpretation considered the equivalent of prophecy?

The analysis showed 71.62 percent of the sample believe that an utterance in tongues followed with inspired interpretation is the equivalent of prophecy (table 6.14). The literature review earlier described a mixture of views on this issue within the Pentecostal movement. It is evident that the view on equivalence is dominant within the AGS. This result validates the inclusion of the items for tongues and its interpretation in the Prophetic Activity Scale.

Table 6.14 Understanding of prophecy

Item	Missing (%)	Strongly Disagree (%)	Disagree (%)	Neutral (%)	Agree (%)	Strongly Agree (%)
All believers can prophesy.	0.00	2.70	10.81	4.05	48.65	33.78
An utterance in tongues followed with interpretation is the equivalent of prophecy.	0.68	1.35	10.81	15.54	50.00	21.62
Inspired preaching or teaching is the equivalent of prophecy	2.03	3.38	27.70	23.65	33.11	10.14
Prophecy carries more authority than the Bible.	0.68	67.57	26.35	3.38	0.68	1.35
Prophecy sometimes contradicts the Bible.	3.38	61.49	19.59	7.43	6.08	2.03
Prophecy sometimes brings a fresh perspective to Bible teachings.	1.35	5.41	8.11	18.92	51.35	14.86
Prophecy carries more authority than pastors.	2.03	42.57	37.16	12.84	4.73	0.68
Prophecy sometimes critiques church leadership and direction.	3.38	20.95	18.92	19.59	33.78	3.38

6.8.1.2 D_2: Is inspired preaching considered the equivalent of prophecy?

The sample has less consistent views on the equivalence of inspired preaching with prophecy. The results show 43.25 percent felt they are equivalent, 31.08 percent felt that they are not equivalent, and 23.65 percent were neutral on this (table 6.14). The earlier interviews had already highlighted instances when pastors received revelatory insight while they were preaching. The result suggests some willingness within the sample to attribute inspiration during the preaching event to prophetic activity. However, the spontaneous nature of prophecy indicates that it should not be confused with the routine preparation and delivery of biblical messages.

6.8.1.3 D_3: What authority do recipients accord to prophecy?

The survey sought to determine the relative authority accorded to prophecy in comparison to the Bible and to pastors (table 6.14). First, the results show an overwhelming majority of the sample (93.92 percent) did not consider prophecy to have more authority than the Bible. Second, 81.09 percent felt that prophecy should not contradict the Bible. These two results indicate a high regard for Scripture and its authority within the AGS. Third, there were 66.21 percent who felt that prophecy might sometimes bring a fresh perspective to Bible teachings. This sentiment is much in line with Pentecostal spirituality which is open to allow the Holy Spirit to guide the interpretation and understanding of Scripture.[28]

Further analysis was done on the minority (2.03 percent) who claimed prophecy carries more authority than Scripture and the minority (8.11 percent) who claimed prophecy sometimes contradicts the Bible. There was nothing statistically atypical about the background characteristics of these respondents. A cross-tab comparison was then performed on the two groups and the results can be seen in table 6.15 and table 6.16. Table 6.15 shows that the three respondents who agree prophecy is more authoritative than the Bible all disagree that prophecy contradicts the Bible. This suggests the respondents do not see contemporary prophecy as new authoritative revelation that competes with or contradicts the Bible. Furthermore, the table also shows that the twelve respondents who agree prophecy sometimes contradicts the Bible do not consider prophecy as more authoritative. Table 6.16 presents more information on these twelve respondents. It shows they all agree that prophecy sometimes contains error. These findings suggest the group may be reporting their actual encounters with prophetic messages that contradict established biblical teaching. The group regards these messages as less authoritative than Scripture and that these contradictory prophecies contain error.

Table 6.15 Cross-tab for prophecy and the authority of the Bible

		Prophecy sometimes contradicts the Bible.			Total
		Disagree	Neutral	Agree	
Prophecy is more authoritative than the Bible.	Disagree	114	9	12	135
	Neutral	3	2	0	5
	Agree	3	0	0	3
Total		120	11	12	143

---

28. Village, *Bible and Lay People*, 151–54.

Table 6.16 Cross-tab for prophecy contradicts the Bible

		Prophecy sometimes contradicts the Bible.			Total
		Disagree	Neutral	Agree	
Prophecy sometimes contains errors.	Disagree	8	0	0	8
	Neutral	8	0	0	8
	Agree	103	10	12	125
Total		119	10	12	141

The survey also showed a high regard for pastoral authority in comparison with prophecy (table 6.14). The large majority (79.73 percent) felt that prophecy did not carry more authority than pastors. Further analysis did not reveal anything statistically atypical about the background of the 5.41 percent who agreed prophecy carried more authority than pastors. Interestingly, all except one respondent in this group is serving as a pastor. Another cross-tab analysis showed that none of the survey respondents considered prophecy to be more authoritative than both the Bible and pastors.

The survey showed a more mixed opinion about prophecy critiquing church leadership and direction (table 6.14). The results show 37.16 percent accepted that this sometimes occurs whereas 39.87 percent disagreed.

6.8.2 The Reception of Prophecy

6.8.2.1 D_4: What spiritual experiences initiate prophecy and how common are these spiritual experiences in relation to prophecy?

The study asked respondents to indicate on a scale of one to five the frequency in which prophecy is initiated by a certain spiritual experience. The mean score was calculated and table 6.17 lists these experiences in descending frequency. The four most common spiritual experiences were found to have very close mean scores. This indicates that prophecy usually occurs by a sentence coming to mind, a general impression, a Scripture verse, or an internal picture. At the other end, the data sample reported that prophecy almost never comes through an angelic visitation. Similarly, prophecies initiated by an external vision or an external audible voice are extremely rare.

Table 6.17 Spiritual experiences initiating prophecy

The prophecy comes in the form of . . .	Mean	Std. deviation
a word or sentence coming to my mind	3.77	0.78
a general impression of what the message is	3.71	0.88
a Scripture verse coming to my mind	3.55	0.87
an internal picture in my mind	3.52	0.83
an internal voice speaking to me	3.06	0.99
a physical sensation	2.44	1.03
a dream	2.21	1.01
an external vision before my eyes	2.06	1.01
others	1.83	1.29
an external audible voice speaking to me	1.79	0.93
an angelic visitation	1.35	0.72

6.8.2.2 D_5: How is the prophetic message revealed to the person prophesying?

More respondents reported receiving the prophetic message progressively as they deliver the prophecy rather than receiving it entirely before they speak. The results show 52.7 percent of the sample reported that they often or almost always receive the prophetic message progressively (table 6.18). Similarly, 37.8 percent reported that they rarely or almost never receive the entire prophetic message before they speak. The analysis did not show anything statistically significant about the background demographics between those who receive prophetic messages progressively and those who receive the entire message before speaking.

Table 6.18 Reception of prophecy

Item	Missing (%)	Almost Never (%)	Rarely (%)	Sometimes (%)	Often (%)	Almost Always (%)
I receive the message *progressively* as I speak.	15.54	3.38	6.08	22.30	38.51	14.19
I receive the entire prophetic message *before* I start speaking.	16.89	5.41	32.43	33.11	10.14	2.03
The prophecy comes in a figurative and symbolic message.	17.57	6.76	12.16	37.84	22.97	2.70
The prophecy comes in a plain and direct instruction.	14.86	0.68	12.84	36.49	29.73	5.41

A one-way analysis of variance (ANOVA) was conducted to explore the relationship between respondents receiving the entire prophetic message before speaking and their ProphAct scores (table 6.19). Respondents were divided into three groups based on how frequently they reported receiving the entire prophetic message before speaking (Group A: "Almost never" and "Rarely"; Group B: "Sometimes"; Group C: "Often" and "Almost always"). The significance value for Levene's test is larger than 0.05 indicating that the assumption of equal variances between groups was not violated. The ANOVA indicates there is a statistically significant difference in the mean ProphAct scores for the different groups (F = 8.922, p = 0.000). The effect size, eta squared, is 0.13 indicating a moderate effect size. The Hochberg GT2 post-hoc test was used due to the different group sizes and it indicates that the mean ProphAct score is higher for groups which report greater frequency in receiving the entire prophetic message before speaking (table 6.20). The results suggest that believers who prophesy more frequently tend to receive the entire prophetic message before speaking. This may possibly be due to their greater experience with prophecy leading to a greater sensitivity to divine communication.

Table 6.19 One-way ANOVA: Receiving entire prophetic message by ProphAct

Group	Mean	Std. deviation	Std. error
Group A	2.973	.939	.127
Group B	3.681	1.100	.159
Group C	4.056	1.494	.352
Total	3.415	1.169	.106
F = 8.922, p = 0.000			

Note: Group A: Almost never and Rarely; Group B: Sometimes; Group C: Often and Almost Always

Table 6.20 Hochberg GT2 post-hoc: Receiving entire prophetic message by ProphAct

Comparison		Mean difference	Std. error	Sig.
Group A	Group B	-.708*	.217	.004
	Group C	-1.083*	.298	.001
Group B	Group A	.708*	.217	.004
	Group C	-.375	.304	.522
Group C	Group A	1.083*	.298	.001
	Group B	.375	.304	.522

The survey also asked respondents if the prophetic message comes in a figurative and symbolic form or in a plain and direct instruction. Table 6.18 shows that both occur with roughly equal frequency.

6.8.3 The Delivery of Prophecy

6.8.3.1 D_6: What is the psychological state of the person prophesying?

From the survey, 70.27 percent reported that they are almost never in a trance while prophesying (table 6.21). Significantly, no respondent claimed that they always prophesied while in a trance. Furthermore, 60.13 percent of respondents are often or almost always able to cease prophesying at will. There was nothing statistically significant about the background demographics of the various groups. These results point towards believers being in a high state of self-control while prophesying.

Table 6.21 Delivery of prophecy

Item	Missing (%)	Almost Never (%)	Rarely (%)	Sometimes (%)	Often (%)	Almost Always (%)
I am in a trance when I prophesy.	15.54	70.27	10.14	3.38	.68	.00
I can choose to stop prophesying at my own will.	16.89	3.38	7.43	12.16	21.62	38.51
I use my own words to express the prophecy.	15.54	2.70	4.05	22.30	43.92	11.49
God gives me the exact words to express the prophecy.	14.86	6.76	23.65	39.19	12.84	2.70

6.8.3.2 D_7: How are the actual words to express the prophecy determined?

The data shows that prophecy is usually expressed in words selected by the one speaking rather than in words divinely given by God. Table 6.21 shows that 55.41 percent of the sample often or almost always express prophecy in their own words. Similarly, the table shows only 15.54 percent reported that God almost always or often gives them the exact words to express the prophecy.

6.8.4 The Judging of Prophecy

The survey showed an acknowledgement of the need to judge prophecy. The data showed 86.49 percent of the sample agreed or strongly agreed that prophecy may contain errors and inaccuracies (table 6.22). Another aspect of the evaluation of prophecy involves the interpretation and application of the prophetic message. 86.48 percent of the sample agreed that this was necessary. In fact, only 1.35 percent disagreed with the need for interpretation and application. The importance of judging prophecy is further highlighted by 59.46 percent of the respondents who agree that personal prophecy may result in abuse.

Table 6.22 Judging of prophecy

Item	Missing (%)	Strongly Disagree (%)	Disagree (%)	Neutral (%)	Agree (%)	Strongly Agree (%)
Prophecy sometimes contains errors or inaccuracies.	2.70	3.38	2.03	5.41	66.22	20.27
Prophecy requires interpretation and application.	0.68	0.00	1.35	11.49	57.43	29.05
Personal prophecy may result in abuse.	3.38	1.35	7.43	28.38	42.57	16.89

6.8.4.1 What criteria are used to judge prophecy and who is involved in the evaluation of prophecy?

The survey asked respondents to select the three most important criteria for judging prophecy from a list. The frequency of respondents selecting each of the criteria is shown in table 6.23. The results show the most common criteria are adherence to the Bible, spiritual discernment, and the character of the one prophesying.

Table 6.23 Criteria for judging prophecy

Item	Indicated as criteria for judging (%)
Adherence to the Bible	95.95
Spiritual discernment	77.03
Character of the one prophesying	60.14
Result of the prophecy	38.51
Adherence to church direction	14.86
Other prophecies	3.38
Other criteria	3.38

The survey also listed various groups of people and asked respondents to indicate those groups who are involved in evaluating congregational prophecy (table 6.24) and personal prophecy (table 6.25). The huge majority of the sample (85.14 percent) indicated that pastors are involved in the evaluation of congregational prophecy in a worship service, prayer meeting, or cell meeting. For personal prophecy, 66.22 percent indicated that a pastor is involved in the evaluation of the prophecy. Almost an equal proportion (64.19 percent) reported that the person receiving the prophecy is also involved in the evaluation. This may be because personal prophecy contains particularistic information for the recipient and so the recipient plays some role in the evaluation.

Church leaders other than pastors are also reported to be involved in both types of prophecy, though this is less common. Interestingly, the person prophesying is reported to be more involved in evaluating personal prophecy (28.38 percent) as compared to congregational prophecy (20.73 percent). A very small percentage of the sample indicated that congregational prophecy (1.35 percent) and personal prophecy (2.03 percent) are not judged by anyone.

Table 6.24 Evaluation of congregational prophecy

Item	Proportion of sample (%)
Prophecy judged by a pastor or pastors	85.14
Prophecy judged by leaders other than pastors	41.89
Prophecy judged by other prophets present	33.11
Prophecy judged by everyone in the meeting	29.73
Prophecy judged by the one prophesying	20.27
Prophecy not judged	1.35

Table 6.25 Evaluation of personal prophecy

Item	Proportion of sample (%)
Prophecy judged by a pastor or pastors	66.22
Prophecy judged by the recipient	64.19
Prophecy judged by leaders other than pastors	36.49
Prophecy judged by the one delivering the prophecy	28.38
Prophecy not judged	2.03

In reviewing the results above, it is a concern that pastors are less frequently involved in evaluating personal prophecy as compared with congregational prophecy. This may possibly be due to the private setting in which personal prophecy takes place where pastors or church leaders are not present. However, there is great potential for abuse and manipulation if only the recipient and the one prophesying are involved in the evaluation.

6.8.5 The Purpose of Prophecy

6.8.5.1 D_9: What is the content of prophecy?

The purpose of prophecy is inextricably linked with the content of prophecy. The survey asked respondents how often congregational and personal prophecy contained various content categories. The content categories were then ranked in terms of their mean frequency as shown in table 6.26 and table 6.27. Both types of prophecy were found to have similar content. Prophecy most commonly contains encouragement and comfort, with similar mean values obtained for congregational and personal prophecy. Both forms of prophecy rarely contained judgment, doctrinal teaching, or rebuke. The sample also reported that prophecy rarely involves the prediction of future events.

The data points towards the same understanding observed in the literature review and earlier interviews. The content of prophecy suggests its purpose is to bring encouragement and comfort to the recipients. In addition, it is fairly common for prophecy to provide guidance in decision-making or to affirm a decision made in the past. The data shows that prophecy rarely consists of prediction, which is a finding consistent with Pentecostal literature. Prophecy also rarely consists of doctrinal teaching. This result complements the earlier data in section 6.8.1.3 showing that prophecy should not contradict the Bible and does not carry more authority than the Bible.

Table 6.26 Content of congregational prophecy

How often does congregational prophecy contain the following?	Mean	Std. deviation
Encouragement	4.22	.68
Comfort	4.10	.71
A call for physical healing	3.10	.68
A message for a specific individual	3.08	.82
Affirmation of a decision made in the past	2.96	.88
Correction	2.80	.82
Guidance to make a specific decision	2.79	.86
An exhortation to receive salvation	2.75	.94
Warnings	2.46	.80
Rebuke	2.26	.79
Doctrinal teaching	2.25	.94
Prediction of future events	2.22	.85
Judgment	1.92	.82

Table 6.27 Content of personal prophecy

How often does personal prophecy (to another person) contain the following?	Mean	Std. deviation
Encouragement	4.22	.64
Comfort	4.15	.63
Affirmation of a decision made in the past	3.04	.90
Guidance to make a specific decision	3.02	.79
A call for physical healing	2.83	.93
Correction	2.70	.87
Prediction of future events	2.58	.96
Warnings	2.35	.86
An exhortation to receive salvation	2.27	1.04
Rebuke	2.19	.93
Doctrinal teaching	2.11	.91
Judgment	1.84	.90

6.8.5.2 D_{10}: What is the effect of prophecy on the church?

The literature review discussed the Pentecostal affections of gratitude, compassion and courage as proposed by Steven Land.[29] It was also posited that prophecy stirs and cultivates these affections within the community of faith. For the survey, a series of statements were developed describing the expression of each of these affections based on Land's proposal. Respondents were then asked to rate each of these statements on a scale of one to five, indicating the impact of prophecy. Quality control was ensured through the random arrangement of statements and the inclusion of three control items. The mean score for each of the statements was calculated and the data are presented in the following tables.

---

29. Land, *Pentecostal Spirituality*.

Table 6.28 Influence of prophecy on gratitude

What is the impact of prophecy on a congregation?	Mean	Std. deviation
Prophecy brings praise to God.	4.34	.75
Prophecy reminds believers of God's mercy and grace.	4.30	.75
Prophecy results in thanksgiving to God.	4.22	.80
Prophecy emphasizes God's righteousness.	4.14	.88
Prophecy creates a sense of belonging to God's church.	3.63	1.06

Table 6.29 Influence of prophecy on compassion

What is the impact of prophecy on a congregation?	Mean	Std. deviation
Prophecy brings a sense of God drawing near.	4.39	.68
Prophecy emphasizes God's love.	4.21	.84
Prophecy motivates believers to live in holiness.	4.12	.86
Prophecy creates desire for Christ-likeness.	3.81	1.02
Prophecy stirs compassion for the "lost."	3.76	.99

Table 6.30 Influence of prophecy on courage

What is the impact of prophecy on a congregation?	Mean	Std. deviation
Prophecy brings trust in God.	4.36	.70
Prophecy stirs courage to overcome challenges.	4.32	.70
Prophecy brings hope for the future.	4.30	.68
Prophecy emphasizes God's power.	4.27	.77
Prophecy creates desire to witness for Christ.	3.61	1.08

Table 6.31 Items for quality control

What is the impact of prophecy on a congregation?	Mean	Std. deviation
Prophecy creates hostility towards God	1.47	.87
Prophecy emphasizes God as strict and controlling	1.68	1.02
Prophecy weakens believers' spiritual faith	1.48	.94

The results show a high mean score for all statements related with the Pentecostal affections. The low scores for the control items indicate that the respondents were accurately answering the survey. These results support the view that prophecy plays an active role in the formation and expression of Pentecostal affections. The similar mean scores suggest that prophecy has an equally significant influence across these affections.

6.9 SURVEY RESULTS: HYPOTHESIS-TESTING

6.9.1 Correlation Analysis

6.9.1.1 H_1: Background variables are correlated with prophetic activity

An independent-samples t-test was conducted to compare the ProphAct scores and CharExp scores for males and females (table 6.32). Levene's test was not statistically significant indicating that the assumption of equal variances between the groups was not violated. The study found no significant difference between males and females for the mean ProphAct scores (t = -0.342, p > 0.05) or the mean CharExp scores (t = -1.948, p > 0.05). The result shows that prophetic activity and personal charismatic experience are not correlated with the sex of the believer.

Table 6.32 Independent-sample t-test: ProphAct and CharExp by sex

	ProphAct		CharExp	
Sex	Mean	Std. deviation	Mean	Std. deviation
Male	3.213	1.161	4.168	1.073
Female	3.287	1.426	4.542	1.213
	t = -.342, p >.05		t = -1.948, p > .05	

Table 6.33 shows the result of an independent-samples t-test to compare the ProphAct scores and CharExp scores for single and married respondents.[30] Levene's test was not statistically significant indicating that the assumption of equal variances between the groups was not violated. The test shows no significant difference between the mean ProphAct scores (t = -0.142, p > 0.05) and the mean CharExp scores (t = -1.154, p > 0.05) for respondents who are single or married. Thus, prophetic activity and personal charismatic experience are not correlated with the marital status of the believer.

---

30. The survey questionnaire provided three options for marital status but all respondents only selected "married" or "single." The third option, "others," was not selected.

Table 6.33 Independent-sample t-test: ProphAct and CharExp by marital status

	ProphAct		CharExp	
Marital status	Mean	Std. deviation	Mean	Std. deviation
Single	3.224	1.258	4.161	1.171
Married	3.259	1.307	4.412	1.135
	$t = -.142, p > .05$		$t = -1.154, p > .05$	

A one-way ANOVA was performed to explore the relationship between the ProphAct scores and the respondents' educational level (table 6.34). This analysis was also performed with the CharExp scores for comparison. The respondents' educational level was recoded into the groups non-degree, bachelor degree, and master degree so as to produce groups of similar size. Levene's test was not statistically significant for both the ProphAct and the CharExp indicating that the assumption of equal variances between groups was not violated. There is no significant difference in the mean ProphAct scores ($F = 2.846$, $p > 0.05$) and the mean CharExp scores ($F = 0.97$, $p > 0.05$) for the different groups. Thus, there is no correlation between prophetic activity and educational level. Likewise, there is no correlation between personal charismatic experience and educational level. In fact, there is very little difference in the mean CharExp scores for all educational levels, suggesting that education has very little influence on personal charismatic experience.

Table 6.34 One-way ANOVA: ProphAct and CharExp by educational level

	ProphAct		CharExp	
Educational qualification	Mean	Std. deviation	Mean	Std. deviation
Non-degree	2.863	1.246	4.294	1.134
Bachelor	3.475	1.141	4.383	1.096
Master and above	3.316	1.390	4.296	1.226
	$F = 2.846, p > .05$		$F = .97, p > .05$	

Table 6.35 shows a one-way ANOVA to explore the relationship between the ProphAct scores and the respondents' role in the church. The analysis was repeated with the CharExp scores. Survey data was recoded into the four groups listed in the table. Levene's test revealed that the assumption of equal variances between groups was not violated. There were no significant differences between the groups for the mean ProphAct scores ($F = 0.680$, $p > 0.05$) and CharExp scores ($F = 0.350$, $p > 0.05$). These results

show there is no correlation between the respondent's role in the church and prophetic activity or personal charismatic experience.

Table 6.35 One-way ANOVA: ProphAct and CharExp by role in church

	ProphAct		CharExp	
	Mean	Std. deviation	Mean	Std. deviation
Group A	2.875	1.454	4.297	1.145
Group B	3.333	1.027	4.521	1.028
Group C	3.279	1.256	4.257	1.141
Group D	3.406	1.401	4.500	1.389
	F = .680, p > .05		F = .350, p > .05	
Note: Group A: Congregation member, ministry leader, and cell-group leader; Group B: Ministry staff; Group C: Pastor; Group D: Itinerant minister and missionary				

The relationship between the ProphAct scores and the respondents' age and DevoFreq scores were investigated using the Pearson product-moment correlation.[31] The correlation matrix can be seen in table 6.36. The results show that prophetic activity is not correlated with either age or devotion frequency. However, there is a medium positive correlation ($r = 0.304$, $p < 0.01$) between personal charismatic experience and devotion frequency.[32]

The results reject the hypothesis that prophetic activity is correlated with any of the background variables of sex, marital status, educational level, role in the church, age, or devotional frequency. This finding corresponds with the earlier result where 82.43 percent of the sample agree or strongly agree that all believers can prophesy. The results corroborate the general understanding among Pentecostals that the practice of prophecy is available to all believers regardless of their background.

A similar result was obtained showing personal charismatic experience to be unrelated with almost all background variables. Only devotion frequency showed a positive correlation with personal charismatic experience. This result differs from the study by Poloma, which showed charismatic experiences were positively correlated with sex, educational level, and age.[33] However, this study's results are consistent with Poloma's finding of

---

31. Instrument scales are treated as interval variables in this study. Bryman and Cramer, *Quantitative Data Analysis*, 70–71.

32. Cohen provides the following guidelines for interpreting the effect size of product-moment correlation: Small correlation $|r| = 0.10$ to 0.29; Medium correlation $|r| = 0.30$ to 0.49; Large correlation $|r| = 0.50$ to 1.00. Cohen, "A Power Primer."

33. Poloma, *Assemblies of God at the Crossroads*, 29–30.

a strong positive correlation between devotional activities and charismatic experiences. This correlation is expected since devotional activities often serve as the context for experiencing charismatic phenomena. Hence believers who engage more frequently in devotional activities should encounter more charismatic experiences. Surprisingly, this direct correlation was not found for prophetic activity. This finding will be discussed again in the later section on path analysis.

Table 6.36 Pearson correlation matrix

		1	2	3	4	5	6	7	8	9	10	11	12	13	14	15	16	17	18
1	Age																		
2	DevoFreq	ns																	
3	Psychoticism	ns	-.189*																
4	Extraversion	ns	ns	ns															
5	Neuroticism	ns	ns	ns	ns														
6	Lie	.280**	ns	ns	ns	-.299**													
7	ExamPray	ns	.179*	ns	ns	ns	ns												
8	TearsPray	ns	ns	ns	ns	.233**	ns	.286**											
9	SacraPray	ns	ns	ns	ns	.169*	ns	ns	.166*										
10	RestPray	.170*	.167*	ns	ns	ns	.166*	.502**	ns	ns									
11	RadPray	ns	ns	ns	.226**	.168*	ns	.454**	.291**	ns	ns								
12	SuffPray	.221**	ns	ns	ns	ns	ns	.461**	.455**	ns	.260**	.443**							
13	InterPray	ns	ns	ns	ns	ns	ns	.419**	.164*	ns	.201*	.445**	.612**						
14	PetPray	-.213*	ns	ns	ns	.343**	-.242**	.313**	ns	ns	ns	.426**	ns	.414**					
15	CharExp	ns	.304**	ns	.279**	ns	ns	.267**	ns	ns	.237**	.279**	.168*	ns	.215*				
16	FMS-V	.230**	.424**	ns	.270**	ns	ns	.362**	ns	ns	.308**	.276**	ns	.281**	.166*	.452**			
17	FMS-H	.250**	.182*	ns	.203*	ns	ns	.250**	ns	ns	ns	.314**	.383**	.406**	ns	.281**	.513**		
18	ProphAct	ns	ns	.171*	.268**	ns	ns	.171*	ns	ns	.174*	.186*	ns	ns	ns	.552**	.286**	.294**	
19	EvangAct	ns	.327**	ns	.287**	ns	ns	.336**	ns	ns	.222**	.260**	.228**	.326**	ns	.430**	.397**	.404**	.324**

ns: not significant
** Correlation is significant at the 0.01 level (2-tailed).
* Correlation is significant at the 0.05 level (2-tailed).

6.9.1.2 H_2: *Personality types are correlated with prophetic activity*

The personality types measured in the survey are psychoticism, extraversion, and neuroticism, together with the Lie Scale. The Pearson product-moment correlation matrix for the variables is shown in table 6.36. The results did not show neuroticism to have any correlation with prophetic activity, personal charismatic experiences, or evangelistic activity. Likewise, the Lie Scale did not demonstrate any correlation with these variables. However, extraversion has a small positive correlation with ProphAct ($r = 0.268$), with CharExp ($r = 0.279$), and with EvangAct ($r = 0.287$). These results suggest that believers with higher scores for extraversion tend to engage more in prophetic activity, encounter personal charismatic experiences, and engage more in evangelism. The effect sizes for all three correlations are about the same, showing that the strengths of the correlations are similar. The results also show that extraversion is positively correlated with the FMS-V ($r = 0.270$) and FMS-H ($r = 0.203$), indicating a positive correlation with Godward love and neighborly love respectively.

The results corroborate the hypothesis that extraversion is positively correlated with prophetic activity. The results also show that extraversion is positively correlated with personal charismatic experiences. These findings are consistent with other studies reviewed in the literature that demonstrate a positive correlation between extraversion and charismatic phenomena.[34] This relationship may be due to the attraction that sensation-seeking extraverts have towards the expressiveness of charismatic spirituality. In the case of prophecy, it is possible that extraverts are more willing to speak in public and share impressions that they sense come from God. Likewise, the positive correlation between extraversion and evangelism may be explained by the more sociable and assertive nature of extraverts.

Extraversion was also noted to have a positive correlation with Godward love and neighborly love. These correlations point towards a relationship between extraversion and spirituality.[35] Indeed, Maltby and Day have noted that a highly spiritual individual reflects the open, optimistic, and

---

34. Francis and Kay, "Personality Characteristics of Pentecostal Ministry Candidates"; Francis and Jones, "Personality and Charismatic Experience among Adult Christians."; Francis and Thomas, "Are Charismatic Ministers Less Stable?"; Kay, *Pentecostals in Britain*; Francis and Robbins, "Personality and Glossolalia."

35. Other studies have found a similar relationship. For example, see Maltby and Day, "Relationship between Spirituality and Eysenck's Personality Dimensions"; Maltby and Day, "Spiritual Involvement and Belief"; Rahanaiah, Rielage, and Sharpe, "Spiritual Well-Being and Personality"; Simpson, Newman, and Fuqua, "Spirituality and Personality."

carefree nature of the extravert.[36] In particular, the positive correlation with neighborly love is not surprising since extraverts tend to seek social interaction with others.

The results indicate a small positive correlation between psychoticism and prophetic activity (r = 0.171) though this is only significant at $p < 0.05$. This may indicate that believers who prophesy tend to be non-conforming and tough-minded. These traits would certainly be necessary when a believer delivers a prophecy calling for changes to the status quo or a prophecy that confronts the current behavior of believers. However, the earlier analysis showed the Psychoticism Scale lacked statistical reliability with a Cronbach alpha of only 0.30. Hence definitive conclusions should not be drawn from these results.

This study did not find a correlation between neuroticism and prophetic activity or between neuroticism and personal charismatic experience. Significantly, there is no evidence that prophetic activity and personal charismatic experience are related to emotionally unstable personalities. The literature survey earlier noted that some studies had found a negative correlation between charismatic activity and neuroticism while other studies showed they were unrelated. From these results, it is affirmed that prophetic activity and personal charismatic experience should not be related with psychopathology.

6.9.1.3 H_3: Prayer types are correlated with prophetic activity

Table 6.36 shows that ProphAct is positively correlated with RadPray (r = 0.186), RestPray (r = 0.174), and ExamPray (r = 0.171). This indicates that believers who engage in radical, rest, and examination prayers tend to report more prophetic activity. The effect size is similar for all three prayer types indicating similar strengths in correlation. In contrast, CharExp is positively correlated with the five prayer types RadPray (r = 0.279), ExamPray (r = 0.267), RestPray (r = 0.237), PetPray (r = 0.215), and SuffPray (r = 0.168). Thus, personal charismatic experience is correlated with petition and suffering prayers in addition to the prayer types which are correlated with prophecy.

The results corroborate the hypotheses that the radical, rest, and examination prayer types are positively correlated with prophetic activity. The rest of the prayer types did not show any statistically significant correlation. Radical prayers consist of bold, assertive prayers that seek to enact spiritual

---

36. Maltby and Day, "Spiritual Involvement and Belief," 190.

change.[37] Likewise, prophetic activity can be described as bold and assertive proclamations that call for a definite response from the recipients of the prophecy. Thus, the correlation may be explained by the consistent nature of both spiritual activities. The correlation also corresponds with the theme of courage that was identified in section 3.4.5.2. Courage was previously said to enhance the practice of prophecy. This theme may be expressed through radical prayer.

The examination prayer type describes inward soul-searching and evaluation whereas the rest prayer type emphasizes quietness and stillness in the presence of the divine.[38] Both prayer types bear strong similarity with the Pentecostal practice of "tarrying" before God.[39] This practice involves deep personal introspection, spiritual purification, and waiting for a fresh encounter with the Holy Spirit. Tarrying often results in charismatic manifestations and this practice may explain the positive correlation between examination and rest prayers with personal charismatic experiences as well as prophecy. In addition, Pentecostals hold a firm expectation that God speaks directly to those who seek God.[40] The posture presented by examination and rest prayers enables the believer to receive a prophetic message or revelation. These results corroborate the findings of another study where believers who practice what was termed "meditative prayer" were more likely to perceive communication from God (section 5.6.1).[41] Both types of prayer also correspond with the theme of intimacy that was identified in section 3.4.5.3. Examination and rest prayer increase spiritual intimacy that then enhances the practice of prophecy.

6.9.1.4 H_4: Personal charismatic experience is correlated with prophetic activity

The data shows a strong positive correlation between CharExp and ProphAct ($r = 0.552$). In fact, this is one of the strongest correlations in table 6.36. Thus, the results corroborate the hypothesis that personal charismatic

37. Ladd and Spilka, "Inward, Outward, and Upward," 479.

38. Ibid.

39. Castelo describes Pentecostal "tarrying" as "travailing, waiting, prostrating, and submitting oneself before the presence of God in hopes that God's presence might break forth in the mundane and profane circumstances of life." See Castelo, "Tarrying on the Lord," 50. Also see Albrecht, *Rites in the Spirit*, 183–84; Synan, *Century of the Holy Spirit*, 280; Tan, "Pentecostals and Charismatics in Malaysia and Singapore," 283.

40. Warrington, *Pentecostal Theology*, 216–18.

41. Poloma and Gallup, *Varieties of Prayer*, 61–63. This was discussed in section 5.6.1.

experience is correlated with prophetic activity. This correlation is expected since prophecy is itself a charismatic phenomenon. However, it is again emphasized that the CharExp scale items were limited to personal, individual experiences. Items that describe charismatic ministry to others were excluded to avoid overlap between the constructs for CharExp and ProphAct. The result indicates that charismatic experiences in private are positively correlated with prophetic ministry in public. Perhaps when believers are open to charismatic encounters for themselves, they are also open to engaging in charismatic ministry to others.

As previously mentioned, speaking in tongues (*glossolalia*) was not included as one of the CharExp scale items. This is not to suggest that *glossolalia* is unimportant to prophetic activity. It is possible that the high frequency of *glossolalia* among all respondents was foundational for the respondents to engage in prophecy and other charismatic phenomena. Indeed some have suggested that the Baptism of the Holy Spirit as evidenced by *glossolalia* serves as a doorway to prophetic-type gifts or that it confers more spiritual power for exercising these gifts.[42] Further investigation can be carried out on a data sample with varying frequencies of *glossolalia* in order to test these assertions.

6.9.1.5 H_5: *God-ward love and neighborly love are correlated with prophetic activity*

Table 6.36 shows that ProphAct has a small positive correlation with FMS-V ($r = 0.286$) and a small positive correlation with FMS-H ($r = 0.294$). Similarly, CharExp has a small positive correlation with FMS-H ($r = 0.281$) and a much stronger positive correlation with FMS-V ($r = 0.452$). These results corroborate the hypothesis that both God-ward love and neighborly love are correlated with prophetic activity. Likewise, God-ward love and neighborly love are also positively correlated with personal charismatic experience. These findings support studies reviewed in section 5.6.3 that postulate charismatic experiences as channels for the vertical flow of "love energy" into the believer that then flows out horizontally as compassion towards others. When understood from this perspective, prophetic activity becomes an expression of love and compassion. The believer who prophesies does so motivated by a compassion for others. The one prophesying also serves as a channel of divine love flowing from God to the recipients of the prophecy. Since God-ward love can be broadly understood as spiritual intimacy and

---

42. Anderson, "Baptism in the Holy Spirit," 8–10; Menzies and Menzies, *Spirit and Power*, 189–97.

neighborly love would likely include compassion, the themes identified in section 3.4.5 are affirmed through this quantitative study.

There are three other interesting observations that can be made from the correlation matrix concerning God-ward and neighborly love. First, the analysis shows that age is positively correlated with God-ward love ($r = 0.230$) and neighborly love ($r = 0.250$). Since physical age is likely a parallel to how long a respondent has been a believer, this positive correlation suggests natural spiritual growth and maturity taking place.

Second, the results show a positive correlation between devotional frequency and God-ward love ($r = 0.424$) as well as devotional frequency and neighborly love ($r = 0.182$). Thus, engaging in devotional activities like prayer and reading the Bible cultivates a love for God and for people. Interestingly, the results show the effect size is stronger for God-ward love than for neighborly love. This may be due to the items in the DevoFreq scale that focus on spiritual disciplines between the believer and God rather than between the believer and other people. Still, the results show that private spiritual disciplines between the believer and God results in an increase in love for other people.

Third, there are different prayer types which correlate with God-ward love and neighborly love. One would expect prayer types that emphasize the personal relationship between a believer and God would correlate strongly with God-ward love. The results show this is true with examination prayer ($r = 0.362$) and rest prayer ($r = 0.308$) demonstrating the two strongest correlations. Correspondingly, prayer types that emphasize the relationship between a believer and other people would be expected to show stronger correlations with neighborly love. The results again corroborate this with intercession prayer ($r = 0.406$) and suffering prayer ($r = 0.383$) showing the strongest correlations with neighborly love. It is also interesting to note the types of prayers that correlate with one type of love but not the other. Suffering prayer, which shows a connection with others experiencing distress, is only correlated with neighborly love. Petition prayer, comprising requests for personal physical and material needs, is only correlated with God-ward love. Likewise rest prayer correlates only with God-ward love since it emphasizes quietness and stillness in the presence of God. These direct correlations between prayer types and the types of love suggest that prayer activities cultivate the love relationships that a believer has with God and with others.

6.9.1.6 H_6: Evangelistic activity is correlated with prophetic activity

The results in table 6.36 show that ProphAct has a medium positive correlation with EvangAct (r = 0.324). In addition, EvangAct is positively correlated with CharExp (r = 0.430), FMS-V (r = 0.397), FMS-H (r = 0.404), and DevoFreq (r = 0.327). The results corroborate the hypothesis that evangelistic activity is correlated with prophetic activity. The results also indicate a direct positive correlation between evangelistic activity and personal charismatic experience, God-ward love, neighborly love, and devotional frequency.

The correlation between prophecy and evangelism was previously noted in the section 5.6.2. The studies that were discussed focused on charismatic phenomena in general though their instrument scales included items describing prophetic activity.[43] One possible reason for the relationship may be that evangelism is one of the purposes of prophecy. Certainly 1 Corinthians 14:24–25 suggests this relationship exists. Furthermore, Pentecostals understand the supernatural empowerment of the Holy Spirit to be an enablement specifically for evangelism (Acts 1:8). A second possible reason may be inferred from the rapid growth of the Pentecostal movement due to its strong emphasis on evangelism. Believers who embrace the practice of charismatic spirituality would also naturally embrace a lifestyle of evangelism. A third possible reason may be deduced from evangelistic activity's positive correlation with God-ward love and neighborly love. Similar correlations were previously noted for prophetic activity. This suggests that both God-ward love and neighborly love are functioning as the underlying motivations driving both prophetic activity and evangelistic activity. This possibility will be assessed in the next section using path analysis.

6.9.2 Path Analysis

The direct correlation analysis in the previous section did not assume causation or the direction of the correlations. In this section, path analysis will be performed to evaluate the previously proposed theological-conceptual model. This model assumes causation based on theory drawn from the earlier phases of this study.[44]

---

43. Poloma, *Assemblies of God at the Crossroads*, 31–33; Kay, *Pentecostals in Britain*, 245–64.

44. Bryman and Cramer, *Quantitative Data Analysis*, 313–14.

6.9.2.1 H_7: Independent variables influence prophetic activity and are mediated through the intervening variables personal charismatic experience, God-ward love, and neighborly love

A series of stepwise linear regression analyses were done based on the theological-conceptual model with prophetic activity as the dependent variable. The independent and intervening variables listed in table 6.37 were used as inputs for the multiple regression. Dichotomous variables (sex, marital status) were included in the analysis. Categorical data (role in the church, educational level) were excluded so as to reduce the number of input variables. While categorical data could be recoded into dichotomous variables so as to include them in the analysis, it was felt that this would have introduced too many input variables.[45] In any case, the excluded variables did not show any significant correlation with prophetic activity in the previous sections. The Psychoticism Scale was also excluded due to its poor statistical reliability.

A separate analysis revealed that the background variables of age, sex, and marital status did not show any significant correlation with extraversion and neuroticism. Hence, background variables and personality types were grouped together as independent variables. The earlier results showed some correlation between prayer types but they are still grouped together as independent variables to simplify the analysis. The input variables were selected based on previous theory and so stepwise regression was performed to obtain the fewest number of predictors for the model. In any case, performing a standard regression on the data produced the same statistically significant predictors for the model.

The results from the stepwise multiple regression are shown in table 6.38. The beta values provide the standardized regression coefficients and the R^2 values describe the amount of variance accounted for in the output variable. Issues with multicollinearity were avoided by checking the tolerance and variance inflation factor.[46] The path diagram in figure 6.2 was constructed from these results. The variables FMS-V and FMS-H were deemed as correlates due to their strong bivariate correlation and also because they actually form two sub-scales of the Faith Maturity Scale. A curved, dotted line was drawn to indicate the bivariate correlation between FMS-V and FMS-H (r = 0.513).[47] This curved line has arrowheads at either end to emphasize that causality may be in both directions.

---

45. Field, *Discovering Statistics Using SPSS*, 208–9.
46. Ibid., 196.
47. Bryman and Cramer, *Quantitative Data Analysis*, 318.

A QUANTITATIVE STUDY ON PROPHECY 203

Table 6.37 Variables for multiple regression with ProphAct and EvangAct

Independent variables	Intervening variables	Dependent variable
Age	Personal charismatic activity	Prophetic activity
Sex		Evangelistic activity
Marital status	God-ward love	
Devotional frequency	Neighborly love	
Extraversion		
Neuroticism		
Examination prayer		
Tears prayer		
Sacramental prayer		
Rest prayer		
Radical prayer		
Suffering prayer		
Intercession prayer		
Petition prayer		

Table 6.38 Stepwise multiple regression with ProphAct

Output	Resulting predictors	B	β	Sig.	R^2	F	Sig.
ProphAct	CharExp	.566	.510	.000	.326	32.144	.000
	FMS-H	.228	.151	.044			
FMS-H	InterPray	.296	.348	.000	.262	15.562	.000
	CharExp	.174	.237	.002			
	Age	.018	.219	.004			
FMS-V	CharExp	.135	.273	.000	.409	17.975	.000
	DevoFreq	.233	.265	.000			
	Age	.012	.215	.002			
	ExamPray	.158	.212	.003			
	Extraversion	.031	.172	.016			
CharExp	DevoFreq	.392	.220	.006	.229	9.713	.000
	Extraversion	.080	.219	.006			
	RestPray	.270	.200	.011			
	RadPray	.246	.191	.018			

Figure 6.2 Path diagram for ProphAct

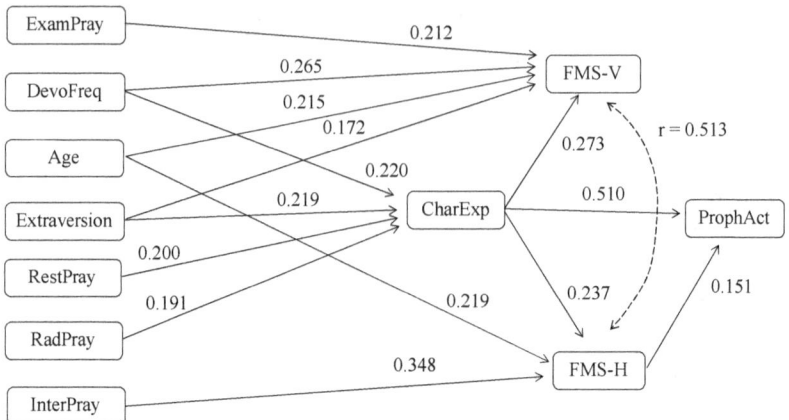

Results show that prophetic activity is primarily influenced by personal charismatic experience and neighborly love. These two explanatory variables account for 32.6 percent of the variance for prophetic activity. Significantly, none of the independent variables were found to have a direct influence on prophetic activity. This is in contrast to the earlier bivariate correlation analysis (table 6.36) that suggested several direct correlations. The path analysis shows that these independent variables indirectly influence prophetic activity through intervening variables.

The strongest predictor of prophetic activity is personal charismatic experience with a direct effect of 0.510 and an indirect effect of 0.036 through neighborly love. The other predictor of prophetic activity is neighborly love with a direct effect of 0.151. This result further supports the theory that prophetic activity serves as an expression of neighborly love and compassion. Alternatively, the pathway suggests that prophetic activity is motivated by the neighborly love of the believer. For neighborly love, the direct predictors are intercession prayer, personal charismatic experience, and age. These explanatory variables account for 26.2 percent of the variance in neighborly love. Both intercession prayer and personal charismatic experience may be interpreted as spiritual encounters where divine "love energy" is transferred from God into the believer. This "love energy" then manifests itself as neighborly love towards others in the form of practical ministry. Age also serves as an explanatory variable since neighborly love should grow with age as a mark of spiritual maturity. Surprisingly, extraversion does not have a direct influence with neighborly love though there is an indirect pathway through personal charismatic experience and possibly through God-ward love.

The results show that devotional frequency, extraversion, rest prayer, and radical prayer serve as explanatory variables for personal charismatic experience, accounting for 22.9 percent of the variance. The relationship between extraversion and personal charismatic experience was discussed earlier in section 6.9.1.2 and also observed in the literature survey. The earlier discussion also reasoned that devotional activities like prayer and reading the Bible functions as the context for believers to engage in personal charismatic activity. In particular, the model demonstrates that two types of prayer influence charismatic experience. Rest prayer, which emphasizes stillness and quietude, puts the believer in the posture to experience God through charismatic manifestations. Similarly, radical prayer, which is bold and assertive, is characteristic of Pentecostal prayer, especially when the believer is praying in tongues. These two types of prayer may seem to conflict with each other but both types are embraced within Pentecostal spirituality.

The intervening variable God-ward love was not found to have a direct influence on prophetic activity. This is surprising since the earlier analysis showed a bivariate correlation of $r = 0.286$. The path analysis shows that this apparent correlation was actually due to the confounding influence of personal charismatic activity and neighborly love. However, this study proposes that God-ward love serves as a correlate with neighborly love. This seems likely since an increase in a believer's love for God should likewise increase the believer's love for other people. If this were true, there would be an indirect pathway from God-ward love to prophetic activity. The predictors for God-ward love are devotion frequency, age, examination prayer, and extraversion. Age likely serves as an indication of spiritual maturity while devotional activities allow believers to grow in their relationship with God. Examination prayer emphasizes personal examination, evaluation, and devoting oneself to God; therefore increasing one's God-ward love. Other studies have noted the correlation between extraversion and spirituality and were discussed in section 5.5.3.

In summary, the results corroborate the hypothesis that personal charismatic experience and neighborly love serve as intervening variables in the theological-conceptual model. God-ward love was not found to have a direct influence on prophetic activity but may have an indirect pathway through neighborly love. Multiple regression identified the independent variables which indirectly influence the practice of prophecy through these intervening variables.

6.9.2.2 H_8: Independent variables influence evangelistic activity and are mediated through the intervening variables personal charismatic experience, God-ward love, and neighborly love

Stepwise multiple regression was performed based on the theological-conceptual model with evangelistic activity as the dependent variable. The same independent and intervening variables were used as in the previous section (table 6.37). The proposed model postulates that prophetic activity is not an explanatory variable for evangelistic activity. The regression result for evangelistic activity is seen in table 6.39. The regression results for the intervening variables remain the same as in table 6.38. The path diagram in figure 6.3 was constructed from these results.

Table 6.39 Stepwise multiple regression with EvangAct

Output	Resulting predictors	B	β	Sig.	R^2	F	Sig.
EvangAct	CharExp	.291	.274	.001	.304	13.298	.000
	FMS-H	.302	.221	.014			
	InterPray	.221	.187	.022			
	DevoFreq	.321	.174	.033			

The regression analysis was repeated a second time including ProphAct as one of the input variables. However, the result showed that ProphAct is not a predictor for EvangAct. This indicates that prophetic activity does not have an influence on evangelistic activity when controlling for the influences of the rest of the variables. Instead, the positive bivariate correlation between prophetic activity and evangelistic activity (section 6.9.1.6) is due to the effects of similar explanatory variables.

The predictors for evangelistic activity are personal charismatic experience, neighborly love, intercession prayer, and devotional frequency. Personal charismatic experience is the strongest predictor with a direct effect of 0.274 and an indirect effect of 0.052. Two reasons were previously suggested in section 6.9.1.6 for the direct relationship. First, supernatural empowering through charismatic manifestations is understood by Pentecostals to be an enablement for evangelism. Second, believers who embrace charismatic spirituality also embrace the Pentecostal movement's emphasis on evangelism. The indirect pathway through neighborly love suggests that personal charismatic experience causes an increase in neighborly love which is then expressed in evangelistic activity. This same pathway was observed for prophetic activity, suggesting that both prophetic activity and evangelistic activity are motivated by neighborly love within a believer.

Intercession prayer emphasizes seeking divine assistance for others. The path diagram suggests that believers who practice this type of prayer likewise experience a growth in neighborly love that then expresses itself in prophetic activity. The direct pathway from intercession to evangelism suggests that believers who pray to help others have a natural tendency to share the gospel for others' benefit. Devotional frequency also leads to more evangelistic activity as prayer and reading the Bible influences believers to obey the evangelistic mandate in Scripture.

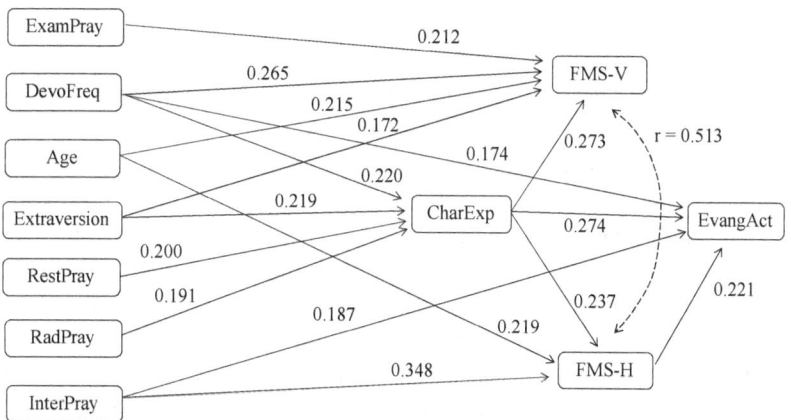

Figure 6.3 Path diagram for EvangAct

In summary, the results corroborate the hypothesis that personal charismatic experience and neighborly love serve as intervening variables for evangelistic activity. The analysis showed that prophetic activity is not a predictor for evangelistic activity but rather both prophecy and evangelism are influenced by similar explanatory variables. Thus, the correlation between prophecy and evangelism should not be interpreted as causative. Multiple regression has also identified the independent variables which have direct and indirect influences on evangelistic activity.

6.10 SUMMARY

This chapter has described the phase of empirical-theological testing in the study on the practice of prophecy. The chapter presents the details of a quantitative survey that was conducted among 148 AGS ministers. This sample forms 46.11 percent of the population under study and enables generalizations to be made for the population. The survey aimed to provide descriptive data and to test various hypotheses drawn from a proposed theological-conceptual model.

6.10.1 Summary of Descriptive Results

The large majority of the data sample considers an utterance in tongues followed by an inspired interpretation to be the equivalent of prophecy. There are mixed views on the equivalence of inspired preaching and prophecy with most considering them to be equivalent. However, there are a number who disagree or hold a neutral position. An overwhelming majority does not consider prophecy to have more authority than the Bible and thinks that prophecy should not contradict the Bible. The majority also does not think that prophecy carries more authority than pastors.

The most common spiritual experience initiating prophecy is when something comes to the mind of the believer. This may be in the form of a word or sentence, a general impression, a Scripture verse, or an internal picture. Most respondents report receiving the prophetic message progressively as they deliver the prophecy rather than receiving the entire message before they speak. The survey also reported roughly equal occurrences of prophetic messages in symbolic form and in plain and direct instruction. The large majority of respondents are not in a trance when they prophesy and are able to stop prophesying at will. Prophecy is usually expressed in words chosen by the one prophesying rather than in words divinely supplied by God.

The majority of respondents think that prophecy may contain errors and that it requires interpretation and application. Most also agree that prophecy can result in abuse. The most common criteria selected by respondents for judging prophecy are adherence to the Bible, spiritual discernment, and the character of the one prophesying. In judging prophecy, most feel that the evaluation should involve pastors. This applies to both congregational prophecy as well as personal prophecy.

The main content of both congregational and personal prophecy were reported to contain encouragement and comfort. Both forms of prophecy rarely contained judgment, doctrinal teaching, or rebuke. The survey also showed that the practice of prophecy both cultivates and expresses the Pentecostal affections of gratitude, compassion, and courage.

6.10.2 Summary of Hypothesis-testing

First, the hypothesis that prophetic activity is correlated with the background variables of sex, marital status, educational level, role in the church, age, or devotional frequency is rejected. This affirms the majority view of the respondents that all believers are able to engage in prophecy.

Second, the hypothesis that personality types are correlated with prophetic activity is partially corroborated. A small positive correlation was found between extraversion and prophetic activity but no correlation was found for either neuroticism or the Lie Scale. Psychoticism was found to have a small negative correlation but the Psychoticism Scale was deemed statistically unreliable for this sample.

Third, the results partially corroborate the hypothesis that prayer types are correlated with prophetic activity. Positive correlations were found between prophetic activity and the prayer types radical, rest, and examination. No correlations were found for the rest of the prayer types. These results correspond with the themes of intimacy and courage identified in section 3.4.5 of this study.

Fourth, the hypothesis that personal charismatic experience is correlated with prophetic activity is corroborated. The results show a strong positive correlation between these two variables. This is not surprising since prophecy is itself considered a charismatic phenomenon.

Fifth, the hypotheses that God-ward love and neighborly love are correlated with prophetic activity are partially corroborated. Both types of love show a positive correlation with almost the same effect size. However, the later analysis using multiple regression showed that God-ward love does not have a direct influence on prophetic activity when the effects of other explanatory variables are controlled. The apparent direct correlation is actually due to the confounding influence of personal charismatic experience and neighborly love. The correlation with neighborly love corresponds with the theme of compassion identified in section 3.4.5.1 of this study.

Sixth, the results corroborate the hypothesis that evangelistic activity is correlated with prophetic activity. The subsequent multiple regression showed that this correlation is due to the influence of similar predictors rather than any direct causation between prophecy and evangelism.

Seventh, the hypothesis that independent variables influence prophetic activity and are mediated through the intervening variables personal charismatic experience, God-ward love, and neighborly love was partially corroborated. The results show that personal charismatic experience and neighborly love function as intervening variables but not God-ward love. However, this study has proposed that God-ward love may still have an indirect influence through neighborly love. The results show there are indirect causal pathways for devotion frequency, extraversion, rest prayer, and radical prayer through personal charismatic experience to prophetic activity. There are also indirect causal pathways from intercession prayer and age through neighborly love to prophetic activity.

Eighth, the results partially corroborate the hypothesis that independent variables influence evangelistic activity and are mediated through the intervening variables personal charismatic experience, God-ward love, and neighborly love. Personal charismatic experience and neighborly love were found to be intervening variables but not God-ward love. Instead, God-ward love was again found to be a spurious variable due to the confounding influence of other variables. Evangelistic activity is also directly influenced by the independent variables intercession prayer and devotional frequency. Prophetic activity was not found to be a predictor of evangelistic activity.

6.10.3 Conclusion

The results of the empirical-theological testing have provided significant data in understanding the practice of prophecy within the AGS. This data serves to answer the research questions posed at the beginning of this chapter. The proposed theological-conceptual model has also been refined through stepwise multiple regression to arrive at the model shown in the path diagrams for prophetic activity and evangelistic activity. The next chapter will discuss and reflect theologically on the results to make proposals for an empirical-theological understanding of prophecy.

7

Theological Reflection and Conclusion

7.1 INTRODUCTION

This study has followed the empirical-theological cycle proposed by Van der Ven to examine the practice of prophecy within the AGS. The four phases of theological problem and goal development, theological induction, theological deduction, and empirical testing have been completed. This chapter continues with the final phase of theological evaluation consisting of theological reflection as well as methodological reflection. The study has provided a rich understanding of the practice of prophecy from the qualitative interviews, literature review, and the quantitative analysis of survey results. This data will now be brought together and points of convergence will be reflected upon in terms of their meaning, significance, and relevance. Specifically, the nature, purpose, and practice of prophecy will be discussed. The study will then seek to situate the practice of prophecy within the larger context of Pentecostal spirituality. Finally, this chapter will reflect and evaluate the research methodology adopted by this study.

7.2 THE NATURE AND CHARACTERISTICS OF PROPHECY

7.2.1 Summary of Findings

The data from this study shows a convergence in understanding contemporary prophecy as the reception and communication of a spontaneous revelation that is believed to originate from God. The study of Pentecostal literature showed an emphasis on understanding prophecy in the New Testament in relation with ἀποκάλυψις. This revelation brings a divine message that is not solely meant for the person receiving it but must be communicated to other intended recipients.

Within Pentecostalism, prophecy is distinguished from preaching and charismatic exegesis. Preaching and teaching involve study, reflection, and composition of a message. In contrast, prophecy arises spontaneously and communicates an immediate revelation. This understanding was seen in the interviews with AGS senior pastors. The interviews reported in section 3.4.2 described spontaneous prophecies occurring in a corporate service and in personal settings. In addition, respondents in section 6.8.2 reported that prophecy was initiated by spiritual experiences where a word, sentence, impression, image, or Scripture verse spontaneously came to their minds. The majority of survey respondents also reported receiving the prophetic message while they were delivering it; again emphasizing its spontaneous nature. This agrees with the interview accounts where prophecy was described as a "torrential rain" of words or a "flow" of words while prophesying.

While the spontaneous nature of prophecy led to the interruption—though not disruption—of congregational services, the study also found accounts where prophetic messages came after a period of "waiting on God" (section 3.4.3.1). The time spent "waiting" would involve the believer engaging in the examination and rest prayer types as outlined in section 6.9.1.3. Both these prayer types were found to correlate positively with prophetic activity. While these instances entail a period of seeking and waiting, the prophetic message still arises spontaneously and is not a message produced from study and reflection.

The study shows that Pentecostals consider prophecy to be subject to the authority of Scripture. While Pentecostals acknowledge prophecy as revelation, they do not accept contemporary prophecy to be the equivalent of Scripture in their praxis. The literature review showed a wide variety of prophecy in the Bible and that not all prophecy resulted in the writing of Scripture. Furthermore, Pentecostal literature contains strong exhortations to evaluate prophetic messages by testing it against the Bible. This practice was well attested to in both the interviews with AGS senior pastors and also in the quantitative survey results. Almost all respondents cited adherence to the Bible as the most important criterion for evaluating prophecy (section 6.8.1.3). Furthermore, the majority of respondents explicitly state that the Bible and pastors are superior in authority to prophecy. Respondents also reported that it was very rare for prophecy to contain any doctrinal teaching that might be confused with biblical instruction. In cases where the content does contain doctrinal teaching, the prophecy would still be subject to evaluation based on the established teachings of Scripture. Within this study, there was no evidence to suggest that the contemporary practice of prophecy adds to the biblical canon, challenges Scripture, or is accorded the same authority as Scripture.

Another point of convergence in the study is the finding that all believers have the potential to prophesy. This potential is in line with the "prophethood" of believers discussed in section 4.2.1 where all believers are charismatically empowered for vocational ministry. This understanding is also attested to in the survey where 82.43 percent held that all believers are able to prophesy. The empirical data adds support to this view since no significant correlations were found between prophecy and sex, marital status, educational level, role in the church, or age (section 6.9.1.1). In considering personality traits, only extraversion was found to be positively correlated with prophecy. No significant correlation was found for neuroticism while a definitive result for psychoticism was not possible due to the lack of scale reliability. Thus, the results suggest that believers who score lower on the Extraversion Scale are less likely to engage in prophecy. It was suggested that believers who are extraverts might simply be more comfortable with public speaking and hence engage in public prophecy more frequently. It seems unlikely that God only gives prophetic messages to the extraverts. The negative correlation with introversion may simply be the lack of courage to speak up in public rather than an innate inability to engage in prophecy. Based on the above findings, this study concludes that the ability to prophesy is independent of background factors and most personality traits. An important qualification here is that while all believers can prophesy, not all believers will actually engage in prophecy; ultimately, spiritual gifts are the sovereign activity of the Holy Spirit (1 Cor 12:11).

While prophetic activity is independent of a believer's background, the empirical data shows that prophecy is influenced by a believer's spiritual maturity. The results show a positive correlation between prophecy and the FMS-V and the FMS-H. Both these scales are sub-scales of the Faith Maturity Scale and were used in this study to operationalize God-ward love and neighborly love. As described in section 6.7.1, the scales measure the degree in which the respondent embodies a vibrant and life-transforming faith. Hence, the positive correlation explicitly shows a correlation between prophecy and spiritual maturity. The path analysis also showed that devotional frequency and prayer had a positive effect on the FMS-V and the FMS-H, which in turn influenced prophecy. Greater devotional frequency and an active prayer life are characteristic of spiritual maturity and so the path analysis again highlights a positive relationship between spiritual maturity and prophetic activity. Closely related with this, the interview data recorded in section 3.4.5.3 also speak of intimacy with God as a factor enabling the practice of prophecy.

There are two other ways in which spiritual maturity influences the practice of prophecy. The first way is in the regular use of Scripture in the practice of prophecy. Section 6.8.2.1 showed that the third most common means of initiating prophecy was a Scripture verse coming to the mind of the believer. This presumes that the believer is familiar with Scripture and is able to correctly interpret it. Scripture is further reported to be the most important criterion used to judge prophecy. While pastors normally do the evaluation, the one prophesying should likewise have a knowledge of the Bible and Christian doctrine to judge for oneself what is being proclaimed. Since Bible knowledge is characteristic of spiritual maturity, it seems reasonable that spiritually mature believers are more involved in prophecy. Less spiritually mature believers who lack Bible knowledge may still prophesy. However, the process of evaluating prophecies would likely reveal issues and the believer would probably be restricted from prophesying by the church leadership.

A second way in which prophecy is influenced by spiritual maturity is seen in the criteria used for evaluating prophecy. A majority of respondents cited the character of the one prophesying as an important criterion (section 6.8.4.1). This suggests that those who prophesy should be spiritually mature believers who are actively participating in the community of faith. New believers or those who are less spiritually mature would be less engaged in the faith community. Hence the process of evaluating prophecies would likely restrict them from prophesying till they are more active within the church and the church leadership is more assured of their character and maturity. This was described in the interviews in section 3.4.4. Furthermore, the concern for the abuse of prophecy would restrict the actual practice of prophecy to believers who are familiar to and trusted by the faith community.

This study has also demonstrated that love plays an important role in the practice of prophecy. The theme of love was first identified in the interviews in section 3.4.5.1. This theme was then studied in the quantitative analysis that then showed God-ward love and neighborly love functioning as mediating variables between predictor variables and prophecy. The path analysis indicated that devotional frequency, prayer, and personal charismatic experiences lead to increases in both forms of love. While only neighborly love was found to have a direct influence with prophetic activity, God-ward love was postulated to have an indirect influence through neighborly love. The pathway identified in this study highlights the importance of vertical love and horizontal love as a motivation behind prophecy and evangelism.

7.2.2 Theological Reflection

7.2.2.1 *Prophecy within the Theo-dramatic Hermeneutic*

This study has used the theo-dramatic proposal of Vanhoozer to serve as the hermeneutical framework for practical theology.[1] Within this framework, practical theology serves to facilitate a dialectic between Scripture as the canonical script and contemporary praxis which is the church's performance of the faith. The playwright and producer of the drama are analogous to God the Father while Jesus Christ is analogous to the lead actor. Within this metaphor, the Holy Spirit is analogous to the director. Applying this theo-dramatic hermeneutic to this study yields several insights.

First, the study emphasizes the role of the Holy Spirit as the director of the performance of the faith. The Holy Spirit divinely inspired the canonical authors in the writing of Scripture. The data from this study also show that the Holy Spirit is at work within the community of faith, illuminating the study of Scripture, prompting and directing prayer activity, and renewing believers in charismatic encounters. Prophecy is described in 1 Corinthians 12:1 and 14:1 as among matters concerning the Holy Spirit (πνευματικά). 1 Corinthians 12:7 continues to describe prophecy as one of the φανέρωσις of the Holy Spirit. This clearly shows a biblical understanding of the relationship between prophecy and the Holy Spirit. Thus, prophecy may be considered the voice of the Holy Spirit as the theo-dramatic director, guiding the church towards a faithful and critical performance. The Holy Spirit already works within believers through promptings and impressions, guiding them in their spiritual walk. Prophecy extends that into the corporate community and gives tangible voice to the Spirit's promptings. Vanhoozer's concept of "transposing praxis" makes the role of prophecy even more crucial to ensure consistency and correspondence between the praxis of Scripture and the praxis of the church today. Prophecy is the voice of the divine director in

---

1. Vanhoozer, *Drama of Doctrine*.

guiding, encouraging, exhorting, and correcting the community of faith. As suggested by Vanhoozer, the Holy Spirit can also be viewed as the prop master, clothing or accessorizing the church with the gift of prophecy so that it is equipped for a fitting performance.[2] However, prophecy and all improvisations in the performance remain under the authority of the canonical script as empirically demonstrated in this study.

Second, this study demonstrates the continuity that Pentecostals see between Scriptural narratives and their present lives. Pentecostals were earlier noted in section 2.5.2.2.1 to embrace a fusion between the horizons of Scripture and their present world.[3] While Vanhoozer notes a gulf between Scripture and Christian praxis, Pentecostals have readily accepted the narratives within Scripture to be their own. There is an enthusiastic expectation for the contemporary life of the church to be a continuation of the narratives of the early church. Pentecostals generally understand themselves to be a community of prophets who bear Spirit-inspired witness to Christ and engage in Spirit-empowered ministry.[4] The practice of prophecy discussed in this study is one example of this posture. Since prophecy is common in the narratives of Scripture, prophecy should likewise be common in the life of the contemporary church.[5] Thus, a theo-dramatic hermeneutic is a fitting framework for examining Pentecostal praxis and may be useful for other investigations on Pentecostalism.

In addition, Village provides an interesting perspective on the relationship between Scripture and Pentecostal praxis. His empirical study shows a close relationship between charismatic experience and a literal interpretation of Scripture.[6] While caution should be exercised in suggesting cause and effect, it seems reasonable that believers who personally experience miraculous manifestations such as prophecy would lean towards a literal interpretation of miraculous manifestations in Scripture. This suggests a somewhat iterative influence between Pentecostal hermeneutics and Pentecostal praxis.[7] A Pentecostal reading of Scripture creates an expectation of charismatic manifestations today.[8] Charismatic encounters in turn lead the

2. Ibid., 448.

3. Martin, "Introduction to Pentecostal Hermeneutics," 5–7; Menzies, *Pentecost*, 21–39.

4. Menzies, *Pentecost*, 27–31; Petts, *Body Builders*, 44; Stronstad, *Prophethood of All Believers*.

5. Ellington, "Locating Pentecostals at the Hermeneutical Round Table," 217; Warrington, *Pentecostal Theology*, 193.

6. Village, *Bible and Lay People*, 149–51.

7. Ellington, "Locating Pentecostals at the Hermeneutical Round Table," 214–17.

8. The Pentecostal movement is essentially restorationist in viewing the biblical

believer to hold a literal interpretation of the Bible and this perpetuates the Pentecostal hermeneutic. Once again, the metaphor of theo-drama captures this on-going dialectic between the canonical script and contemporary praxis.

7.2.2.2 Prophecy and Love

The theme of love within Pentecostalism was earlier discussed in section 5.6.3. In particular, the diamond-model of "godly love" was noted to propose that dynamic interaction between God and believers leads to a flow of "love energy" from God into believers and subsequently flows outwards to others in the form of ministry such as prophecy and evangelism.[9] The findings of this current study were already noted to agree with this basic proposal. This study has shown personal charismatic experiences as one of the main channels through which the dynamic interaction takes place. It is these charismatic encounters with God that result in the cultivation of divine love in the life of the believer. Once again, it is emphasized that the Personal Charismatic Experience Scale employed in this study was limited to personal experiences between the individual and God. It excluded items related to charismatic ministry to others. This enabled the study to focus on how a vertical interaction between the believer and God influences the horizontal interaction between the believer and others. The results show that charismatic experiences play a crucial role within the Pentecostal church in the cultivation of a *habitus* of love. Other spiritual disciplines such as Bible-reading and certain types of prayer are also empirically shown to cultivate love within the believer, hence influencing the practice of prophecy. However, it is charismatic encounters that distinguish the Pentecostal church from others within the Christian family. It is also these charismatic encounters that result in the strongest influence on the practice of prophecy.

Theologically, the relationships outlined above can be explained by the proposals discussed in section 5.6.3. God-ward love and neighborly love encompass the Pentecostal affections of gratitude and compassion respectively. Personal charismatic experiences like singing in tongues, experiencing a fresh infilling of the Spirit, being "slain in the Spirit," and receiving personal divine guidance results in the stirring and cultivation of

---

narratives, particularly the book of Acts, as the ideal model for the church today. Hence patterns found in Scripture are considered repeatable in contemporary church life. See Martin, "Introduction to Pentecostal Hermeneutics," 7.

9. Poloma and Hood, *Blood and Fire*; Lee and Poloma, *Sociological Study of the Great Commandment*.

these Pentecostal affections. The charismatic encounters lead the believer deeper into the *koinonia* of God, resulting in growth in intimacy with God and sharing in God's compassion for humanity. Compassion is expressed through prophecy so as to bring edification, encouragement, and comfort to others in the faith community. Prophecy brings the love of God into specific contexts through a divinely inspired message so that recipients sense God's love and concern for them individually and collectively. Significantly, the path analysis also shows that neighborly love reaches out to unbelievers through evangelistic practices. Believers who are touched by the love of God will naturally seek to bring others into the faith community so that they too can enter into a redemptive relationship with Christ and so enter into the *koinonia* of God.

When considering the activity of the Spirit, Pentecostals have tended to focus on the charismatic dimension and viewed Spirit baptism as a vocational empowerment for ministry.[10] This has led Pentecostals to focus on the theme of power when discussing the ministry of spiritual gifts. Pentecostals see the Holy Spirit empowering the church with spiritual gifts so that the church may serve as a powerful witness to the world and to see evangelism and church growth take place. Unfortunately, this emphasis has resulted in a lack of discussion on love as a central theme in the activity of the Spirit and in spiritual gifts.

One possible reason for this separation between the themes of love and power is due to the distinction often made between a Pauline and Lukan perspective of Spirit-baptism.[11] Pentecostals have clung to this distinction, in part, to argue for their position that the Baptism of the Holy Spirit is a subsequent and separate event from salvation. Unfortunately, this distinction has also resulted in the compartmentalization of the work of the Holy Spirit and the themes accompanying it. The end result is a separation between the soteriological theme of love associated with the Pauline perspective and the charismatic theme of power associated with the Lukan perspective.

A second possible reason may be found in the historical development of the Pentecostal movement in North America. Pentecostalism was birthed in the context of a Wesleyan-Holiness revival that interpreted the baptism of the Holy Spirit as "entire sanctification" or "perfect love."[12] Subsequently, a schism in the movement took place with one group led by William Durham

---

10. Palma, *Holy Spirit*, 164–66; Wyckoff, "Baptism in the Holy Spirit," 447–51.

11. Hart, "Spirit-Baptism"; Keener, *Gift & Giver*, 147–69; Macchia, *Baptized in the Spirit*, 28–29.

12. Anderson, *Introduction to Pentecostalism*, 29.

holding to the view of progressive sanctification and rejecting the concept of "entire sanctification."[13] Those who held to Durham's "finished work" theology understood the baptism of the Holy Spirit in purely charismatic terms. Some of the churches aligned with this position eventually birthed the AG denomination with Durham's view becoming the dominant position within the Pentecostal movement. Thus, the separation of sanctification from Spirit-baptism caused the Pentecostal church to focus on the concept of power rather than love.

This present study has provided an important insight into the relationship between prophecy and love. The results lend support to Macchia's proposal for Spirit-baptism to be understood as a baptism in divine love.[14] This expands the Pentecostal understanding of Spirit-baptism to integrate both soteriological and charismatic perspectives, integrating the themes of love and power. For Macchia, Spirit-baptism is primarily relational in that it brings the believer into fellowship with the Trinitarian God-head.[15] The experience of divine love results in the transformation of the believer and divine love then reaches out through the believer in the form of empowered ministry. This approach integrates love with power in the activity of spiritual gifts like prophecy, as demonstrated in the results of this present empirical study.

The integration of love and power in the practice of prophecy finds strong biblical support in 1 Corinthians 13. While discussing spiritual gifts from 1 Corinthians 12 to 14, the apostle Paul felt it important to locate an exposition on love right at the heart of the discourse. Paul's teaching indicates that love is meant to be the motivating force guiding prophecy and all other spiritual gifts. The empirical data from this study shows that this assertion is indeed occurring within the research context. Locating prophecy firmly within the themes of both love and power prevents spiritual gifts from being wrongly perceived as simply "raw power" without guidance or context.[16] However, this is not to suggest that prophetic activity serves as a measure of compassion among believers. Paul's correction of the church at Corinth who were wrongly exercising spiritual gifts should serve as sufficient caution against this assumption.

Locating prophecy within the theme of love provides an additional insight for the theo-dramatic metaphor discussed in the previous section.

---

13. Ibid., 45–47; Anderson, "Varieties, Taxonomies, and Definitions," 17; Macchia, *Baptized in the Spirit*, 28–33; Synan, *Century of the Holy Spirit*, 123–24.

14. Macchia, *Baptized in the Spirit*.

15. Ibid., 259–61.

16. Ibid., 18.

Prophecy and other spiritual gifts may be viewed as the theo-dramatic performance of divine love within the drama of redemption. The Holy Spirit brings an infilling of divine love into the hearts of all believers (Rom 5:5). Believers who live by the Spirit bear the fruit of the Spirit which includes love (Gal 6:22). The empirical evidence from this study suggests that love is cultivated in believers as they study the canonical script, engage in prayer activities, and encounter the Spirit of love. The path analysis shows all these activities bring about the growth in God-ward love and neighborly love. Applying Vanhoozer's metaphor of theo-drama, these activities result in the shaping of the believer's *habitus* and identity to take after the God of love (1 John 4:7–8, 16). To be clear, Vanhoozer's proposal is limited only to the church's identity formation through the study of Scripture. Still, it is useful to stretch the metaphor in discussing the effect of prayer and charismatic experiences. The shaping of the *habitus* results in the believer becoming an incarnation of divine love. Divine love leads to and is expressed through prophecy so that others both within and without the church experience Christ. Thus, a fresh perspective of prophecy as the theo-dramatic performance of love is proposed by this study.

7.2.2.3 Prophecy and Spontaneity

The spontaneous nature of prophecy is an embodiment of the spontaneity that is characteristic of Pentecostalism.[17] Pentecostals believe that God is dynamic, active, and immanent, intervening in this world to address the church and to direct its activities. Pentecostals do not see a worship service as merely consisting of human-led activities. There is an ardent expectation to encounter the living God through manifestations of the Holy Spirit such as prophecy. Pastors are expected to be "led by the Spirit" in their conduct of the worship service, allowing prophecy to change the order of the service or even the whole direction of ministry. Albrecht has described the "waiting" or "tarrying" before God as a mode of contemplation where believers adopt deep receptivity and openness for the manifestation of the Holy Spirit in their midst.[18] He explains: "The 'tarry until' attitude of the Pentecostal mode of contemplation generally holds sway, that is, it waits as a preparation for what it cannot control."[19] It is precisely this surrender of control that brings about the characteristic spontaneity.

---

17. Ma, "Pentecostal Worship in Asia," 145–47.
18. Albrecht, *Rites in the Spirit*, 183–84.
19. Ibid., 184. Also see Castelo, "Tarrying on the Lord," 50.

There seems to be an inherent tension between the spontaneous nature of prophecy and the need to maintain order within a congregational service. Often, prophecy is restricted to specific points within the order of service. Pentecostal services usually begin with a time of singing and testimonies dominated by what Albrecht describes as the mode of celebration.[20] This often turns into a period of "free worship" where believers are able to freely express themselves through singing or through shouts of praise, in their own language or in tongues. Next, the mode of contemplation becomes dominant and it is within this portion of the service that opportunity is given for believers to prophesy.[21] Pastors would normally be able to prophesy at any point during the service since they are directing the service from the front. However, congregational members would generally be limited to prophesy only during this portion of time so as to avoid disruption and disorder. As this practice becomes ritualized, the result might be the loss of spontaneity in the practice of prophecy. More importantly, the practice may communicate that believers have some element of control over the Holy Spirit and are able to invoke spiritual gifts when desired.

The need to evaluate prophecy so as to prevent abuse also leads to tension with the spontaneity of prophecy. The interviews recorded in section 3.4.4 showed that some churches require believers to seek permission before prophesying. This allows the pastor to briefly evaluate the prophecy as well as the believer who wishes to prophesy. This further limits when and how prophecy might take place in a congregation. In some cases where the congregation size is large, prophecies cannot even be heard without the use of a microphone and sound system. Again, the spontaneity for prophecy to occur seems curtailed at the congregational service platform.

In view of the issues raised above, there is a necessity for practical guidelines to encourage and yet regulate spiritual gifts like prophecy. This includes educating the congregation about prophecy, providing space in the order of service for manifestations, and having clear guidelines on how to evaluate and respond to prophecy. This will be discussed further in section 7.4.2.1.

7.2.2.4 Prophecy and Biblical Authority

The literature review showed that Pentecostals have a high regard for the authority of Scripture and insist that all prophecies do not supersede the Bible. The results from this study certainly bear testimony to this reality. While

---

20. Albrecht, *Rites in the Spirit*, 183–85.
21. Ibid., 183–84.

Pentecostals may prize spiritual experiences, this study suggests that there is a firm belief in Scripture as objective truth by which impressions from the Holy Spirit must be judged. Furthermore, since prophecy is reported to rarely contain doctrinal teaching, it would be unlikely for prophecy to challenge the Bible.

Some scholars who believe in the cessation of prophecy suggest that the contemporary practice leads to claims of revelation that are on par with the biblical canon.[22] This is not true for the phenomenon that is the focus of this study. Criticisms against Pentecostals seem to portray a regular occurrence of church leaders depending on prophecy for their doctrinal teaching. The empirical reality shows this is not taking place and that prophecy holds a much lower level of authority, below both the Bible and pastoral leadership. Prophecy within this study functions mainly to bring encouragement and comfort. Therefore, there seems little cause for concern as raised by critics unless this is considered usurping the authority of the Bible.

At least one critic of prophecy has shared that guidance and direction from the Holy Spirit must remain anchored upon Scripture.[23] In this regard, it may actually be possible for some critics to accept one form of prophecy occurring within the AGS. The study showed that prophecy might occur when a Scripture verse arises spontaneously in the mind of the minister who then proclaims it as a message for practical application within the congregation. In fact, this was the third most common spiritual experience reported to initiate prophecy in this study. Perhaps this form of prophecy would be acceptable to critics as it remains anchored on guidance from the truth of Scripture. However, it is likely that critics would define this phenomenon as divine guidance, discernment, or inspired preaching rather than as prophecy. If this were the case then the argument would move on to the definition of phenomena rather than on what is actually practiced. It is hoped that empirical studies like this present one helps to demonstrate what charismatic phenomena are in reality and bring greater clarity for discussion and reflection.

7.3 THE PURPOSE OF PROPHECY

7.3.1 Summary of Findings

The phase of theological induction earlier identified four purposes of prophecy as edification of the church, sign of God's attitude, evangelism and

---

22. Gaffin, "A Cessationist View," 46–47, 51–54; MacArthur, *Charismatic Chaos*, 82.
23. Gaffin, "A Cessationist Response to Robert L. Saucy," 154–55.

church growth, and personal guidance. The phase of empirical-theological testing found empirical support for all these purposes in terms of corporate and personal prophecy. A fifth purpose was later identified as the cultivation of the Pentecostal affections. In one sense, all these purposes can be broadly categorized as edification. However, distinctions have been made so as to allow further discussion of each area.

First, the study found that prophecy results in edification of the church. Prophecy may contain a wide range of content as shown in section 6.8.5.1. Some of the more common content include encouragement, comfort, a call for physical healing, affirmation of a decision made previously, and guidance for decision-making. Regardless of the content, the purpose in all these instances is to bring spiritual growth to believers' lives. Equally important, this study shows that prophecy rarely contains doctrinal teaching or judgment.

Prophecy also results in edification as its practice implicitly communicates a message of unity within the faith community. The activity of spiritual gifts emphasizes the *koinonia* within the community as believers minister one to another (Rom 12:4-8; Eph 4:11-13). Furthermore, the study shows that spiritual gifts depend on each other for proper functioning. For example, a message in tongues needs the interpretation of tongues for the message to be understood; a prophecy which calls on sick believers to receive divine healing requires the activity of the gift of healing so that people can receive ministry. All this emphasizes the interdependence of believers within the faith community and underscores the emphasis of Paul in 1 Corinthians 12:12-30 and Romans 12:4-8. Believers need one another to exercise their different spiritual gifts to fully minister to the faith community and to ensure health and wholeness. Such interdependence emphasizes the community life that is characteristic of the church. It also prevents believers from growing proud and exalting their spiritual gifts above others as they recognize their mutual need for each other (Rom 12:3).

A second purpose of prophecy is to function as a sign of God's attitude towards the faith community (section 4.3.2). The manifestation of prophecy reveals that God is present, active, and concerned about the congregation. The results in section 6.8.5.2 show awareness of God's presence, power, and provision through prophecy. Thus, the presence of charismatic manifestations such as prophecy, tongues, and divine healing may be interpreted to function as a sign of God's blessing upon a local congregation (1 Cor 14:22-25). These manifestations reinforce the identity of the faith community as one that is charismatically empowered for life and ministry.

The third purpose of prophecy is to bring about evangelism and church growth. The study found a correlation between prophecy and evangelism and proposed possible reasons for this relationship (section 6.9.1.6). Prophecy brings the reality of God to non-believers and this may lead to their conversion to the Christian faith. The study also found that prophecy and evangelism were related through neighborly love serving as a common motivating force.

The fourth purpose of prophecy is to provide guidance for making decisions. Prophecy may guide believers in decisions that lie before them or it may provide affirmation of decisions that were made in the past. Interestingly, this role was found to be more common in personal prophecy than in corporate prophecy (section 6.8.5.1).

A fifth purpose of prophecy identified during empirical-theological testing was the cultivation of Pentecostal affections. The survey results in section 6.8.5.2 showed widespread affirmation of statements reflecting prophecy's impact on the Pentecostal affections of gratitude, compassion, and courage. Furthermore, this study has already proposed that prophecy functions as an extension of prayer. Thus, the results lend credence to the proposal that Pentecostal affections are primarily formed and expressed through prayer.[24]

7.3.2 Theological Reflection

7.3.2.1 Prophecy and Personal Guidance

The results showing that both corporate and personal prophecy function to encourage and comfort believers is well supported in Scripture and in the literature review. However, the role of prophecy in providing guidance for decision-making is of concern. The literature review had earlier raised questions on prophecy functioning in this role (section 4.3.4). As Gee points out, Scripture lacks evidence of prophecy functioning in the role of personal guidance.[25] Instead, the early church relied on Scripture, natural judgment, and corporate agreement when making decisions. Hence, it appears that prophecy has assumed a role in the church today that is more than what Scripture can substantiate.

This issue is made more acute within the research context since Asian religions in Singapore are known to practice divination and fortune-telling (section 3.4.1). The interviews showed that the senior pastors were clear on the distinction between Christian prophecy and the practices of other religions. However, Christian converts from other religions may perceive

---

24. Land, *Pentecostal Spirituality*, 163–72.
25. Gee, *Spiritual Gifts in the Work of the Ministry Today*, 50–51.

personal prophecy in the church to be merely another form of fortune-telling similar to what they had experienced in other religions. This study did not explore the possible confusion and does not assert that there is evidence of confusion actually occurring. However, the church may need to re-consider advocating the role of prophecy in providing personal guidance. Proper teaching within the Singapore church is essential to prevent any possible misunderstanding of prophecy and its role.

The survey results also showed that prophecy frequently provides affirmation of a decision made in the past. One such occurrence was described in section 3.4.2.2 where there was an account of this taking place at the corporate church level. While the interviews and the survey results show a general acceptance of this practice, there is always the potential danger of believers misinterpreting a prophecy as affirming their decisions. This is especially in cases where believers are eagerly expecting God to provide affirmation of their personal decisions. There is even greater potential for misinterpretation if the prophetic message comes in a figurative and symbolic form. In any case, the New Testament does not provide examples of prophecy functioning to affirm a decision which the early church had already made and hence the church today may need to re-consider advocating this practice.

Closely related to the issue of guidance is the practice of personal prophecy. The biblical discussion on prophecy places its function within the corporate setting. While there is no explicit biblical evidence forbidding personal prophecy, there is also little support for prophecy to function extensively at a personal level. Section 3.4.4 showed senior pastors voicing concern over how prophecies given in one-to-one settings should be evaluated. The survey results also showed widespread awareness of the possible abuse of prophecy. Moreover, the results showed a common understanding that prophecy requires interpretation and application and may sometimes contain errors (section 6.8.4). It is thus surprising that 62.16 percent of respondents reported that their churches encouraged personal prophecies (section 6.8). It is hoped that the AGS churches have enforced sound protocols regulating the practice of personal prophecy. In all instances, there needs to be an objective evaluation of prophecy by mature spiritual leaders, especially when prophecy brings guidance or confirmation to specific individuals. This permits corporate accountability for the practice of prophecy and prevents prophecy from being judged solely by the one prophesying and the one receiving it.

7.3.2.2 Prophecy and Courage

The role of prophecy in stirring and cultivating the Pentecostal affections have been corroborated through this empirical investigation. The direct divine communication afforded through prophecy serves to convey a vision of God's kingdom grounded in God's righteousness, love, and power.[26] This births a yearning in believers manifest as a passion for God's kingdom and characterized by the affections of gratitude, compassion, and courage. The Pentecostal affection of compassion was discussed at some length under the theme of love in section 7.2.2.2. This section will focus instead on the Pentecostal affection of courage. While it was earlier noted that more attention should be placed on the theme of love, this is not to ignore the significant themes of power and courage that are a part of the Pentecostal movement.

There are at least three ways in which the affection of courage is evident in the practice of prophecy. First, prophecy was noted to provide encouragement and strengthening of the church. As believers experience this divine encouragement and strengthening, they become infused with courage to overcome obstacles and challenges in their lives. Furthermore, prophecy shows that God is active, present, and concerned with the lives of congregation members. This naturally evokes the affection of courage as believers understand that they are not alone in their spiritual journey but that the Almighty God is working on their behalf. The results recorded in table 6.30 show evidence of this, indicating that prophecy brings trust in God, hope for the future, and an emphasis on God's power.

Second, the practice of prophecy within the congregation conveys the reality that all believers are charismatically empowered for ministry. The manifestation of spiritual gifts occurs not only among clergy but also among laity. This brings two results to the Pentecostal church. The first result is that the laity recognizes that ministry is not solely for clergy and so they take courage to engage in serving within the church. This has led to the high participation of laity within Pentecostal churches.[27] In fact, prophecy even permits God to use laity to lead and direct a congregational service. The second result is that believers not only understand their important role in the church but also realize that God has given them the spiritual power to fulfil that role. The activity of spiritual gifts stirs up courage within believers to step into charismatic ministry as they embrace their key role in building and establishing God's kingdom. In this sense, the Pentecostal affections

---

26. Land, *Pentecostal Spirituality*, 135–59.
27. Ma, "Pentecostal Worship in Asia," 143–45.

release a yearning for the kingdom that causes them to take an active role in bringing about its realization.

Third, the radical prayer type was found to be positively correlated with the practice of prophecy. This prayer type was already noted to consist of bold, assertive prayers that seek to effect spiritual change through prayer. This form of prayer is clearly an expression of the Pentecostal affection of courage, passionately seeking the establishment of God's eschatological reign. As previously suggested, prophecy then becomes an extension of the radical prayer type and is likewise characterized by the same affection of courage. Prophecy becomes a bold declaration of what God's kingdom should be like and exhorts other believers to press forward in that direction. It challenges the status quo and instills faith and courage within the congregation. In this way, prophecy serves to express the affection of courage as well as to grow it within the church.

The nurturing of courage through charismatic manifestations like prophecy will also result in a positive influence on evangelism and church growth. The literature review in section 4.3.3 already noted that the *charismata* stir courage and perseverance within the church and this study has found empirical evidence in support of such a relationship. Courage and perseverance are essential virtues for the practice of evangelism, church planting, and church growth.[28] This enables the church to fulfill missional faithfulness in the face of opposition, suffering, and even persecution. The earlier discussion showed that the affection of compassion linked the practice of prophecy with evangelism. This section now adds the affection of courage as an important connection. Thus, this study suggests that the relationship between prophecy and evangelism occurs primarily through the Pentecostal affections.

7.4 THE PRACTICE OF PROPHECY

7.4.1 Summary of Findings

This study found that prophecy was initiated by a range of spiritual experiences in the AGS churches. The literature review described these experiences (section 5.3.1) and most of them were found to occur in the research context (section 6.8.2.1). More importantly, the data indicated that some of these experiences are far more predominant than others. Prophecy is most often initiated when a word, sentence, or impression arises in the mind of

---

28. Tan-Chow, *Pentecostal Theology*, 92–93; Tyra, *Holy Spirit in Mission*.

believers. In this sense, the spiritual experiences appear to be an extension of the promptings and impressions common within Christian prayer.

The prophetic message may come in either a plain or figurative form. The message is usually revealed progressively as the believer speaks, though believers who prophesy more frequently tend to receive the entire prophetic message even before they speak. This may be due to the greater sensitivity of these believers to this *charisma*. The prophecy is usually coded in words chosen by the one prophesying. In this sense, prophecy is "speaking merely human words to report something which God brings to mind."[29] This then indicates a need for the interpretation, evaluation, and application of prophecy. This was described within the literature (section 5.3.2) and was also found to be practiced within the research context (section 6.8.4).

There was widespread acknowledgement in the literature and the research data that prophecy may contain errors. There was also recognition that people may try to abuse the practice of prophecy. Thus, both the literature and the empirical data described the importance of judging prophecy and highlighted adherence to Scripture as the most important criterion for this task. Pastors or church leaders usually did the actual judging of prophecy, though the study raises questions on how this is done for personal prophecy. There is also an issue of who evaluates the prophecy when the pastor is the one prophesying, though it seems likely that other church leaders would be involved in this case.

The literature contained discussion on the psychological state of the one prophesying. This study did not find indication that prophecy was related with psychopathology. The one prophesying retains a high degree of self-control and self-awareness. Believers are able to choose when to start and stop prophesying or even to refuse to speak in the first place. Prophecy did not involve the believer entering into a trance or prophesying in the midst of an ecstatic frenzy. This is in contrast with the activities of other religions in Singapore that display such behavior.[30]

Another finding on the practice of prophecy is that it functions as an extension of prayer. Earlier in section 5.6.1, it was noted that prayer is a dialogue where the believer both speaks to and listens to God. For the one prophesying, the phenomenon serves as an extension to prayerfully listening to what God wants to say to others. For the ones receiving the prophecy, the phenomenon functions as God's response to their prayers. Various studies within literature were noted to have made this assertion that prophecy is an extension of prayer. The descriptions from the interviews showed that

---

29. Grudem, *Gift of Prophecy in the New Testament and Today*, 71.
30. Choong, "Chinese Divination"; Ju, "Chinese Spirit-Mediums in Singapore."

prophecy usually occurred in the context of a corporate worship service as believers were singing and praying to God. The data analysis of the survey showed certain forms of prayer were correlated with prophetic activity (section 6.9.1.3). Specifically, prophecy was found to be influenced by the rest, examination, intercession, and radical prayer types. The first two prayer types enhance a believer's spiritual sensitivity to God's communication. It follows that believers who frequently make effort to pray and listen to God would be able to hear God better and hence prophesy. The next prayer type of intercession involves praying to God for the needs of others. The study suggests that God responds to the intercession by using the believer to prophesy to the people in need. The radical prayer type was already discussed in section 7.3.2.2.

This study has provided insights into the reception, delivery, and judging of prophecy within the context of the AGS. These insights are significant as there is a lack of empirical data on the actual practice of prophecy in literature. Much of the literature was limited to discussion of biblical material or based on anecdotal accounts of prophecy from churches in the West rather than based on a systematic, scholarly investigation. This study has sought to fill this gap in the literature and to provide data for practical-theological reflection.

7.4.2 Theological Reflection

7.4.2.1 *Prophecy and Ministry Training*

There are several insights that may be drawn from the results of this study for the purpose of training ministers and leaders within Pentecostal churches. First, the nature of the *charisma* of prophecy should be emphasized, especially its relationship with Scripture and the authority which it carries in the church. Church leaders must understand that Scripture remains supreme over all *charismata* and that supernatural manifestations must never usurp its position. This also applies to church leaders who may claim the activity of *charismata* as validation of their ministry and hence of their authority over the local church. The faith community must be instructed to judge all prophetic proclamations against the established teachings of the Bible and to exercise spiritual discernment.

A second insight is that believers who wish to grow in the practice of prophecy should first focus on their own spiritual growth. This study has already shown that spiritual maturity bears an important influence on the practice of prophecy. Personal devotion, the study of Scripture, and prayer are all important disciplines in spiritual growth and this study has demonstrated that they bear a positive influence on the practice of prophecy. Believers must also assess their personal motivation for seeking to engage in prophecy. This study indicates that prophecy functions as a channel of divine love and an expression of human compassion. It appears that believers who have an honest desire to serve and bless their faith community would be the most likely people who actually prophesy. Believers motivated by self-interest or self-glorification would be unlikely channels for true prophecy. Hence, believers should be focused on growing in God-ward love and neighborly love and on expressing this through humble acts of service to the faith community.[31] Believers can also serve the needs of others by engaging in intercessory prayer to bring these needs before God. The path analysis showed that intercessory prayer had an indirect influence on the practice of prophecy. In any case, believers who serve the faith community through acts of service or through intercession bring edification to the church. This is precisely the purpose of prophecy and so believers should focus on achieving this purpose even as they seek to prophesy.

A third insight concerns factors that serve to enhance the practice of prophecy. These factors include personal charismatic experience and certain types of prayer. Personal charismatic experience was found to have the strongest influence on prophecy. Adopting a posture of openness to hear God through examination and rest prayers was also noted to enhance prophecy. This indicates that churches that seek to encourage prophecy within congregational meetings may wish to teach their members how to engage in these practices. Time can be set aside in meetings for believers to prayerfully wait before God, expecting God to speak directly to them. The church may also wish to facilitate charismatic encounters within congregational meetings and to provide adequate teaching on the dynamics of such experiences. This will allow greater opportunity for the manifestation of prophecy through the creation of an environment where believers expect to encounter God and to hear directly from God.[32]

A fourth insight has been provided on the mechanics of prophecy. Teaching on prophecy should avoid emphasizing the strange and bizarre in the reception and delivery of prophecy.[33] This study has shown little evidence of bizarre practices and has instead shown that the entire mechanics is far more mundane. Specifically, teaching on the reception of prophecy

---

31. Deere, *Surprised by the Voice of God*, 317–20.

32. Cooke, *Developing Your Prophetic Gifting*, 50–57; Pytches, *Prophecy in the Local Church*, 110–11.

33. Deere, *Beginner's Guide to the Gift of Prophecy*, 103–12.

should stress that audible voices, dreams, and external visions are rare and, in the case of angelic visitations, almost never occur. While the Bible may contain accounts of these occurrences, it does not suggest that this is the norm for initiating prophecy. Instead the empirical evidence reports God speaking through impressions or Scripture verses arising within a believer. Likewise, the delivery of prophecy did not consist of ecstatic proclamations made by believers in a trance. Instead, it simply entails speaking forth what a believer senses God is wanting to say to the congregation. Proper teaching on prophecy avoids a pre-occupation with the bizarre and prevents the church from becoming enamored by supernatural manifestations. Instead, the church should focus on the message being communicated through prophecy.

A fifth insight concerns the purpose and content of prophecy. The study shows that prophecy regularly contains a message of comfort or encouragement and so believers who receive such prophetic impressions may feel more confident that it is indeed a message from God. However, believers should exercise caution if the prophetic impression contains a message of rebuke or judgment. These types of prophecy were reported to be rare and so believers should seek pastoral counsel before making such proclamations in the corporate setting. There is always the possibility that these believers are mistaken in their impressions. Furthermore, believers should refrain from delivering prophecies that contain doctrinal teaching so as to protect congregation members from stumbling into error.

The sixth insight is that churches need to establish and enforce a strict protocol on the practice of prophecy. This should include who is permitted to prophesy, how it should be done in a corporate setting, who should evaluate the prophecy, and how should a congregational response be made. The literature already contains guidelines for how churches might practically facilitate prophecy.[34] The main intent behind such protocols is to ensure order within the church (1 Cor 14:40) and also to prevent abuse (1 Thess 5:19–22). In private one-to-one settings, a believer who receives a prophetic message for someone else should refrain from delivering that prophecy. Instead the prophecy should only be delivered in the presence of pastoral leaders so that there is proper evaluation and accountability.

Finally, it may be better for believers to start exploring prophecy within a small-group setting rather than in a larger corporate setting. This study shows that prophecy has great potential to build up the local church. It is an important spiritual gift and there is even a biblical exhortation for believers

---

34. Cooke, *Developing Your Prophetic Gifting*, 265–80; Gentile, *Your Sons and Daughters Shall Prophesy*, 363–75; Pytches, *Prophecy in the Local Church*, 110–16.

to seek this gift (1 Cor 14:1). However, this study also notes that great harm may come to the church as a result of the improper use of prophecy or from false prophecy. It should be expected that believers would make mistakes when they start prophesying. Hence, it seems wise for churches to restrict believers who are learning to prophesy to do so only within a small-group setting such as in a prayer meeting or in a home cell group. Proper pastoral supervision can be ensured and mentoring provided to such believers so that they can gain proficiency in prophesying. The church can provide teaching at these platforms so that they become a safe context for believers to make mistakes, learn, and grow. These settings are also less structured and provide greater freedom for the spontaneous nature of prophecy.

7.4.2.2 Prophecy and Pentecostal Spirituality

The central feature of Pentecostal spirituality was earlier noted to be the ardent expectation of an encounter with God (section 5.6). For Pentecostals, it is the experience with the divine that results in orthodoxy, orthopraxy, and orthopathy.[35] Prophecy can be located within the search-encounter-transformation framework that describes this feature of Pentecostal spirituality.[36]

The search phase includes the spiritual disciplines of Bible study, prayer, and worship. For the Pentecostal, these practices are not an end in themselves but are meant to move the believer into an almost tangible experience with God. Within this study, the examination and rest prayer types may be seen as attempts to facilitate this encounter by adopting a posture of receptivity. These prayer types also express the passionate expectation that God can be encountered and will respond to believers who wait patiently to meet with God. Intercessory and radical prayer may likewise be viewed in this manner where the believer seeks to encounter God so as to bring supernatural intervention in the situations that prompted their prayers.

The path analysis in this study reveals that these practices within the search phase have a direct bearing on personal charismatic experience within the encounter phase. Believers meet with God and experience a fresh infilling of the Spirit, sing in tongues, or get "slain in the Spirit." The practice of prophecy also falls within the encounter phase of the framework. Within a church service, the congregation moves past the search phase, usually characterized by praise and prayer, then waits expectantly for an encounter

---

35. Land, *Pentecostal Spirituality*, 30–31. Also note Castelo's discussion on the relationship between Pentecostal affections and theological ethics. See Castelo, "Tarrying on the Lord."

36. Cartledge, *Encountering the Spirit*, 25–27.

with the divine. A believer then spontaneously releases a prophecy and the congregation receives a direct word from God through an inspired human intermediary. The prophecy brings edification to the congregation and signifies that God is indeed present in the gathering; that God is fully engaged in the life of the faith community. It is important to stress that charismatic experiences such as tongues or prophecy do not totally define the encounter phase. This phase mainly consists of the felt presence of the divine occurring in both private settings as well as corporate platforms.[37] However, the activity of the *charismata* serves to induce and enhance such an experience.

Prophecy brings a message of encouragement and comfort to the recipients. Believers are transformed as they receive courage, hope, and spiritual strength in their Christian walk. The prophecy may contain an invitation to receive physical or emotional healing and this leads to physical as well as emotional transformation. The prophecy may also give an exhortation for believers to turn away from sin or spiritual distractions and to give priority to the worship of God. Believers then respond by renewing their commitment to the Lordship of Christ. Further transformation occurs as believers recognize that they are divinely empowered for ministry. This leads to believers ministering to one another within the church as well as through evangelism and social ministry to those outside the faith community.

In addition, the encounter yields a transformation within the believer that leads to the nurturing of the Pentecostal affections of gratitude, compassion, and courage. Within this study, the correlation with God-ward love and neighborly love was empirically observed. These affections represent a passion for God's eschatological kingdom to be realized in the present. These affections thus create a yearning that perpetuates the search for further encounters with God so as to further experience the in-breaking of the kingdom.

The reflection above presents the practice of prophecy from the perspective of Pentecostal spirituality. Prophecy and the other *charismata* affirm, reinforce, and perpetuate this spirituality. Their activity serves as evidence of the reality of God and the possibility of encountering God. The testimonies of transformation resulting from these experiences then serve as evidence of the fruit of these God-encounters.

7.5 METHODOLOGICAL REFLECTION

This study has found the model proposed by Van der Ven to be a valuable approach to practical theology. The model has enabled the empirical tools

37. Albrecht, *Rites in the Spirit*, 142.

and methods from the social sciences to be used in the service of theology. However, the hypotheses that are formulated and tested in the study remain theological and so the exercise remains a theological endeavor. Furthermore, the empirical tools are not utilized uncritically but this study has sought to augment Van der Ven's proposal with the Chalcedonian pattern. Social science and its methods are transformed into sub-sciences within theology so that theology retains logical priority over other disciplines. Furthermore, the hermeneutical model of Vanhoozer was incorporated and this has significantly enabled critical theological reflection through the metaphor of theo-drama. Without empirical tools and methods, theology is limited to only the loci of the Bible and human history. Thus, Van der Ven's model has helped expand theology by equipping it with the tools for the rigorous exploration of actual Christian praxis.

This study has also demonstrated the importance of theological perception of the research phenomenon in the phase of theological induction. This occurs prior to a detailed study of the literature so as to prevent the literature from influencing the perception of the researcher. The qualitative interviews conducted in this study permitted themes to arise through the analysis and these themes were then investigated in the literature review and formulated into hypotheses in the phase of theological deduction. The theme of love was one significant theme that was studied as a result of this approach. If this study had begun with a literature review, it is possible that the theme of power would have dominated the research investigation and the theme of love would have been overlooked. Thus, the current approach demonstrates the value of engaging with the empirical reality twice during both theological induction and empirical-theological testing. This spiral between theory and praxis also demonstrates the dialectic that must take place in the pursuit of practical theology. However, the requirement for two distinct empirical investigations places greater demands on time and resources and may seem unfavorable for some.[38]

7.6 SUMMARY

This study has completed an empirical-theological examination of prophecy within the AGS. The investigation has examined the nature, purpose, significance, and characteristics of contemporary prophecy, and identified and explained theological variables that are correlated with its practice. The empirical-theological approach of Van der Ven was employed with the augmentation of the Chalcedonian pattern and the use of Vanhoozer's

---

38. Cartledge, *Testimony in the Spirit*, 15.

hermeneutical framework. The phenomenon of prophecy was first investigated through interviews conducted with ten AGS senior pastors. The data from these interviews were qualitatively analyzed to produce a case description around the process of receiving, delivering, and judging prophecy. Content analysis led to the identification of the significant themes of compassion, courage, and intimacy with God, leading to further research on these themes. A literature review was conducted to obtain information on how Pentecostals understood the nature and purpose of prophecy as well as to determine how it was actually practiced. The information from the interviews and the literature review were reflected upon and led to the development of descriptive goals and theological hypotheses for the next phase of empirical-theological testing.

An empirical-theological model was proposed and this was operationalized through the use of various survey instruments. Some of these instruments were drawn from literature to measure God-ward love, neighborly love, personality types, and prayer types. Other instruments were constructed to measure prophetic activity, personal charismatic experience, evangelistic activity, and devotional frequency. A survey of AGS credentialed ministers was conducted and responses were obtained from 46.11 percent of the survey population. The data from this survey produced a rich description of the practice of prophecy. Quantitative analysis produced an understanding of variables which are correlated with the practice of prophecy. The study went further with path analysis to determine how the different variables interact with each other and suggestions were made on how they influence the practice of prophecy. These findings are reflected upon in this chapter and points of convergence were identified from all the information gathered from the study. Finally, the significance and relevance of the findings were discussed together with the themes that characterize the phenomenon of prophecy.

This book began with the words of Donald Gee and now returns to this Pentecostal pioneer in closing. Gee exhorts the church to seek the *charisma* of prophecy when he writes:

> One of the greatest responsibilities entrusted to us today is the preservation of the *actual exercise* of these gifts of inspired utterance in the church. We emphasize the "actual exercise," because it is so very easy to stand for these things theoretically and doctrinally without actually manifesting them. It is sure to cost something to stand for the real gift of prophecy and to give its lawful place in our assemblies today; but unless we do so we are

persuaded that one very big part of the purpose of God in the outpouring of the Spirit will be frustrated.[39]

This book hopes that it has met a small part of the desire expressed by Gee. The work makes a contribution to research on prophecy—specifically the actual practice of the phenomenon in a Singaporean context. More importantly, it is hoped that this book will stir up and guide the actual manifestation of prophecy within the church today.

---

39. Gee, *Concerning Spiritual Gifts*, 61. Italics in original.

Appendix A
Qualitative Interview Questions

Date:
Time started:
Place:
Interviewee Name:
Church:
Position in church:
Gender: M / F
Age: 21–30 / 31–40 / 41–50 / 51–60 / 61–70

1. Warm-up question: Briefly tell me how long you have been serving in your church and the various ministries you have been involved in.
2. What do you understand about the spiritual gift of prophecy?
3. What is the purpose of prophecy?
4. How does prophecy in the New Testament compare with the Old Testament? Are there any differences?
5. Have you prophesied before? Describe a typical experience and an example of a prophecy you delivered.
6. Have you received or witnessed a prophecy before? Describe a typical experience and an example of a prophecy you received or witnessed.
7. When prophesying, how does the person receive the message?
8. Are you in control of yourself when you prophesy?
9. Can you stop prophesying whenever you want to?
10. Can someone "learn" to prophesy?
11. What hinders a person from prophesying?

12. What helps a person to prophesy?
13. What is the content of prophecy?
14. How often does prophecy occur in your church?
15. When does prophecy usually occur?
16. What effect does prophecy have on the meeting?
17. How is prophecy judged? Who judges the prophecy?
18. How does Christian prophecy compare with forms of non-Christian prophecy in Singapore?
19. What resources (books, people) are useful to you in understanding prophecy?
20. Open-ended question: Is there anything you would like to add to what you have told me?

Time ended:

Appendix B
Survey Instruments

PROPHETIC ACTIVITY SCALE (PROPHACT)

INSTRUCTIONS: PLEASE READ THE following statements and circle the number that best describes your experience. (1 = Never, 2 = Rarely, 3 = Once in a year, 4 = Once every 6 months, 5 = Once every 3 months, 6 = Once a month, 7 = Once or more a week)

How often do you . . .
- prophesy in a church service or group setting?
- prophesy to an individual in private?
- sing out a prophetic message?
- utter a message in tongues (glossolalia) which is then interpreted?
- interpret an utterance of tongues (glossolalia)?
- receive a message or impression from God for someone else?

PERSONAL CHARISMATIC EXPERIENCE SCALE (CHAREXP)

Instructions: Please read the following statements and circle the number that best describes your experience. (1 = Never, 2 = Rarely, 3 = Once in a year, 4 = Once every 6 months, 5 = Once every 3 months, 6 = Once a month, 7 = Once or more a week)

How often do you . . .
- experience being "slain in the Spirit"?
- experience a fresh "infilling" of the Spirit?
- experience a miracle from God?
- sing in tongues (glossolalia)?
- receive divine knowledge for yourself about something you did not know previously?
- receive divine guidance for yourself to make a specific decision?

EVANGELISTIC ACTIVITY SCALE (EVANGACT)

Instructions: Please read the following statements and circle the number that best describes your experience. (1 = Never, 2 = Rarely, 3 = Once in a year, 4 = Once every 6 months, 5 = Once every 3 months, 6 = Once a month, 7 = Once or more a week)

How often do you engage in the following activities with non-Christian or "back-slided" Christians?
- Invite them to Christian events or activities
- Share about Christianity with them
- Share a testimony with them
- Pray with them
- Give them Christian resources (books, music, sermons)

FAITH MATURITY SCALE (FMS)

This study modified some questions and the instructions for the scale due to feedback from participants in a pilot study.

Instructions: How true are each of these statements for you? (1 = Never true, 2 = Rarely true, 3 = True once in a while, 4 = Sometimes, 5 = Often true, 6 = Almost always true, 7 = Always true)

1. I am concerned that our country is not doing enough to help the poor.
2. I know that Jesus Christ is the Son of God who died on a cross and rose again.

3. My faith shapes how I think and act each and every day.
4. I help others with their religious questions and struggles.
5. I tend to be critical of other people.
6. In my free time, I help people who have problems or needs.
7. My faith helps me know right from wrong.
8. I do things to help protect the environment.
9. I devote time to reading and studying the Bible.
10. I have a hard time accepting myself.
11. Every day I see evidence that God is active in the world.
12. I take excellent care of my physical health.
13. I am active in efforts to promote social justice.
14. I seek out opportunities to help me grow spiritually.
15. I take time for periods of prayer or meditation.
16. I am active in efforts to promote world peace.
17. I accept people whose religious beliefs are different from mine.
18. I feel a deep sense of responsibility for reducing pain and suffering in the world.
19. As I grow older, my understanding of God changes.
20. I feel overwhelmed by all the responsibilities and obligations I have.
21. I give significant portions of time and money to help other people.
22. I speak out for equality for the underprivileged.
23. I feel God's presence in my relationships with other people.
24. My life is filled with meaning and purpose.
25. I do not understand how a loving God can allow so much pain and suffering in the world.
26. I believe that I must obey God's rules and commandments in order to be saved.
27. I am confident that I can overcome any problem or crisis no matter how serious.
28. I care a great deal about reducing poverty in my country and throughout the world.
29. I try to apply my faith to national and social issues.

30. My life is committed to Jesus Christ.
31. I talk with other people about my faith.
32. My life is filled with stress and anxiety.
33. I go out of my way to show love to people I meet.
34. I have a real sense that God is guiding me.
35. I do not want the churches getting involved in national issues.
36. I like to worship and pray with others.
37. I think Christians must be about the business of creating international understanding and harmony.
38. I am spiritually moved by the beauty of God's creation.

Items 5, 10, 20, 25, 26, 32 and 35 should be reverse scored.

The vertical subscale (FMS-V) comprises items 3, 7, 9, 11, 14, 15, 19, 24, 31, 34, 36, 38.

The horizontal subscale (FMS-H) comprises items 1, 6, 8, 13, 16, 18, 21, 22, 28, 29, 33, 37.

DEVOTION FREQUENCY SCALE (DEVOFREQ)

Instructions: How frequently do you engage in the following devotional activities in an average week? (1 = None; 2 = 1–2 days a week; 3 = 3–4 days a week; 4 = 5–6 days a week; 5 = Everyday)

How often do you . . .
- Pray
- Read the Bible
- Read Christian materials other than the Bible

PRAYER SCALES

Instructions: Please use the scale of 1 to 6 to indicate the degree to which you think about each of the following words or phrases during your own prayers.

Examination (ExamPray)

- Devoting myself
- Examining myself
- Committing
- Judging myself
- Evaluating my inner life

Tears (TearsPray)
- Misery
- Grieving
- Sadness

Sacramental (SacraPray)
- Engaging rituals
- Connecting with traditions
- Exploring sacraments

Rest (RestPray)
- Stillness
- Silence
- Quietude
- Private experiences

Radical (RadPray)
- Radical approaching
- Assertiveness
- Seeking to be revolutionary
- Boldness

Suffering (SuffPray)
- Accepting the pain of others
- Agonizing with others
- Carrying the distress of people

Intercession (InterPray)
- Seeking assistance for others
- Asking for help for other people
- Searching on behalf of someone else

Petition (PetPray)
- Making personal appeals
- Requesting material things
- Asking for things I need
- Asking that physical needs be met

Bibliography

Abeysekera, Fred. *The History of the Assemblies of God of Singapore.* Singapore: Abundant, 1992.
Ahn, Yongnan Jeon. "Prophecy in the Pauline Communities." *The Spirit and Church* 3, no. 1 (2001) 71–95.
Aker, Benny C. "Charismata: Gifts, Enablements, or Ministries?" *Journal of Pentecostal Theology* 11, no. 1 (2002) 53–69.
———. "The Gift of Tongues in 1 Corinthians 14:1–5." *Paraclete* 29, no. 1 (1995) 13–21.
———. "The Gospel in Action." In *Signs and Wonders in Ministry Today*, edited by Benny C. Aker and Gary B. McGee, 34–46. Springfield, MO: Gospel, 1996.
Akin, Daniel L. *1, 2, 3 John.* New American Commentary. Nashville: Broadman & Holman, 2001.
Albrecht, Daniel E. *Rites in the Spirit: A Ritual Approach to Pentecostal/Charismatic Spirituality.* Sheffield, UK: Sheffield Academic Press, 1999.
Alden, Robert L. "Ecstasy and the Prophets." *Bulletin of the Evangelical Theological Society* 9, no. 3 (1966) 149–56.
Alexander, Carol Anne. "Missional Leadership: A Christian Response to Cultural Shifts, Authority Structures and Moral Ambiguities in Contemporary Western Society." PhD diss., University of Wales, 2009.
Alexander, Estrelda, and Amos Yong, eds. *Philip's Daughters: Women in Pentecostal-Charismatic Leadership.* Eugene, OR: Pickwick, 2009.
Alexander, Paul. *Signs and Wonders: Why Pentecostalism Is the World's Fastest-Growing Faith.* San Francisco, CA: Jossey-Bass, 2009.
Anderson, Allan. *An Introduction to Pentecostalism: Global Charismatic Christianity.* Cambridge: Cambridge University Press, 2004.
———. "Varieties, Taxonomies, and Definitions." In *Studying Global Pentecostalism: Theories and Methods*, edited by Allan Anderson, Michael Bergunder, Andre Droogers, and Cornelis van der Laan, 13–29. Berkeley, CA: University of California Press, 2010.
Anderson, Allan, Michael Bergunder, Andre Droogers, and Cornelis van der Laan, eds. *Studying Global Pentecostalism: Theories and Methods.* Berkeley: University of California Press, 2010.
Anderson, Allan, and Edmond Tang, eds. *Asian and Pentecostal: The Charismatic Face of Christianity in Asia.* Oxford: Regnum, 2005.
Anderson, Gordon L. "Baptism in the Holy Spirit, Initial Evidence, and a New Model." *Paraclete* 27, no. 4 (1993) 1–10.

Archer, Kenneth J. *A Pentecostal Hermeneutic for the Twenty-First Century: Spirit, Scripture, and Community.* London: T. & T. Clark, 2004.
Armstrong, Michael Robert. "Lay Christian Views of Life After Death: A Qualitative Study and Theological Appraisal of the Ordinary Eschatology of Some Congregational Christians." ThD diss., University of Durham, 2011.
Aune, David Edward. *Prophecy in Early Christianity and the Ancient Mediterranean World.* Grand Rapids: Eerdmans, 1983.
Ballard, Paul H., and John Pritchard. *Practical Theology in Action: Christian Thinking in the Service of Church and Society.* 2nd ed. London: SPCK, 2006.
Balthasar, Hans Urs von. *Theo-Drama: Theological Dramatic Theory.* San Francisco: Ignatius, 1994.
Barrett, C. K. *A Commentary on the First Epistle to the Corinthians.* 2nd ed. Black's New Testament Commentaries. London: Adam & Charles Black, 1971.
Barrett, P. T., K. V. Petrides, S. B. G. Eysenck, and H. J. Eysenck. "The Eysenck Personality Questionnaire: An Examination of the Factorial Similarity of P, E, N, and L across 34 Countries." *Personality and Individual Differences* 25, no. 5 (1998) 805–19.
Barth, Karl. *The Doctrine of Creation, Part Two.* Vol. 3 of *Church Dogmatics.* Edited by Geoffrey Bromiley et al. Edinburgh: T. & T. Clark, 1980.
———. *The Doctrine of the Word of God, Part Two.* Vol. 2 of *Church Dogmatics.* Edited by Geoffrey Bromiley et al. Edinburgh: T. & T. Clark, 1980.
Bartholomew, Craig G. *The Drama of Scripture: Finding Our Place in the Biblical Story.* Grand Rapids: Baker, 2004.
Bennett, Dennis J., and Rita Bennett. *The Holy Spirit and You.* London: Coverdale, 1974.
Benson, Peter, Michael Donahue, and Joseph Erickson. "The Faith Maturity Scale: Conceptualization, Measurement and Empirical Validation." In *Research in the Social Scientific Study of Religion*, vol. 5, edited by Monty Lynn and David Moberg, 1–26. Greenwich, CT: JAI, 1993.
Berding, Kenneth. *What Are Spiritual Gifts? Rethinking the Conventional View.* Grand Rapids: Kregel, 2006.
Bickle, Mike. *Growing in the Prophetic.* Rev. ed. Lake Mary, FL: Charisma, 2008.
Blasi, Jean Krisle. *Prophetic Fishing: Evangelism in the Power of the Spirit.* Grand Rapids: Chosen, 2008.
Blenkinsopp, Joseph. *A History of Prophecy in Israel.* Rev. ed. Louisville, KY: Westminster John Knox, 1996.
Blomberg, Craig. *1 Corinthians.* The NIV Application Commentary. Grand Rapids: Zondervan, 1994.
Blumhofer, Edith W. *The Assemblies of God: A Chapter in the Story of American Pentecostalism.* 2 vols. Springfield, MO: Gospel, 1989.
Boff, Leonardo, and Clodovis Boff. *Introducing Liberation Theology.* Maryknoll, NY: Orbis, 1987.
Boring, M. Eugene. *The Continuing Voice of Jesus: Christian Prophecy and the Gospel Tradition.* Louisville, KY: Westminster John Knox, 1991.
Brems, Christiane. "Dimensionality of Empathy and Its Correlates." *Journal of Psychology* 123, no. 4 (1989) 329–37.
Browning, Don S. *A Fundamental Practical Theology: Descriptive and Strategic Proposals.* Minneapolis, MN: Fortress, 1996.
Bruce, F. F. *1 and 2 Corinthians.* New Century Bible Commentary. Grand Rapids: Eerdmans, 1980.

———. *The Book of Acts*. Rev. ed. New International Commentary on the New Testament. Grand Rapids: Eerdmans, 1988.

Bryman, Alan, and Duncan Cramer. *Quantitative Data Analysis with SPSS Release 12 and 13: A Guide for Social Scientists*. London: Routledge, 2005.

Burgess, Stanley M., and Eduard M. van der Maas, eds. "Introduction." In *The New International Dictionary of Pentecostal and Charismatic Movements*, xvii–xxiii. Rev. and exp. Grand Rapids: Zondervan, 2002.

Calvin, John. *Commentaries on the Epistles to the Corinthians*. Vol. 1. Grand Rapids: Baker, 1981.

———. *Commentaries on the Epistles to the Philippians, Colossians and Thessalonians*. Grand Rapids: Baker, 1981.

Carlson, G. Raymond. *Spiritual Dynamics: The Holy Spirit in Human Experience*. Springfield, MO: Gospel, 1976.

Carson, D. A. *Showing the Spirit: A Theological Exposition of 1 Corinthians 12-14*. Milton Keynes, UK: Authentic, 2010.

Carter, Howard. *Spiritual Gifts and Their Operation*. Springfield, MO: Gospel, 1968.

Cartledge, David. *The Apostolic Revolution: The Restoration of Apostles and Prophets in the Assemblies of God in Australia*. Chester Hill, Australia: Paraclete Institute, 2000.

Cartledge, Mark J. *Charismatic Glossolalia: An Empirical-Theological Study*. Aldershot, UK: Ashgate, 2002.

———. "Charismatic Prophecy." *Journal of Empirical Theology* 8, no. 1 (1995) 71–88.

———. "Charismatic Prophecy: A Definition and Description." *Journal of Pentecostal Theology*, no. 5 (1994) 79–120.

———. *Encountering the Spirit: The Charismatic Tradition*. Maryknoll, NY: Orbis, 2007.

———. *Practical Theology: Charismatic and Empirical Perspectives*. Carlisle, UK: Paternoster, 2003.

———, ed. *Speaking in Tongues: Multidisciplinary Perspectives*. Milton Keynes, UK: Paternoster, 2006.

———. *Testimony in the Spirit: Rescripting Ordinary Pentecostal Theology*. Farnham, UK: Ashgate, 2010.

Castelo, Daniel. "Tarrying on the Lord: Affections, Virtues and Theological Ethics in Pentecostal Perspective." *Journal of Pentecostal Theology* 13, no. 1 (2004) 31–56.

Cettolin, Angelo. "AOG Pentecostal Spirituality in Australia: A Comparative Study of the Phenomenon of Historic Pentecostal Spirituality and Its Contemporary Developments within the Assemblies of God in Australia." DMin diss., Australian College of Theology, 2007.

Chan, Chee-Keong. "Urban Evangelistic Strategies of Pentecostals in Singapore." MTh diss., The Southern Baptist Theological Seminary, 1995.

Chan, Simon. "Prophecy and Discernment." *Church and Society* 6, no. 3 (2003) 114–26.

Chen, Ruoyu. "新約教會中的先知恩賜 [The Gift of Prophecy in the New Testament Church]." In 聖靈工作的神學課題 *[Theological Issues on the Work of the Holy Spirit]*, edited by Chen Ruoyu, 85–102. 香港:中國神學研究院 [Hong Kong: China Graduate School of Theology], 1996.

Chia, Anita. "A Biblical Theology on Power Manifestation: A Singaporean Quest." *Asian Journal of Pentecostal Studies* 2, no. 1 (1999) 19–33.

Choong, Ket-Che. "Chinese Divination: An Ethnographic Case Study." In *Studies in Chinese Folk Religion in Singapore and Malaysia*, edited by John R. Clammer, 49–97. Singapore: Contributions to Southeast Asian Ethnography, 1983.

Chopp, Rebecca S. "Practical Theology and Liberation." In *Formation and Reflection: The Promise of Practical Theology*, 120–38. Philadelphia: Fortress, 1987.

Clark, Alexander M. "Critical Realism." In *The SAGE Encyclopedia of Qualitative Research Methods*, edited by Lisa M. Given, 168–71. Thousand Oaks, CA: SAGE, 2008.

Clifton, Shane. "The Spirit and Doctrinal Development: A Functional Analysis of the Traditional Pentecostal Doctrine of the Baptism in the Holy Spirit." *Pneuma* 29, no. 1 (2007) 5–23.

Cohen, Jacob. "A Power Primer." *Psychological Bulletin* 112, no. 1 (1992) 155–59.

Conn, Harvie M. "Theologies of Liberation: Toward a Common View." In *Tensions in Contemporary Theology*, edited by S. N. Gundry and A. F. Johnson, 395–434. Chicago: Moody, 1979.

Conzelmann, Hans. *1 Corinthians: A Commentary on the First Epistle to the Corinthians*. Hermeneia. Philadelphia: Fortress, 1975.

Cooke, Graham. *Developing Your Prophetic Gifting*. Tonbridge, UK: Sovereign World, 1994.

Corduan, Winfried. *Neighboring Faiths*. 2nd ed. Downers Grove, IL: InterVarsity, 2012.

Cotterell, Peter. *Mission and Meaninglessness: The Good News in a World of Suffering and Disorder*. London: SPCK, 1990.

Cox, Harvey. *Fire from Heaven: The Rise of Pentecostal Spirituality and the Reshaping of Religion in the Twenty-First Century*. Cambridge, MA: Da Capo, 1995.

Creswell, John W. *Qualitative Inquiry & Research Design: Choosing among Five Approaches*. 2nd ed. Thousand Oaks, CA: SAGE, 2007.

———. *Research Design: Qualitative, Quantitative, and Mixed Methods Approaches*. 3rd ed. Thousand Oaks, CA: SAGE, 2009.

Creswell, John W., and Vicki L. Plano Clark. *Designing and Conducting Mixed Methods Research*. Thousand Oaks, CA: SAGE, 2007.

Dawson, Jane. "Thick Description." In *Encyclopedia of Case Study Research*, edited by Albert J. Mills, Gabrielle Durepos, and Elden Wiebe, 942–44. Thousand Oaks, CA: SAGE, 2010.

Deere, Jack. *The Beginner's Guide to the Gift of Prophecy*. Ann Arbor, MI: Servant, 2001.

———. *Surprised by the Power of the Spirit: Discovering How God Speaks and Heals Today*. Grand Rapids: Zondervan, 1993.

———. *Surprised by the Voice of God: How God Speaks Today through Prophecies, Dreams, and Visions*. Grand Rapids: Zondervan, 1996.

Department of Statistics. *Census of Singapore 2010*. Singapore: Ministry of Trade and Industry, 2010.

Dingemans, G. D. J. "Practical Theology in the Academy: A Contemporary Overview." *Journal of Religion* 76, no. 1 (1996) 82–96.

Dowling, Maura. "Reflexivity." In *The SAGE Encyclopedia of Qualitative Research Methods*, edited by Lisa M. Given, 748–49. Thousand Oaks, CA: SAGE, 2008.

Dunn, James D. G. *Jesus and the Spirit: A Study of the Religious and Charismatic Experience of Jesus and the First Christians as Reflected in the New Testament*. Philadelphia: Westminster, 1975.

———. *The Theology of Paul the Apostle*. Edinburgh: T. & T. Clark, 1998.

Eckhardt, John. *God Still Speaks: How to Hear and Receive Revelation from God for Your Family, Church, and Community*. Lake Mary, FL: Charisma, 2009.

Edgar, Thomas R. *Satisfied by the Promise of the Spirit: Affirming the Fullness of God's Provision for Spiritual Living*. Grand Rapids: Kregel, 1996.

Ellington, Scott A. "Locating Pentecostals at the Hermeneutical Round Table." *Journal of Pentecostal Theology* 22, no. 2 (2013) 206–25.

Ellis, Edward Earle. *Prophecy and Hermeneutic in Early Christianity*. Grand Rapids: Baker, 1993.

———. "The Role of the Christian Prophet in Acts." In *Apostolic History and the Gospel*, edited by W. Ward Gasque and Ralph P. Martin, 55–67. Exeter, UK: Paternoster, 1970.

Eysenck, Hans. *The Biological Basis of Personality*. New Brunswick, NJ: Transaction, 2006.

———. *Dimensions of Personality*. New Brunswick, NJ: Transaction, 1998.

Eysenck, Michael W. "Personality and the Psychology of Religion." *Mental Health, Religion & Culture* 1, no. 1 (1998) 11–19.

Eysenck, S. B. G., H. J. Eysenck, and Paul Barrett. "A Revised Version of the Psychoticism Scale." *Personality and Individual Differences* 6, no. 1 (1985) 21–29.

Farley, Edward. "Interpreting Situations: An Inquiry into the Nature of Practical Theology." In *The Blackwell Reader in Pastoral and Practical Theology*, edited by James Woodward, Stephen Pattison, and John Patton, 118–27. Oxford: Blackwell, 2000.

Farnell, F. David. "The Current Debate about New Testament Prophecy." *Bibliotheca Sacra* 149, no. 595 (1992) 277–303.

———. "Does the New Testament Teach Two Prophetic Gifts?" *Bibliotheca Sacra* 150, no. 597 (1993) 62–88.

———. "The Gift of Prophecy in the Old and New Testaments." *Bibliotheca Sacra* 149, no. 596 (1992) 387–410.

———. "When Will the Gift of Prophecy Cease?" *Bibliotheca Sacra* 150, no. 598 (1993) 171–202.

Fee, Gordon D. *The First Epistle to the Corinthians*. New International Commentary on the New Testament. Grand Rapids: Eerdmans, 1987.

———. *God's Empowering Presence: The Holy Spirit in the Letters of Paul*. Peabody, MA: Hendrickson, 1994.

Feist, Jess, and Gregory J. Feist. *Theories of Personality*. 7th ed. Boston: McGraw Hill, 2009.

Field, Andy. *Discovering Statistics Using SPSS*. 3rd ed. London: SAGE, 2009.

Forbes, Christopher. *Prophecy and Inspired Speech in Early Christianity and Its Hellenistic Environment*. Peabody, MA: Hendrickson, 1997.

Forrester, Duncan B. *Truthful Action: Explorations in Practical Theology*. Edinburgh: T. & T. Clark, 2000.

Foster, Richard J. *Prayer: Finding the Heart's True Home*. San Francisco, CA: Harper & Row, 1992.

Fowler, James W. "Practical Theology and Theological Education: Some Models and Questions." *Theology Today* 42, no. 1 (1985) 43–58.

Francis, Leslie J., Laurence B. Brown, and Ronald Philipchalk. "The Development of an Abbreviated Form of the Revised Eysenck Personality Questionnaire (EPQR-A):

Its Use among Students in England, Canada, the U.S.A. and Australia." *Personality and Individual Differences* 13, no. 4 (1992) 443–49.

Francis, Leslie J., and Susan H. Jones. "Personality and Charismatic Experience among Adult Christians." *Pastoral Psychology* 45, no. 6 (1997) 421–28.

Francis, Leslie J., and William K. Kay. "The Personality Characteristics of Pentecostal Ministry Candidates." *Personality and Individual Differences* 18, no. 5 (1995) 581–94.

Francis, Leslie J., and Mandy Robbins. "Personality and Glossolalia: A Study among Male Evangelical Clergy." *Pastoral Psychology* 51, no. 5 (2003) 391–96.

Francis, Leslie J., and Hugh T. Thomas. "Are Charismatic Ministers Less Stable? A Study among Male Anglican Clergy." *Review of Religious Research* 39, no. 1 (1997) 61–69.

Friesen, Aaron T. *Norming the Abnormal: The Development and Function of the Doctrine of Initial Evidence in Classical Pentecostalism*. Eugene, OR: Pickwick, 2013.

Fuchs, Ottmar. "Charismatic Prophecy and Innovation: A Practical-Theological Reflection on the Study by Mark J. Cartledge." *Journal of Empirical Theology* 8, no. 1 (1995) 89–95.

Fung, Ronald Y. K. "Function or Office: A Survey of the New Testament Evidence." *Evangelical Review of Theology* 8, no. 1 (1984) 16–39.

Furseth, Inger, and Pal Repstad. *An Introduction to the Sociology of Religion: Classical and Contemporary Perspectives*. Farnham, UK: Ashgate, 2006.

Gaffin, Richard B. "A Cessationist Response to Robert L. Saucy." In *Are Miraculous Gifts for Today?* edited by Wayne A. Grudem, 149–55. Grand Rapids: Zondervan, 1996.

———. "A Cessationist View." In *Are Miraculous Gifts for Today?* edited by Wayne A. Grudem, 25–64. Grand Rapids: Zondervan, 1996.

———. *Perspectives on Pentecost: Studies in New Testament Teaching on the Gifts of the Holy Spirit*. Nutley, NJ: Presbyterian & Reformed, 1979.

Ganzevoort, R. Ruard. "Van Der Ven's Empirical/Practical Theology and the Theological Encyclopaedia." In *Hermeneutics and Empirical Research in Practical Theology: The Contribution of Empirical Theology by Johannes A. van der Ven*, edited by Chris A. M. Hermans and Mary Elizabeth Moore, 53–74. Leiden: Brill, 2004.

Gee, Donald. *Concerning Spiritual Gifts*. Rev. ed. Springfield, MO: Gospel, 1980.

———. *Fruit of the Spirit*. Springfield, MO: Gospel, 1975.

———. *Pentecostal Experience: The Writings of Donald Gee*. Edited by David A. Womack. Springfield, MO: Gospel, 1993.

———. *Spiritual Gifts in the Work of the Ministry Today*. Springfield, MO: Gospel, 1963.

Geertz, Clifford. "Thick Description: Toward an Interpretive Theory of Culture." In *The Interpretation of Cultures*, 3–30. New York: Basic, 1973.

Gentile, Ernest. *Your Sons and Daughters Shall Prophesy: Prophetic Gifts in Ministry Today*. Grand Rapids: Chosen, 1999.

Gentry, Kenneth L. *The Charismatic Gift of Prophecy*. Eugene, OR: Wipf & Stock, 2000.

Gibbs, Graham. *Analyzing Qualitative Data*. Los Angeles, CA: SAGE, 2007.

Gill, Deborah M., and Barbara L. Cavaness. *God's Women: Then and Now*. Springfield, MO: Grace & Truth, 2004.

Gillespie, Thomas W. *The First Theologians: A Study in Early Christian Prophecy*. Grand Rapids: Eerdmans, 1994.

Gillham, Bill. *Research Interviewing: The Range of Techniques*. Maidenhead, UK: Open University Press, 2005.

Goll, James W., and Michal Ann Goll. *Dream Language: The Prophetic Power of Dreams, Revelations, and the Spirit of Wisdom.* Shippensburg, PA: Destiny Image, 2006.

Grabbe, Lester L. *Priests, Prophets, Diviners, Sages: A Socio-Historical Study of Religious Specialists in Ancient Israel.* Valley Forge, PA: Trinity, 1995.

Grady, J. Lee. "God Spoke through a Man." *Charisma and Christian Life*, September 2004.

Green, Matthew, ed. *Understanding the Fivefold Ministry.* Lake Mary, FL: Charisma, 2005.

Greig, Gary S. "The Purpose of Signs and Wonders in the New Testament." In *The Kingdom and the Power*, edited by Gary S. Greig and Kevin N. Springer, 133–74. Ventura, CA: Regal, 1993.

Greig, Gary S., and Kevin N. Springer, eds. *The Kingdom and the Power.* Ventura, CA: Regal, 1993.

Grenz, Stanley J., and Roger E. Olson. *20th Century Theology: God & the World in a Transitional Age.* Downers Grove, IL: InterVarsity, 1992.

Gritzmacher, Steven A., Brian Bolton, and Richard H. Dana. "Psychological Characteristics of Pentecostals: A Literature Review and Psychodynamic Synthesis." *Journal of Psychology and Theology* 16, no. 3 (1988) 233–45.

Groome, Thomas H. *Christian Religious Education: Sharing Our Story and Vision.* San Francisco: Harper & Row, 1980.

———. "Theology on Our Feet: A Revisionist Pedagogy for Healing the Gap between Academia and Ecclesia." In *Formation and Reflection: The Promise of Practical Theology*, 55–78. Philadelphia: Fortress, 1987.

Grudem, Wayne A., ed. *Are Miraculous Gifts for Today?* Grand Rapids: Zondervan, 1996.

———. *The Gift of Prophecy in 1 Corinthians.* Eugene, OR: Wipf & Stock, 1999.

———. *The Gift of Prophecy in the New Testament and Today.* Rev. ed. Wheaton, IL: Crossway, 2000.

———. *Systematic Theology: An Introduction to Biblical Doctrine.* Leicester, UK: InterVarsity, 1994.

Guba, Egon G., and Yvonna S. Lincoln. "Competing Paradigms in Qualitative Research." In *Handbook of Qualitative Research*, edited by Norman K. Denzin and Yvonna S. Lincoln, 105–17. Thousand Oaks, CA: SAGE, 1994.

Habermas, Jürgen. *The Theory of Communicative Action.* Edited by Mark R. McMinn. London: Heinemann, 1984.

Hair, Joseph F., Rolph E. Anderson, Ronald L. Tatham, and William C. Black. *Multivariate Data Analysis.* 5th ed. Upper Saddle River, NJ: Prentice Hall, 1998.

Hamon, Bill. *Apostles, Prophets, and the Coming Moves of God: God's End-Time Plans for His Church and Planet Earth.* Santa Rosa Beach, FL: Destiny Image, 1997.

———. *Prophets and Personal Prophecy: God's Prophetic Voice Today.* Shippensburg, PA: Destiny Image, 1987.

———. *Prophets, Pitfalls and Principles: God's Prophetic People Today.* Shippensburg, PA: Destiny Image, 1991.

Hanegraaff, Hank. *Christianity in Crisis: The 21st Century.* Nashville: Thomas Nelson, 2009.

Hart, Larry. "Spirit-Baptism." In *Spirit-Empowered Christianity in the Twenty-First Century*, edited by Vinson Synan, 261–86. Lake Mary, FL: Charisma, 2011.

Hayford, Jack W. *The Beauty of Spiritual Language: My Journey toward the Heart of God.* Dallas, TX: Word, 1992.

Heitink, Gerben. *Practical Theology: History, Theory, Action Domains: Manual for Practical Theology.* Grand Rapids: Eerdmans, 1999.

Hemphill, Kenneth S. *You Are Gifted: Your Spiritual Gifts and the Kingdom of God.* Nashville: Broadman & Holman, 2009.

Henry, Carl F. H. "Liberation Theology and the Scriptures." In *Liberation Theology*, edited by Ronald H. Nash, 191–202. Milford, MI: Mott Media, 1984.

Hermans, C. A. M., and Mary Elizabeth Moore, eds. *Hermeneutics and Empirical Research in Practical Theology: The Contribution of Empirical Theology by Johannes A. van der Ven.* Leiden: Brill, 2004.

Higgins, John R. "God's Inspired Word." In *Systematic Theology: A Pentecostal Perspective*, edited by Stanley M. Horton, 61–115. Springfield, MO: Logion, 1994.

Hilber, John W. "Diversity of OT Prophetic Phenomena and NT Prophecy." *Westminster Theological Journal* 56, no. 2 (1994) 243–58.

Hill, David. *New Testament Prophecy.* Atlanta: John Knox, 1979.

———. "Prophecy and Prophets in the Revelation of St. John." *New Testament Studies* 18, no. 4 (1972) 401–18.

Hiu, Elim. *Regulations concerning Tongues and Prophecy in 1 Corinthians 14.26–40: Relevance beyond the Corinthian Church.* London: T. & T. Clark, 2010.

Hollenweger, Walter J. *Pentecostalism: Origins and Developments Worldwide.* Peabody, MA: Hendrickson, 1997.

Holm, Randall, Matthew Wolf, and James K. A. Smith. "New Frontiers in Tongues Research: A Symposium." *Journal of Pentecostal Theology* 20, no. 1 (2011) 122–54.

Hood, Ralph W., Peter C. Hill, and Bernard Spilka. *The Psychology of Religion: An Empirical Approach.* 4th ed. New York: Guilford, 2009.

Horton, Harold. *The Gifts of the Spirit.* Springfield, MO: Gospel, 1975.

Horton, Stanley M. *The Gifts and Fruit of the Spirit.* Springfield, MO: Gospel, n.d.

———. "Review of *The Gift of Prophecy in the New Testament and Today* by Wayne Grudem." *Paraclete* 25, no. 1 (1991) 30–32.

———. *What the Bible Says about the Holy Spirit.* Springfield, MO: Gospel, 1976.

Huber, Stefan, and Odilo W. Huber. "Psychology of Religion." In *Studying Global Pentecostalism: Theories and Methods*, edited by Allan Anderson, Michael Bergunder, Andre F. Droogers, and Cornelis Van der Laan, 133–55. Berkeley, CA: University of California Press, 2010.

Hui, C. Harry, Eddie Chi Wai Ng, Doris Shui Ying Mok, Esther Yuet Ying Lau, and Shu-Fai Cheung. "'Faith Maturity Scale' for Chinese: A Revision and Construct Validation." *International Journal for the Psychology of Religion* 21, no. 4 (2011) 308–22.

Hunsinger, Deborah van Deusen. "An Interdisciplinary Map for Christian Counselors: Theology and Psychology in Pastoral Counseling." In *Care for the Soul: Exploring the Intersection of Psychology and Theology*, edited by Mark R. McMinn and Timothy R. Phillips, 218–40. Leicester, UK: InterVarsity, 2001.

———. *Theology and Pastoral Counseling: A New Interdisciplinary Approach.* Grand Rapids: Eerdmans, 1995.

Hunsinger, George. *Disruptive Grace: Studies in the Theology of Karl Barth.* Grand Rapids: Eerdmans, 2000.

———. *How to Read Karl Barth: The Shape of His Theology.* New York: Oxford University Press, 1991.
Hurley, Susan L. *Natural Reasons: Personality and Polity.* New York: Oxford University Press, 1992.
Hutch, Richard A. "The Personal Ritual of Glossolalia." *Journal for the Scientific Study of Religion* 19, no. 3 (1980) 255–66.
Hvidt, Niels Christian. *Christian Prophecy: The Post-Biblical Tradition.* New York: Oxford University Press, 2007.
Hwa Yung. "Endued with Power: The Pentecostal Charismatic Renewal and the Asian Church in the Twenty-First Century." *Asian Journal of Pentecostal Studies* 6, no. 1 (2003) 63–82.
———. "Recover the Supernatural." *Christianity Today* 54, no. 9 (2010) 32–33.
Iap, Joshua Sian-Chin. 聖靈的洗：路加與五旬宗的聖靈神學 *[Baptism in the Spirit: Lukan and Pentecostal Theology of the Holy Spirit].* 台北市：中原大學宗教研究所 [Taipei: Chung Yuan University Press], 2008.
Jackson, Chris J., and Leslie J. Francis. "Interpreting the Correlation between Neuroticism and Lie Scale Scores." *Personality and Individual Differences* 26, no. 1 (1999) 59–63.
Jacobs, Cindy. *The Voice of God.* Ventura, CA: Regal, 1995.
Janssen, Jacques A. P. J., Maerten H. Prins, Jan M. Van Der Lans, and Cor Baerveldt. "The Structure and Variety of Prayer." *Journal of Empirical Theology* 13, no. 2 (2000) 29–54.
Joyner, Rick. *The Prophetic Ministry.* Fort Mill, SC: Morning Star, 2008.
Ju, Shi-Huey. "Chinese Spirit-Mediums in Singapore: An Ethnographic Study." In *Studies in Chinese Folk Religion in Singapore and Malaysia,* edited by John R. Clammer, 3–48. Singapore: Contributions to Southeast Asian Ethnography, 1983.
Kay, William K. "The Dynamics of the Growth of Pentecostal Churches: Evidence from Key Asian Centres." *Australasian Pentecostal Studies,* no. 15 (2013). http://webjournals.ac.edu.au.
———. "Empirical and Historical Perspectives on the Growth of Pentecostal-Style Churches in Malaysia, Singapore and Hong Kong." *Journal of Beliefs & Values* 34, no. 1 (2013) 14–25.
———. "The Mind, Behaviour, and Glossolalia: A Psychological Perspective." In *Speaking in Tongues: Multi-Disciplinary Perspectives,* edited by Mark J. Cartledge, 174–205. Milton Keynes, UK: Paternoster, 2006.
———. *Pentecostalism.* London: SCM, 2009.
———. *Pentecostals in Britain.* Carlisle, UK: Paternoster, 2000.
———. "Perspectives on Prophecy." *Paraclete* 26, no. 1 (1992) 1–7.
———. *Prophecy!* Nottingham, UK: Life Stream, 1991.
———. "Where the Wind Blows: Pentecostal Christians in Hong Kong and Singapore." *PentecoStudies* 11, no. 2 (2012) 128–48.
Keener, Craig S. *1–2 Corinthians.* New Cambridge Bible Commentary. Cambridge University Press, 2005.
———. *Gift & Giver: The Holy Spirit for Today.* Grand Rapids: Baker, 2001.
———. *Paul, Women & Wives: Marriage and Women's Ministry in the Letters of Paul.* Peabody, MA: Hendrickson, 1992.
Kelsey, Morton T. *Encounter with God: A Theology of Christian Experience.* Minneapolis, MN: Bethany Fellowship, 1975.

———. *Tongue Speaking: An Experiment in Spiritual Experience*. Garden City, NY: Doubleday, 1964.

Kennedy, John W. "J. I. Packer: Knowing God Is a Lifelong Process." *Today's Pentecostal Evangel*, March 23, 2008.

Khoo, Jeffrey. *Charismatism Q&A*. Singapore: Far Eastern Bible College Press, 1999.

Kildahl, John P. "Psychological Observations." In *Speaking in Tongues: A Guide to Research on Glossolalia*, edited by Watson E. Mills, 347–68. Grand Rapids: Eerdmans, 1986.

———. *The Psychology of Speaking in Tongues*. London: Hodder & Stoughton, 1972.

Koning, Juliette, and Heidi Dahles. "Spiritual Power: Ethnic Chinese Managers and the Rise of Charismatic Christianity." *The Copenhagen Journal of Asian Studies* 27, no. 1 (2009) 5–37.

Kruse, Colin G. *John: An Introduction and Commentary*. Tyndale New Testament Commentaries. Downers Grove, IL: InterVarsity, 2003.

Ladd, Kevin L., and Bernard Spilka. "Inward, Outward, and Upward: Cognitive Aspects of Prayer." *Journal for the Scientific Study of Religion* 41, no. 3 (2002) 475–84.

———. "Inward, Outward, Upward Prayer." *Journal for the Scientific Study of Religion* 45, no. 2 (2006) 233–51.

Laird, Steven P., C. R. Snyder, Michael A. Rapoff, and Sam Green. "Measuring Private Prayer: Development, Validation, and Clinical Application of the Multidimensional Prayer Inventory." *International Journal for the Psychology of Religion* 14, no. 4 (2004) 251–72.

Lamb, Matthew L. *Solidarity with Victims: Toward a Theology of Social Transformation*. New York: Crossroad, 1982.

Land, Steven J. *Pentecostal Spirituality: A Passion for the Kingdom*. Cleveland, TN: CPT, 2010.

Lartey, Emmanuel. "Practical Theology as a Theological Form." In *The Blackwell Reader in Pastoral and Practical Theology*, edited by James Woodward, Stephen Pattison, and John Patton, 128–34. Oxford, UK: Blackwell, 2000.

Latham, Steven Foster. "'Is There Any Word from the Lord?': Schools of Contemporary Christian Prophecy." PhD diss., King's College, 1999.

Lee, Dong Y., Jee Y. Lee, and Chul H. Kang. "Development and Validation of an Altruism Scale for Adults." *Psychological Reports* 92, no. 2 (2003) 555–61.

Lee, Matthew T., and Margaret M. Poloma. *A Sociological Study of the Great Commandment in Pentecostalism: The Practice of Godly Love as Benevolent Service*. Lewiston, NY: Mellen, 2009.

Lim, David. *Spiritual Gifts: A Fresh Look*. Springfield, MO: Gospel, 2003.

Lincoln, Andrew T. *Ephesians*. Word Biblical Commentary. Dallas, TX: Word, 2002.

Lindblom, Johannes. *Prophecy in Ancient Israel*. Philadelphia: Fortress, 1962.

Loder, James E. *The Logic of the Spirit: Human Development in Theological Perspective*. San Francisco: Jossey-Bass, 1998.

Logan, James C. "Controversial Aspects of the Movement." In *The Charismatic Movement*, edited by Michael Pollock Hamilton, 33–46. Grand Rapids: Eerdmans, 1975.

Lonergan, Bernard J. *Method in Theology*. Canada: University of Toronto Press, 2003.

Ma, Julie. "Asian Women and Pentecostal Ministry." In *Asian and Pentecostal: The Charismatic Face of Christianity in Asia*, edited by Allan Anderson and Edmond Tang, 129–46. Oxford, UK: Regnum, 2005.

Ma, Julie, and Allan Anderson. "Pentecostals (Renewalists), 1910-2010." In *Atlas of Global Christianity*, edited by Todd M. Johnson and Kenneth R. Ross, 100-101. Edinburgh, UK: Edinburgh University Press, 2009.

Ma, Wonsuk. "Asian Pentecostalism: A Religion Whose Only Limit Is the Sky." *Journal of Beliefs & Values* 25, no. 2 (2004) 191-204.

———. "Pentecostal Worship in Asia: Its Theological Implications and Contributions." *Asian Journal of Pentecostal Studies* 10, no. 1 (2007) 136-52.

MacArthur, John F. *Charismatic Chaos*. Grand Rapids: Zondervan, 1992.

———. *Strange Fire: The Danger of Offending the Holy Spirit with Counterfeit Worship*. Nashville: Thomas Nelson, 2013.

Macchia, Frank D. *Baptized in the Spirit: A Global Pentecostal Theology*. Grand Rapids: Zondervan, 2006.

MacDonald, William Graham. "Biblical Glossolalia: Thesis 7." *Paraclete* 28, no. 2 (1994) 1-12.

Maddox, Randy L. "Practical Theology: A Discipline in Search of a Definition." *Perspectives in Religious Studies* 18, no. 2 (1991) 159-69.

———. "The Recovery of Theology as a Practical Discipline." *Theological Studies* 51, no. 4 (1990) 650-72.

Maltby, John, and Liza Day. "The Relationship between Spirituality and Eysenck's Personality Dimensions: A Replication among English Adults." *Journal of Genetic Psychology* 162, no. 1 (2001) 119-22.

———. "Spiritual Involvement and Belief: The Relationship between Spirituality and Eysenck's Personality Dimensions." *Personality and Individual Differences* 30 (2001) 187-92.

Martin, Lee Roy. "Introduction to Pentecostal Hermeneutics." In *Pentecostal Hermeneutics: A Reader*, edited by Lee Roy Martin, 1-9. Leiden: Brill, 2013.

McGee, Gary B., ed. *Initial Evidence: Historical and Biblical Perspectives on the Pentecostal Doctrine of Spirit Baptism*. Peabody, MA: Hendrickson, 1991.

McGrath, Alister E. *A Scientific Theology: Nature*. London: T. & T. Clark, 2006.

———. *A Scientific Theology: Realism*. London: T. & T. Clark, 2006.

McGuire, Meredith B. "Social Context of Prophecy: 'Word-Gifts' of the Spirit among Catholic Pentecostals." *Review of Religious Research* 18, no. 2 (1977) 134-47.

Menzies, Robert P. "Anti-Charismatic Bias in the Chinese Union Version of the Bible." *Pneuma* 29, no. 1 (2007) 86-101.

———. *The Development of Early Christian Pneumatology: With Special Reference to Luke-Acts*. Sheffield, UK: JSOT, 1991.

———. *Empowered for Witness: The Spirit in Luke-Acts*. Sheffield, UK: Sheffield Academic Press, 1994.

———. *Pentecost: This Is Our Story*. Springfield, MO: Gospel, 2013.

———. "A Pentecostal Perspective on 'Signs and Wonders.'" *Pneuma* 17, no. 2 (1995) 265-78.

Menzies, William W. "Review of *The Gift of Prophecy in 1 Corinthians* by Wayne Grudem." *Paraclete* 17, no. 4 (1983) 29-30.

Menzies, William W., and Stanley M. Horton. *Bible Doctrines: A Pentecostal Perspective*. Rev. and exp. Springfield, MO: Logion, 1993.

Menzies, William W., and Robert P. Menzies. *Spirit and Power: Foundations of Pentecostal Experience*. Grand Rapids: Zondervan, 2000.

Middleton, J. Richard, and Brian J. Walsh. *Truth Is Stranger than It Used to Be: Biblical Faith in a Postmodern Age*. Downers Grove, IL: InterVarsity, 1995.

Mikoski, Gordon S. "Educating and Forming Disciples for the Reign of God: Reflections on Youth Pilgrimages to the Holy Land." In *For Life Abundant: Practical Theology, Theological Education, and Christian Ministry*, edited by Dorothy C. Bass and Craig R. Dykstra, 329–52. Grand Rapids: Eerdmans, 2008.

Miles, Jeremy, and Susanne Hempel. "The Eysenck Personality Scales." In *Comprehensive Handbook of Psychological Assessment: Personality Assessment*, edited by Mark J. Hilsenroth, 99–107. Hoboken, NJ: John Wiley & Sons, 2004.

Miller, Donald E., and Tetsunao Yamamori. *Global Pentecostalism: The New Face of Christian Social Engagement*. Berkeley: University of California Press, 2007.

Mills, Watson E., ed. *Speaking in Tongues: A Guide to Glossolalia*. Grand Rapids: Eerdmans, 1986.

Moo, Douglas J. *The Epistle to the Romans*. New International Commentary on the New Testament. Grand Rapids: Eerdmans, 1996.

Mounce, Robert H. *Romans*. New American Commentary. Nashville: Broadman & Holman, 1995.

Muindi, Samuel L. "The Nature and Significance of Prophecy in Pentecostal-Charismatic Experience: An Empirical-Biblical Study." PhD diss., The University of Birmingham, 2012.

National Council of Churches of Singapore. *A Guide to Churches and Christian Organisations in Singapore 2011–2012*. Singapore: GospelWorks, 2011.

Neuman, William Lawrence. *Social Research Methods: Qualitative and Quantitative Approaches*. 6th ed. Boston: Pearson, 2006.

Neumann, Peter D. *Pentecostal Experience: An Ecumenical Encounter*. Eugene, OR: Pickwick, 2012.

Newton, Jon K. "The Scope of Christian Prophecy." *Australasian Pentecostal Studies* 13 (2010) 59–86.

O'Murchu, Diarmuid. *Quantum Theology*. New York: Crossroad, 1997.

Ong, Andrew. "A Historical Analysis of the Factors of Growth of the Assemblies of God in Singapore and Their Implications in the 21st Century." DMin diss., Asia Graduate School of Theology, 2008.

Osborne, Grant R. *The Hermeneutical Spiral: A Comprehensive Introduction to Biblical Interpretation*. 2nd ed. Downers Grove, IL: InterVarsity, 2006.

Osman, Mohammad Taib. *Malay Folk Beliefs: An Integration of Disparate Elements*. Kuala Lumpur: Dewan Bahasa dan Pustaka, Kementerian Pendidikan Malaysia, 1989.

Osmer, Richard Robert. *Practical Theology: An Introduction*. Grand Rapids: Eerdmans, 2008.

Overholt, Thomas W. *Channels of Prophecy: The Social Dynamics of Prophetic Activity*. Philadelphia: Fortress, 1989.

Packer, James I. *Keep in Step with the Spirit*. Downers Grove, IL: InterVarsity, 1984.

Pallant, Julie. *SPSS Survival Manual*. 2nd ed. Sydney: Allen & Unwin, 2005.

Palma, Anthony D. "The Gift of Prophecy: Its Nature and Scope." *Paraclete* 4, no. 3 (1970) 8–13.

———. "The Gift of Prophecy: Its Regulation and Purpose." *Paraclete* 4, no. 4 (1970) 7–12.

———. *The Holy Spirit: A Pentecostal Perspective*. Springfield, MO: Gospel, 2001.

Pannenberg, Wolfhart. *Theology and the Philosophy of Science*. London: Darton, Longman & Todd, 1976.
Parker, Stephen E. *Led by the Spirit: Toward a Practical Theology of Pentecostal Discernment and Decision Making*. Sheffield, UK: Sheffield Academic Press, 1996.
Patton, Michael Quinn. *Qualitative Research and Evaluation Methods*. 3rd ed. Thousand Oaks, CA: SAGE, 2002.
Paver, John E. *Theological Reflection and Education for Ministry: The Search for Integration in Theology*. Aldershot, UK: Ashgate, 2006.
Penney, John. "The Testing of New Testament Prophecy." *Journal of Pentecostal Theology* 5, no. 10 (1997) 35–84.
Petersen, David L., ed. *Prophecy in Israel*. Philadelphia: Fortress, 1987.
Peterson, Douglas. "The Kingdom of God and the Hermeneutical Circle: Pentecostal Praxis in the Third World." In *Called and Empowered: Global Missions in Pentecostal Perspective*, edited by Murray A. Dempster, Byron D. Klaus, and Douglas Peterson, 44–58. Peabody, MA: Hendrickson, 1991.
Petts, David. *Body Builders: Gifts to Make God's People Grow*. Mattersey, UK: Mattersey Hall, 2002.
Pew Research Center. "Spirit and Power: A 10-Country Survey of Pentecostals." Washington, DC: Pew Forum on Religion & Public Life, 2007.
Pierce, Chuck D., and Rebecca Wagner Sytsema. *When God Speaks: How to Interpret Dreams, Visions, Signs and Wonders*. Ventura, CA: Gospel Light, 2005.
Pilario, Daniel Franklin. *Back to the Rough Grounds of Praxis: Exploring Theological Method with Pierre Bourdieu*. Leuven: Leuven University Press, 2005.
Pixley, George V., and Clodovis Boff. *The Bible, the Church and the Poor*. Maryknoll, NY: Burns & Oates, 1989.
Polhill, John B. *Acts*. New American Commentary. Nashville: Broadman & Holman, 1992.
Polkinghorne, John C. *Belief in God in an Age of Science*. New Haven, CT: Yale University Press, 2003.
Poloma, Margaret M. "Pentecostal Prayer within the Assemblies of God: An Empirical Study." *Pneuma* 31, no. 1 (2009) 47–65.
Poloma, Margaret M. *The Assemblies of God at the Crossroads: Charisma and Institutional Dilemmas*. Knoxville, TN: University of Tennessee Press, 1989.
Poloma, Margaret M., and George H. Gallup. *Varieties of Prayer: A Survey Report*. Philadelphia: Trinity, 1991.
Poloma, Margaret M., and Ralph W. Hood. *Blood and Fire: Godly Love in a Pentecostal Emerging Church*. New York: New York University Press, 2008.
Poloma, Margaret M., and Brian F. Pendleton. "Exploring Types of Prayer and Quality of Life: A Research Note." *Review of Religious Research* 31, no. 1 (1989) 46.
Popper, Karl R. *The Logic of Scientific Discovery*. London: Routledge, 2002.
Poythress, Vern S. "Modern Spiritual Gifts as Analogous to Apostolic Gifts: Affirming Extraordinary Works of the Spirit within Cessationist Theology." *Journal of the Evangelical Theological Society* 39, no. 1 (1996) 71–101.
Pytches, David. *Prophecy in the Local Church: A Practical Handbook and Historical Overview*. London: Hodder and Stoughton, 1993.
Rahanaiah, Nerella V., Jennifer K. Rielage, and J. Patrick Sharpe. "Spiritual Well-Being and Personality." *Psychological Reports* 89 (2001) 659–62.

Resane, Kelebogile Thomas. "A Critical Analysis of the Ecclesiology of the Emerging Apostolic Churches with Special Reference to the Notion of the Fivefold Ministry." PhD diss., University of Pretoria, 2008.

Robbins, Mandy, James Hair, and Leslie J. Francis. "Personality and Attraction to the Charismatic Movement: A Study among Anglican Clergy." *Journal of Beliefs & Values* 20, no. 2 (1999) 239–46.

Robeck, Cecil M., Jr. "The Gift of Prophecy in Acts and Paul Part 1." *Studia Biblica et Theologica* 5, no. 1 (1975) 15–38.

———. "The Gift of Prophecy in Acts and Paul Part 2." *Studia Biblica et Theologica* 5, no. 2 (1975) 37–54.

———. "Prophecy, Gift of." In *The New International Dictionary of Pentecostal and Charismatic Movements*, edited by Stanley M. Burgess and Eduard M. van der Maas, 999–1012. Rev. and exp. Grand Rapids: Zondervan, 2002.

———. "Prophetic Authority in the Charismatic Setting: The Need to Test." *Theological Renewal* 24 (July 1983) 4–10.

———. "The Role and Function of Prophetic Gifts for the Church at Carthage, A.D. 202–258." PhD diss., Fuller Theological Seminary, 1985.

Robertson, O. Palmer. *The Final Word*. Carlisle, PN: Banner of Truth Trust, 1993.

Rodgers, Darrin J. "Assemblies of God." In *Encyclopedia of Christianity*, edited by John Stephen Bowden, 86–88. New York: Oxford University Press, 2005.

Rushton, J. Philippe, Roland D. Chrisjohn, and G. Cynthia Fekken. "The Altruistic Personality and the Self-Report Altruism Scale." *Personality and Individual Differences* 2, no. 4 (1981) 293–302.

Ruthven, Jon. "The 'Foundational Gifts' of Ephesians 2:20." *Journal of Pentecostal Theology* 10, no. 2 (2002) 28–43.

———. *On the Cessation of the Charismata: The Protestant Polemic on Post-Biblical Miracles*. Sheffield, UK: Sheffield Academic Press, 1993.

Salsman, John M., and Charles R. Carlson. "Religious Orientation, Mature Faith, and Psychological Distress: Elements of Positive and Negative Associations." *Journal for the Scientific Study of Religion* 44, no. 2 (2005) 201–9.

Schatzmann, Siegfried S. *A Pauline Theology of Charismata*. Peabody, MA: Hendrickson, 1987.

———. "Purpose and Function of Gifts in 1 Corinthians." *Southwestern Journal of Theology* 45, no. 1 (2002) 53–68.

Schleiermacher, Friedrich. *Brief Outline on the Study of Theology*. Reprint. Richmond, VA: John Knox, 1966.

Shade, W. Robert, and Bruce J. Nicholls. *Acts*. Asia Bible Commentary. Singapore: Asia Theological Association, 2007.

Sheldrake, Philip. *A Brief History of Spirituality*. Malden, MA: Blackwell, 2007.

Sheppard, Gerald T. "Prophecy: From Ancient Israel to Pentecostals at the End of the Modern Age." *The Spirit and Church* 3, no. 1 (2001) 47–70.

Simpson, David B., Jody L. Newman, and Dale R. Fuqua. "Spirituality and Personality: Accumulating Evidence." *Journal of Psychology and Christianity* 26, no. 1 (2007) 33–44.

Singh, Daljeet, and V. T. Arasu, eds. *Singapore: An Illustrated History, 1941–1984*. Singapore: Information Division, Ministry of Culture, 1984.

Sinha, Vineeta. "'Hinduism' and 'Taoism' in Singapore: Seeing Points of Convergence." *Journal of Southeast Asian Studies* 39, no. 1 (2008) 123–47.

Small, Mario Luis. "How to Conduct a Mixed Methods Study: Recent Trends in a Rapidly Growing Literature." *Annual Review of Sociology* 37 (2011) 57–86.

Smith, Chuck. *Charisma vs Charismania*. Irvine, CA: Harvest House, 1983.

Smith, Daniel S., and J. Roland Fleck. "Personality Correlates of Conventional and Unconventional Glossolalia." *Journal of Social Psychology* 114, no. 2 (1981) 209–17.

Smith, James K. A. *Thinking in Tongues: Pentecostal Contributions to Christian Philosophy*. Grand Rapids: Eerdmans, 2010.

Soh, Chin Guan. "Biblical Perspectives on Prophecy." *Church and Society* 6, no. 3 (2003) 101–13.

Sorokin, Pitirim A. *The Ways and Power of Love: Types, Factors, and Techniques of Moral Transformation*. Philadelphia: Templeton Foundation, 2002.

Spilka, Bernard. "Religious Practice, Ritual, and Prayer." In *Handbook of the Psychology of Religion and Spirituality*, edited by Raymond F. Paloutzian and Crystal L. Park, 365–77. New York: Guilford, 2005.

Spittler, Russell P. "Interpretation of Tongues, Gift of." In *The New International Dictionary of Pentecostal and Charismatic Movements*, edited by Stanley M. Burgess and Eduard M. van der Maas, 801–2. Rev. and exp. ed. Grand Rapids: Zondervan, 2002.

———. "Spirituality, Pentecostal and Charismatic." In *The New International Dictionary of Pentecostal and Charismatic Movements*, edited by Stanley M. Burgess and Eduard M. van der Maas, 1096–1102. Rev. and exp. ed. Grand Rapids: Zondervan, 2002.

———. "Suggested Areas for Further Research in Pentecostal Studies." *Pneuma* 5, no. 2 (1983) 39–56.

Sprecher, Susan, and Beverley Fehr. "Compassionate Love for Close Others and Humanity." *Journal of Social & Personal Relationships* 22, no. 5 (2005) 629–51.

Stark, Rodney. "A Taxonomy of Religious Experience." *Journal for the Scientific Study of Religion* 5, no. 1 (1965) 97–116.

Stibbe, Mark. *Know Your Spiritual Gifts*. Grand Rapids: Zondervan, 2000.

———. *Prophetic Evangelism*. Milton Keynes, UK: Authentic Media, 2004.

Stronstad, Roger. "Affirming Diversity: God's People as a Community of Prophets." *Pneuma* 17, no. 2 (1995) 145–57.

———. *The Charismatic Theology of St. Luke*. Peabody, MA: Hendrickson, 1984.

———. *The Prophethood of All Believers: A Study in Luke's Charismatic Theology*. Sheffield, UK: Sheffield Academic Press, 1999.

Suurmond, Jean-Jacques. *Word and Spirit at Play: Towards a Charismatic Theology*. London: SCM, 1994.

Swinton, John, and Harriet Mowat. *Practical Theology and Qualitative Research*. London: SCM, 2006.

Synan, Vinson. *The Century of the Holy Spirit: 100 Years of Pentecostal and Charismatic Renewal, 1901–2001*. Nashville: Thomas Nelson, 2001.

Tan, Derek. "Singapore." In *The New International Dictionary of Pentecostal and Charismatic Movements*, edited by Stanley M. Burgess and Eduard M. van der Maas, 223–25. Rev. and exp. ed. Grand Rapids: Zondervan, 2002.

Tan, Jin Huat. "Pentecostals and Charismatics in Malaysia and Singapore." In *Asian and Pentecostal: The Charismatic Face of Christianity in Asia*, edited by Allan Anderson and Edmond Tang, 281–306. Oxford, UK: Regnum, 2005.

Tan-Chow, May Ling. *Pentecostal Theology for the Twenty-First Century: Engaging with Multi-Faith Singapore*. Aldershot, UK: Ashgate, 2007.

Tappeiner, Daniel A. "A Psychological Paradigm for the Interpretation of the Charismatic Phenomenon of Prophecy." *Journal of Psychology and Theology* 5 (1977) 23–29.

The Assemblies of God of Singapore. *Directory 2010*. Singapore, 2010.

The Assemblies of God USA. "Apostles and Prophets: Official Statement by the General Presbytery of the Assemblies of God." Accessed May 1, 2012. https://ag.org/Beliefs/Topics-Index/Apostles-and-Prophets.

———. "Prophets and Personal Prophecies." Accessed May 1, 2012. https://ag.org/Beliefs/Topics-Index/Prophets-and-Personal-Prophecies.

Thiselton, Anthony C. *The First Epistle to Corinthians: A Commentary on the Greek Text*. New International Greek Testament Commentary. Grand Rapids: Eerdmans, 2000.

———. *New Horizons in Hermeneutics*. Grand Rapids: Zondervan, 1992.

Thomas, Andrew James. "Pathways to Healing: An Empirical-Theological Study of the Healing Praxis of 'The Group' Assemblies of God in Kwazulu-Natal, South Africa." ThD diss., University of South Africa, 2010.

Tian, Jessamyn. "The Pioneering Days: Reminiscences of a Veteran Missionary." *Singapore Evangel*, Special Issue 2008.

Tillich, Paul. *Systematic Theology*. Chicago: University of Chicago Press, 1967.

Torrance, Thomas F. "The Problem of Natural Theology in the Thought of Karl Barth." *Religious Studies* 6 (1970) 121–35.

———. *Space, Time and Resurrection*. Edinburgh: T. & T. Clark, 1998.

Tracy, David. *Blessed Rage for Order: The New Pluralism in Theology*. Chicago: University of Chicago Press, 1996.

———. "The Foundations of Practical Theology." In *Practical Theology: The Emerging Field in Theology, Church, and World*, edited by Don S. Browning, 62–82. New York: Harper & Row, 1983.

Turnbull, Constance Mary. *A History of Modern Singapore: 1819–2005*. Singapore: National University of Singapore, 2009.

Turner, Max. *The Holy Spirit and Spiritual Gifts: Then and Now*. Rev. ed. Milton Keynes, UK: Paternoster, 2006.

———. *Power from on High: The Spirit in Israel's Restoration and Witness in Luke-Acts*. Sheffield, UK: Sheffield Academic Press, 1996.

Twelftree, Graham H. *People of the Spirit: Exploring Luke's View of the Church*. Grand Rapids: Baker, 2009.

Tyra, Gary. *The Holy Spirit in Mission: Prophetic Speech and Action in Christian Witness*. Downers Grove, IL: InterVarsity, 2011.

Van der Ven, Johannes. "An Empirical or a Normative Approach to Practical-Theological Research? A False Dilemma." In *Normativity and Empirical Research in Theology*, edited by Johannes van der Ven and Michael Scherer-Rath, 101–35. Leiden: Brill, 2004.

———. *Practical Theology: An Empirical Approach*. Leuven: Peeters, 1998.

———. "Practical Theology: From Applied to Empirical Theology." *Journal of Empirical Theology* 1, no. 1 (1988) 7–27.

VanderStoep, Scott W., and Deirdre D. Johnston. *Research Methods for Everyday Life: Blending Qualitative and Quantitative Approaches*. Research Methods for the Social Sciences. San Francisco, CA: Jossey-Bass, 2009.

Vanhoozer, Kevin J. *The Drama of Doctrine: A Canonical-Linguistic Approach to Christian Theology*. Louisville, KY: Westminster John Knox, 2005.

———. *Is There a Meaning in This Text? The Bible, the Reader, and the Morality of Literary Knowledge*. Leicester, UK: Apollos, 1998.

———. "Lost in Interpretation? Truth, Scripture, and Hermeneutics." *Journal of the Evangelical Theological Society* 48, no. 1 (2005) 89–114.

Village, Andrew. *The Bible and Lay People: An Empirical Approach to Ordinary Hermeneutics*. Aldershot, UK: Ashgate, 2007.

Vines, Jerry. *Spirit Works: Contemporary Views on the Gifts of the Spirit and the Bible*. Nashville: Broadman & Holman, 1999.

Wagner, C. Peter. "A Church Growth Perspective on Pentecostal Missions." In *Called and Empowered: Global Missions in Pentecostal Perspective*, edited by Murray A. Dempster, Byron D. Klaus, and Douglas Peterson, 265–84. Peabody, MA: Hendrickson, 1991.

———, ed. *The New Apostolic Churches*. Ventura, CA: Regal, 1998.

———. "Third Wave." In *The New International Dictionary of Pentecostal and Charismatic Movements*, edited by Stanley M. Burgess and Eduard M. van der Maas, 1141. Rev. and exp. ed. Grand Rapids: Zondervan, 2002.

———. *Your Spiritual Gifts Can Help Your Church Grow*. Rev. ed. Ventura, CA: Regal, 1994.

Walvoord, John F. "The Holy Spirit and Spiritual Gifts." *Bibliotheca Sacra* 143, no. 570 (1986) 109–22.

Warfield, Benjamin B. *Counterfeit Miracles*. Edinburgh: Banner of Truth Trust, 1918.

Warrington, Keith. *Pentecostal Theology: A Theology of Encounter*. London: T. & T. Clark, 2008.

Wells, Samuel. *Improvisation: The Drama of Christian Ethics*. London: SPCK, 2004.

Wenk, Matthias. "The Creative Power of the Prophetic Dialogue." *Pneuma* 26, no. 1 (2004) 118–29.

Williams, J. Rodman. "Biblical Truth and Experience: A Reply to Charismatic Chaos by John F. MacArthur." *Paraclete* 27, no. 3 (1993) 16–30.

———. *Renewal Theology: Systematic Theology from a Charismatic Perspective*. Grand Rapids: Zondervan, 1996.

Wilson, Robert R. "Prophecy and Ecstasy: A Re-Examination." *Journal of Biblical Literature* 98, no. 3 (1979) 321–37.

———. *Prophecy and Society in Ancient Israel*. Philadelphia: Fortress, 1980.

Wimber, John. *Power Evangelism: Signs and Wonders Today*. London: Hodder & Stoughton, 1985.

Wimber, John, and Kevin Springer. *Power Points*. San Francisco: HarperSanFrancisco, 1991.

Witherington, Ben, III. *Conflict and Community in Corinth: A Socio-Rhetorical Commentary on 1 and 2 Corinthians*. Grand Rapids: Eerdmans, 1995.

Woodward, James, Stephen Pattison, and John Patton, eds. *The Blackwell Reader in Pastoral and Practical Theology*. Oxford: Blackwell, 2000.

Wright, N. T. "How Can the Bible Be Authoritative?" *Vox Evangelica* 21 (1991) 7–32.

———. *The New Testament and the People of God*. London: SPCK, 1992.

Wyckoff, John W. "The Baptism in the Holy Spirit." In *Systematic Theology: A Pentecostal Perspective*, edited by Stanley M. Horton, 423–55. Springfield, MO: Logion, 1994.

Yin, Robert K. *Case Study Research: Design and Methods*. 3rd ed. Thousand Oaks, CA: SAGE, 2003.

Yong, Amos. *Hospitality and the Other: Pentecost, Christian Practices, and the Neighbor*. Maryknoll, NY: Orbis, 2008.

Zhou, Gonghe. "先知恩賜與當代教會 [The Gift of Prophecy and the Contemporary Church]." In 聖靈古今論：從聖經, 歷史, 神學看神的同在 *[The Holy Spirit: Biblical, Historical and Theological Perspectives]*, edited by Xu Hongdu, 317–43. 台北市：中華福音神學院 [Taipei: China Evangelical Seminary Press], 1999.

www.ingramcontent.com/pod-product-compliance
Lightning Source LLC
Chambersburg PA
CBHW071246230426
43668CB00011B/1604